IMAGES of America

FIRST NATIONAL BANK

Hometown Banking Since 1874

On the Cover: Please see page 44.

IMAGES
of America

FIRST NATIONAL BANK

Hometown Banking Since 1874

U.L. "Rusty" Patterson and Barry E. Hambright

ARCADIA
PUBLISHING

ISBN 978-0-7385-1739-1

Published by Arcadia Publishing
Charleston SC, Chicago IL, Portsmouth NH, San Francisco CA

Printed in the United States of America

Library of Congress Catalog Card Number: 2004111530

For all general information contact Arcadia Publishing at:
Telephone 843-853-2070
Fax 843-853-0044
E-mail sales@arcadiapublishing.com
For customer service and orders:
Toll-Free 1-888-313-2665

Visit us on the Internet at www.arcadiapublishing.com

Contents

Acknowledgments 6

Introduction 7

1. Bank History 1874–1947 9

2. Bank History 1947–2004 41

3. A Business Is Only as Good as Its People: The Bank's Extended Family 79

4. A Community-Oriented Bank 97

5. The First National Team in 2004 115

Appendix: Board of Directors, Advisors, and Bank Officers 125

Acknowledgments

The authors wish to thank those who have helped to make this publication possible. Many persons throughout the county have generously and enthusiastically provided photos, stories, and background information, including personal interviews with Nancy Dicks Blanton, Edgar Blanton Hamilton, Adelaide Austell Craver, Mabel Elliott, Bobby Smith, Henry Lee Weathers, and Joe Stockton. Credit has been given at the end of each caption for those images from other sources. Several publications have been instrumental in the development of the book, including *The Living Past of Cleveland County* by Lee B. Weathers; *Our Heritage, A History of Cleveland County* by Henry Lee Weathers; *The Heritage of Cleveland County* by the Cleveland County Historical Association; *Architectural Perspectives of Cleveland County, North Carolina* by Brian R. Eades and J. Daniel Pezzoni; *The Shelby Star*; and bank histories written by George Blanton Jr. and Adelaide Austell Craver.

We wish to thank the following people for their assistance: bank employees Vickie Melton, Phyllis Monteith, Brenda Page, Peggy Paksoy, Bill Plowden, and David Thompson. Thank you also to Wes Chaney, Tommy Forney, Boyd Hendricks, Frankie Patterson, Marion Patterson, Brownie Plaster, and Mike Royster for their contributions. The works of professional photographers Elwin Stilwell and Floyd Willis were a valuable addition. And a very special thank you to our editor, Barbie Langston at Arcadia Publishing, for her technical support and endless patience.

A reasonable effort has been made to gather accurate information about each image within the timeline provided by the publisher. All of these people have helped make this publication possible. None of them is responsible for the errors, which are the authors' alone.

INTRODUCTION

Small towns across the country have changed greatly over the last several decades. Downtowns, or uptowns, have often died as malls opened or businesses moved to "the bypass." When one looks at Shelby, North Carolina, one can see an uptown that has survived. Numerous new restaurants are thriving in Uptown Shelby. The town is no longer deserted at night. The Uptown Shelby Association has played a major role in the survival of the uptown area.

Events are regularly sponsored at night to draw additional people and provide entertainment for the community. Ted Alexander's leadership in this organization resulted in his election as mayor in 2003.

A person who returned to Shelby in 2004 after a 50-year absence would recognize only two businesses that were here in the post–World War II era. The first is the Shelby Café, which has survived for over half a century. The other is First National Bank (FNB), which has survived in the same location for 130 years. It has not only survived but has also grown to include branches across Cleveland County and now into neighboring Gaston County. With mega banks all around, First National has bucked the big bank trend and remained "Your Hometown Bank." It is still the dominant financial institution in Cleveland County.

What is even more striking is the fact that all the presidents and CEOs have been descendants of Burwell Blanton, who was a key figure in the bank's history almost from the beginning in 1874. By the 1890s, the bank was known as B. Blanton & Company, Bankers. In 1903, the company became a federally chartered bank known under the name of First National Bank of Shelby. Burwell Blanton was succeeded by his son, Charles, as president. Charles was then succeeded by his brother, George. In 1947, George Blanton Sr. was replaced by his son, George Blanton Jr. In time, the leadership of the bank passed to two other descendants of Burwell Blanton. Edgar Blanton Hamilton replaced George Blanton Jr., and he would be replaced by Adelaide Austell Craver. Today, Mr. Hamilton is still chairman of the board, and Ms. Craver is president and CEO.

This book will recount the years of personal banking that survived even through the Great Depression of the 1930s. People were and are the focus of the Hometown Bank. Decisions are made locally. CEO Adelaide Craver's office is open—both doors in fact. When Chairman Hamilton is at the bank, he too has an open door and welcomes friends and customers. One can feel a sense of family or team in the atmosphere.

We will trace the many changes that have occurred as banking itself has changed and become more complicated.

Some of the longtime employees at the bank stated that the biggest change over 50 years was technology. We will examine a growing process that not only requires new equipment, but also brings a demand for many people with expertise in different fields of banking. While First National has a large number of veterans who have served over 25 or even 50 years, the bank has regularly integrated valuable new people into its team.

Emphasis will be given to the large set of community activities that the bank is involved in each year. Many people see Christmas floats, fair booths, special events, and activities in the schools, but the money that First National gives to community organizations and charities is not always seen by all. The time given by the employees of the bank cannot be counted, but civic organizations, schools, and charitable organizations benefit greatly by these often unseen contributions. A close look at the contributions of the team at First National and the bank itself reveals that this is more than just a business out to make a profit. It is an integral part of all that happens in its larger community.

The authors have spent many hours in First National over the last several months and have gained a new appreciation of the institution and its people. We had never had a bank CEO ask if we would like tea and then have her walk a block to the Shelby Café and return with three cups of iced tea. As we talked to many employees about this 130-year-old institution, we felt a positive attitude and atmosphere. First National is ready to serve both Cleveland and Gaston Counties in the 21st century.

This book is dedicated to the memory of George Blanton Jr., who served First National Bank and his community for 63 years.

One

Bank History 1874–1947

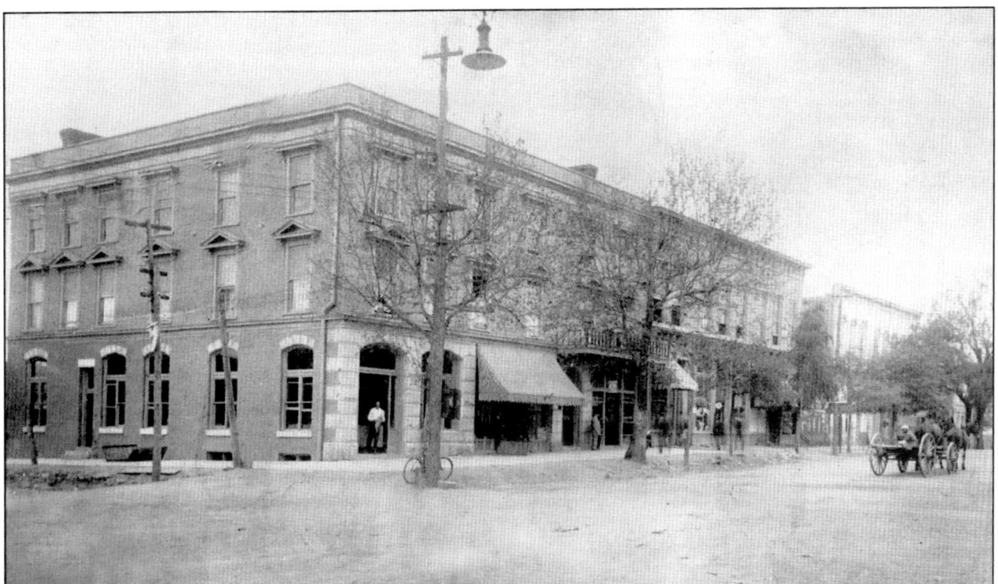

This c. 1895 photograph shows the front of the Central Hotel and Blanton Building. A saloon occupied the corner to the left. The first bank was located in a room in the back center of the Central Hotel building, off of the hotel lobby.

Named for Revolutionary War patriot Col. Benjamin Cleveland, Cleveland County was formed by an act of the North Carolina Legislature on January 11, 1841. Little information was recorded for posterity in the formative years of Cleveland County. The history of First National Bank unfolds through the documented facts and bank records of the day, and in the memories of those citizens who lived the history. The following account of the history of First National Bank includes excerpts from a history of First National Bank written by the late bank president and chairman, George Blanton Jr., and from interviews with current bank president Adelaide Austell Craver and chairman of the board Edgar Blanton Hamilton.

The heritage of First National Bank can be traced to 1874, when Jesse Jenkins and H.D. (DeKalb) Lee first opened J. Jenkins and Company, the county's first bank. For many years, this was the only bank in the territory between Charlotte and Asheville. Shortly after the formation of the bank, Burwell Blanton became an investor and partner with Major Jenkins and Major Lee. The addition of Burwell Blanton as a partner in the bank marked the beginning of the name Blanton becoming synonymous with banking in Cleveland County. We know that in March of 1875, Blanton purchased half of the building where the bank was located (the home office of the bank occupies the same location today). Mr. Lee had previously purchased the other half of the building in December of 1874. It is known also that Burwell Blanton, H.D. Lee, and S.J. Green had other business ventures together in the early years of the bank.

Five years after opening Cleveland County's first bank, Jesse Jenkins, experiencing financial hardships, sold his interest in the bank and moved to Texas. The name of the bank was changed to H.D. Lee and Company, Bankers, with H.D. Lee, Burwell Blanton, and S.J. Greene as partners. At that time, the bank had assets of $136,983.60 and deposits of $98,071.97.

On February 5, 1889, Major Lee transferred all of his interest in the bank, including personal and real property, to Burwell Blanton and moved to Knoxville, Tennessee. Lee gave permission for the H.D. Lee name to be retained, and it was for several years. On May 1, 1895, Major Green appointed Burwell Blanton to wind up the affairs of H.D. Lee and Company, thereby withdrawing as a partner.

On July 10, 1895, the name was changed to B. Blanton & Company, Bankers. This firm was composed of Burwell Blanton and his two sons, Charles Coleman Blanton and George Blanton. Charles Blanton had returned to Shelby from Meridian, Texas, where he had been in the pharmaceutical, cattle, and banking business for 11 years. George Blanton returned to Shelby from Virginia, where he had been selling Singer sewing machines since graduating from Wake Forest College in 1893. On May 9, 1903, B. Blanton & Company, Bankers received their national charter (charter #6776) and became the First National Bank of Shelby. The national charter provided for the United States Treasury to print national currency for the local bank.

During the Great Depression of the 1930s, many banks failed and most encountered severe problems. In March of 1933, President Roosevelt proclaimed a national bank holiday, closing all banks in the United States. Each bank remained closed until banking auditors examined the books to see if they were financially able to continue operation. At the height of the panic, First National Bank officials and board members met with major depositors of the bank. Appeals for patience and confidence in the bank were made first by local Shelbian former governor O. Max Gardner and then by former Congressman Clyde R. Hoey. A vote of confidence was taken after each had spoken, and both times, none of the depositors voted in support of the bank. Then Charles Blanton stood before the group and made what was likely the speech of his life. He told the group, "Now you know me, and I know you. I know your families and I know your horses and dogs, and I stand here before you today to ask for your patience and confidence that with time all will be well with the bank, and I guarantee you that no one will lose any money deposited with First National Bank. Now who is with me?" With that, the entire room jumped to their feet in support of Charles Blanton and First National Bank. When First National Bank emerged from the bank moratorium, Charles Blanton paid $100,000, from his personal assets, to depositors in order that no customer would lose any money in the bank.

George Blanton Sr. succeeded his brother, Charles C. Blanton, as president and chairman of the board in 1937. He held that position for 10 years. George Blanton Jr. succeeded his father as president of the bank in 1947. George Blanton Sr. remained chairman of the board until his death at age 87 in 1959. Throughout its first 73 years, First National Bank and its predecessors experienced both good times and bad. From the very beginning, First National Bank established itself with the following principles: "To provide quality, caring, and personal service to all people." These are the same principles that make it "Your Hometown Bank" today.

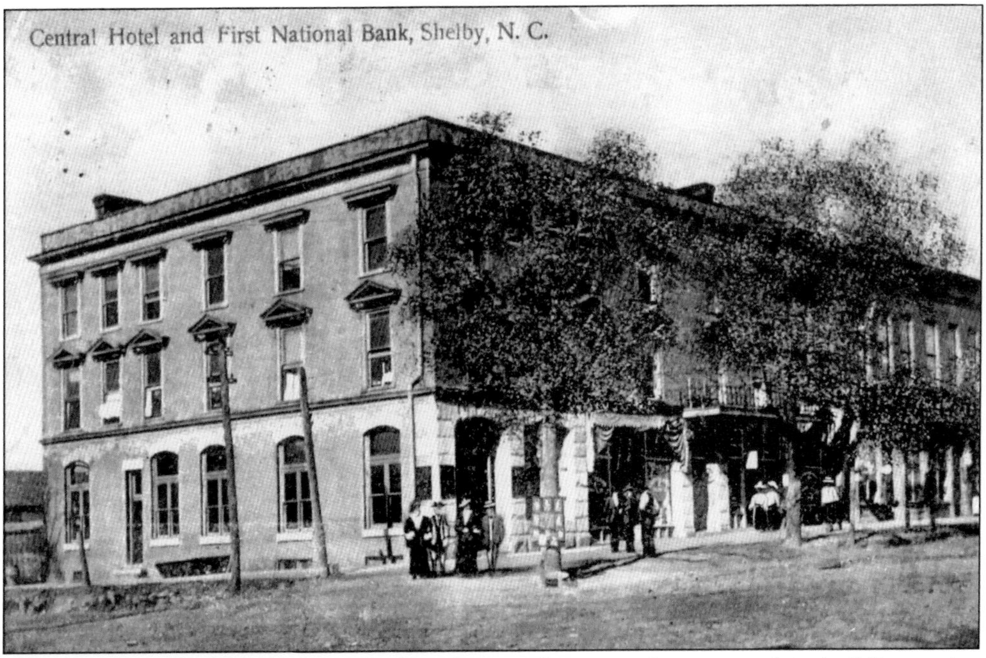

This c. 1910 postcard image shows the large bronze plaques on the corner of the building noting that First National Bank occupied the corner of the building. The doors to the sidewalk freight elevator can be seen on the West Warren Street side of the bank. It was used for deliveries into the basement of the bank building. The doors to the freight elevator are visible on Warren Street today. First National Bank has occupied the same location for 130 years.

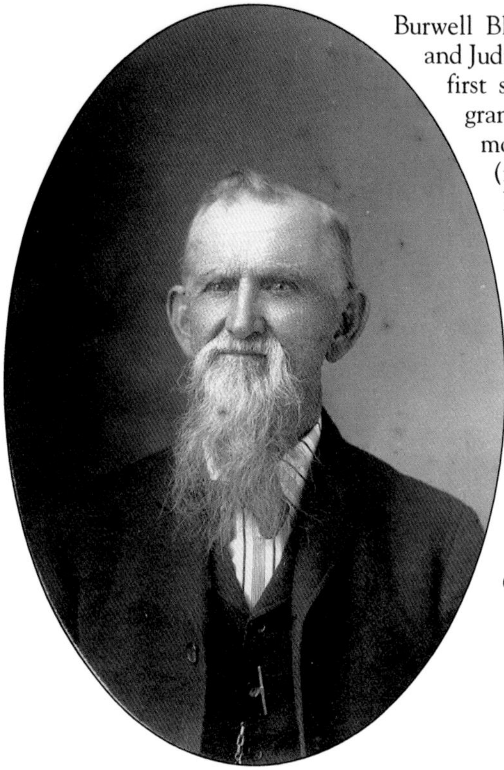

Burwell Blanton (1834–1908) was the son of Charles and Judith Hamrick Blanton. Charles Blanton was the first sheriff of Cleveland County. Burwell's great-grandparents, George and Elvira Lee Blanton, moved from Virginia with their son Burrell (note old spelling) in 1769 and settled in North Carolina along the First Broad River. The records of the day listed George Blanton as a planter. This was some 72 years before Cleveland County was formed. Burrell also became a planter and was called Grandsire Burrell. He lived to be almost 100 years old. His grandson, Burwell (note new spelling), distinguished himself as a successful farmer, miller, and business developer even before his days as a banker. In 1889, Blanton was appointed one of the first trustees of North Carolina College of Agriculture and Mechanical Arts, known today as North Carolina State University.

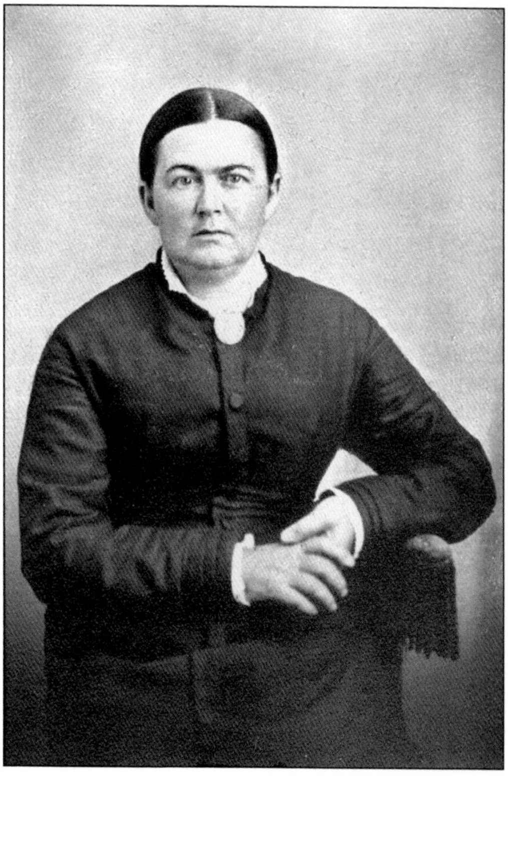

Frances (Fannie) Caroline Doggett (1838–1892) married Burwell Blanton on August 16, 1855. The Blantons had six children: Charles Coleman, Mary Judith (Mrs. Richard Eskridge), Margaret (Mrs. George M. Webb Jr.), Dora (Mrs. Rush Oates), George, and Edgar. One story told about her is that "in 1892 as the family was walking to church past Dr. McBrayer's house at the corner of West Marion and Cemetery Road, the doctor greeted them and said to his wife, 'I must bleed Fannie tomorrow. She is too red.' That night she had a stroke and died."

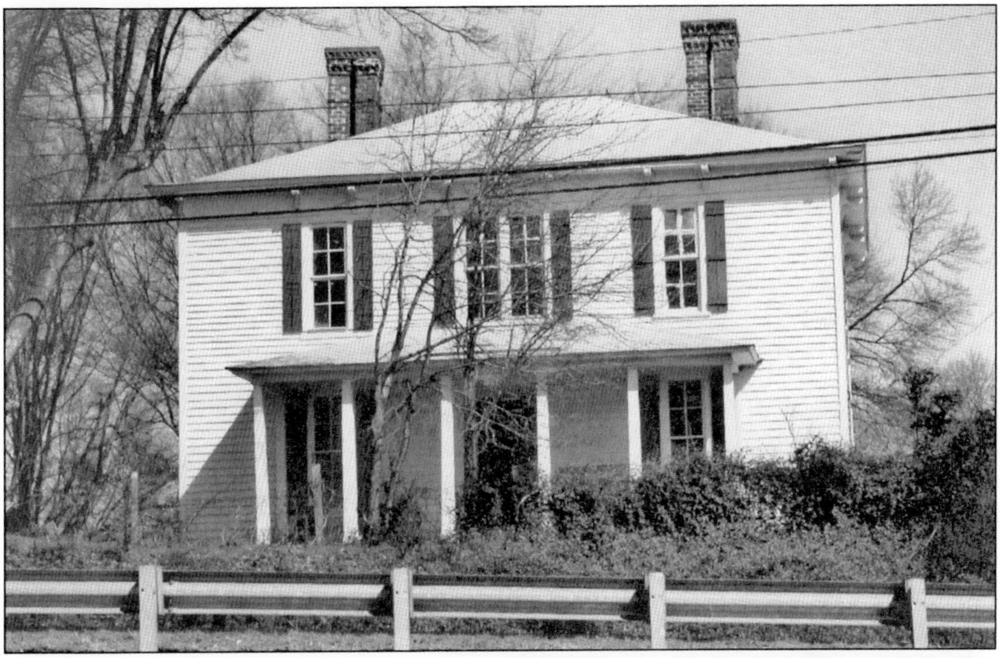

The Burwell Blanton farmhouse was built *c.* 1875 along the Brushy Creek west of Shelby. The house was part of a 271-acre tract. The house stands today just beyond the Shelby city limits on West Dixon Boulevard. (Courtesy of Tommy Forney, *Architectural Perspectives of Cleveland County, North Carolina.)*

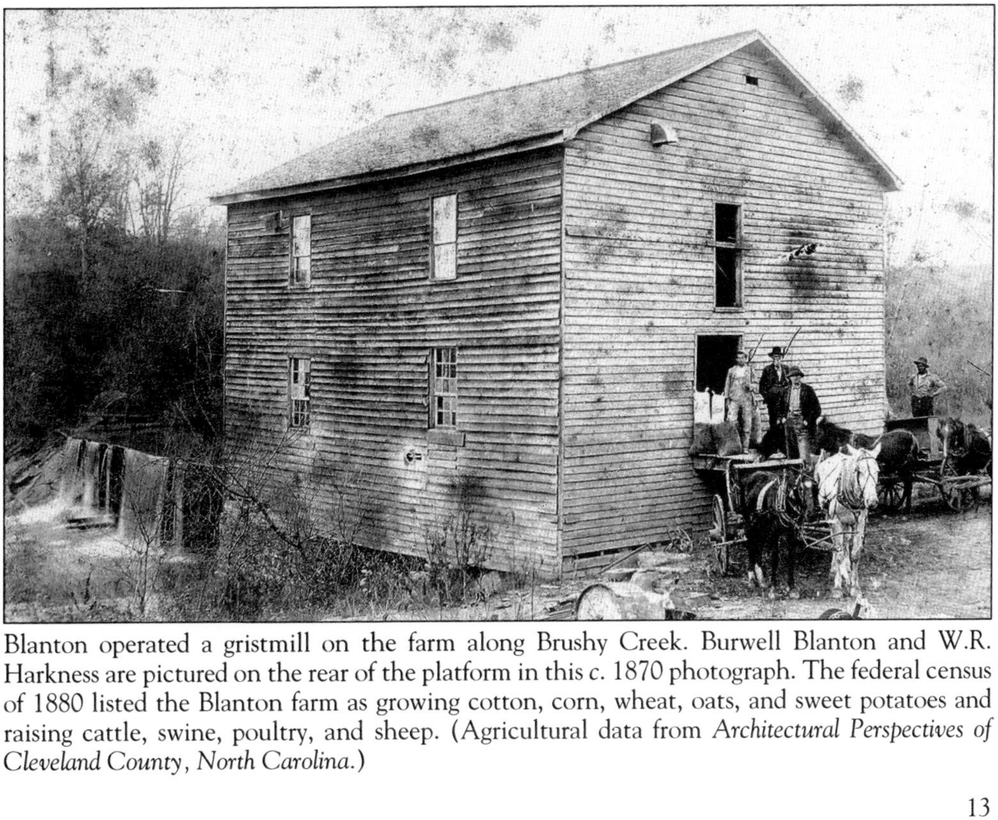

Blanton operated a gristmill on the farm along Brushy Creek. Burwell Blanton and W.R. Harkness are pictured on the rear of the platform in this *c.* 1870 photograph. The federal census of 1880 listed the Blanton farm as growing cotton, corn, wheat, oats, and sweet potatoes and raising cattle, swine, poultry, and sheep. (Agricultural data from *Architectural Perspectives of Cleveland County, North Carolina.*)

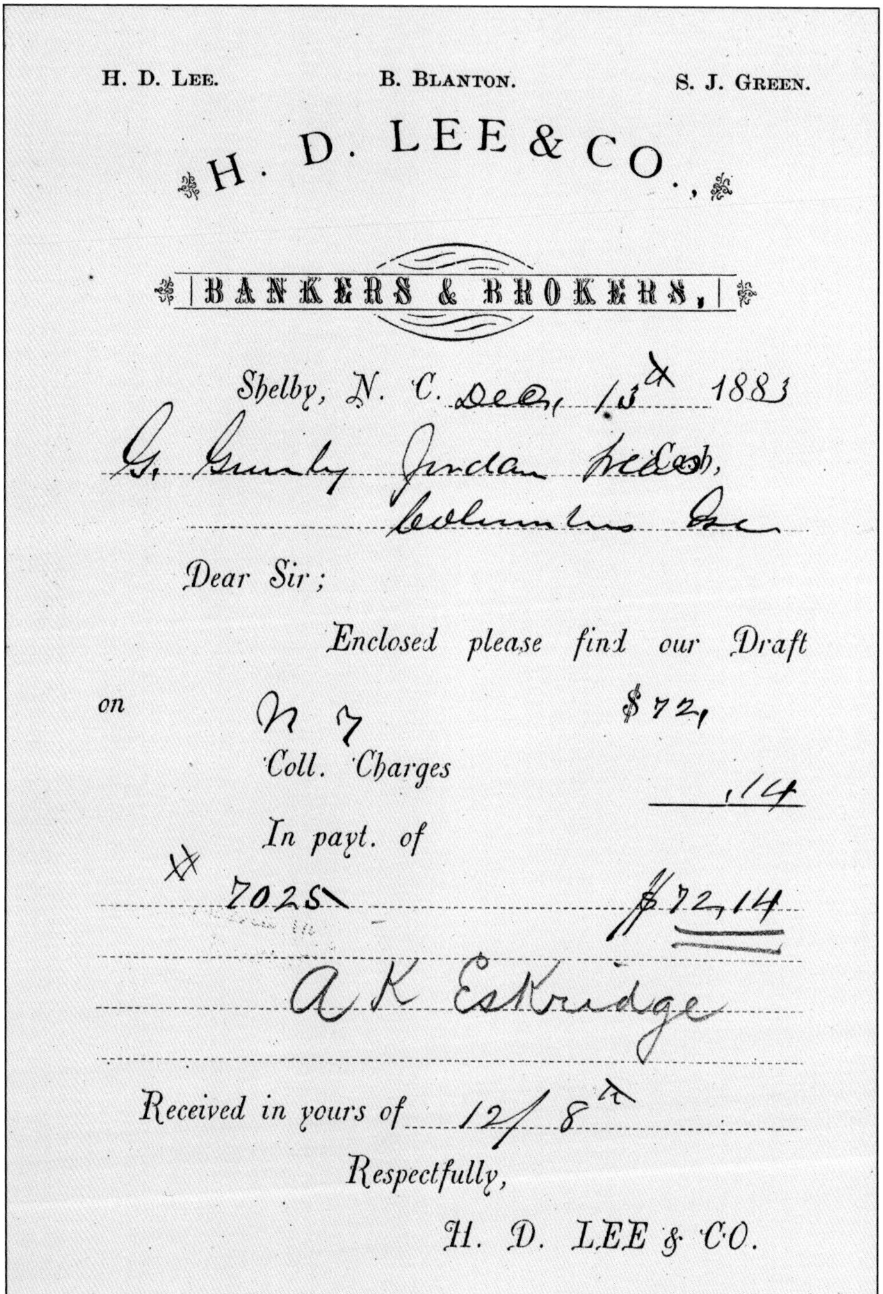

H. D. LEE. B. BLANTON. S. J. GREEN.

H. D. LEE & CO.,

BANKERS & BROKERS,

Shelby, N. C. Dec. 13th 1883

G. Grundy Jordan [illegible],
Columbus [illegible]

Dear Sir;

Enclosed please find our Draft

on N 7 $72,

Coll. Charges .14

In payt. of

7025 $72,14

A K Eskridge

Received in yours of 12/8th

Respectfully,

H. D. LEE & CO.

This statement of a banking transaction was mailed to a customer in Columbus, North Carolina, on December 13, 1883. H.D. Lee, B. Blanton, and S.J. Green are listed as principles in the bank. The statement was signed by A.K. Eskridge.

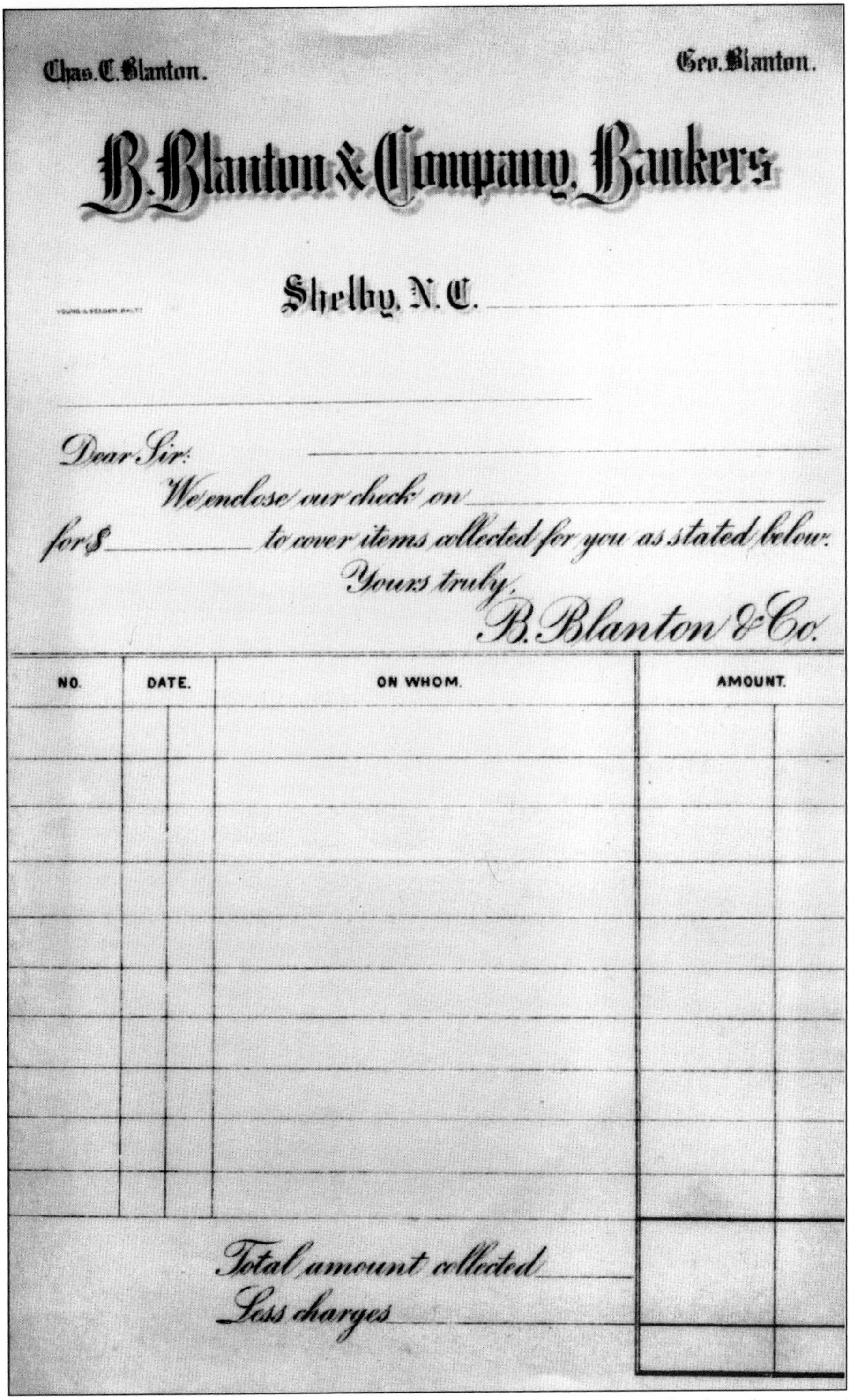
Chas. C. Blanton. Geo. Blanton.

B. Blanton & Company, Bankers

Shelby, N. C. ______

______

Dear Sir: ______

We enclose our check on ______

for $ ______ to cover items collected for you as stated below.

Yours truly,

B. Blanton & Co.

NO.	DATE.	ON WHOM.	AMOUNT.

Total amount collected

Less charges

Here is an example of a statement used by B. Blanton & Company, Bankers between 1895 and 1903.

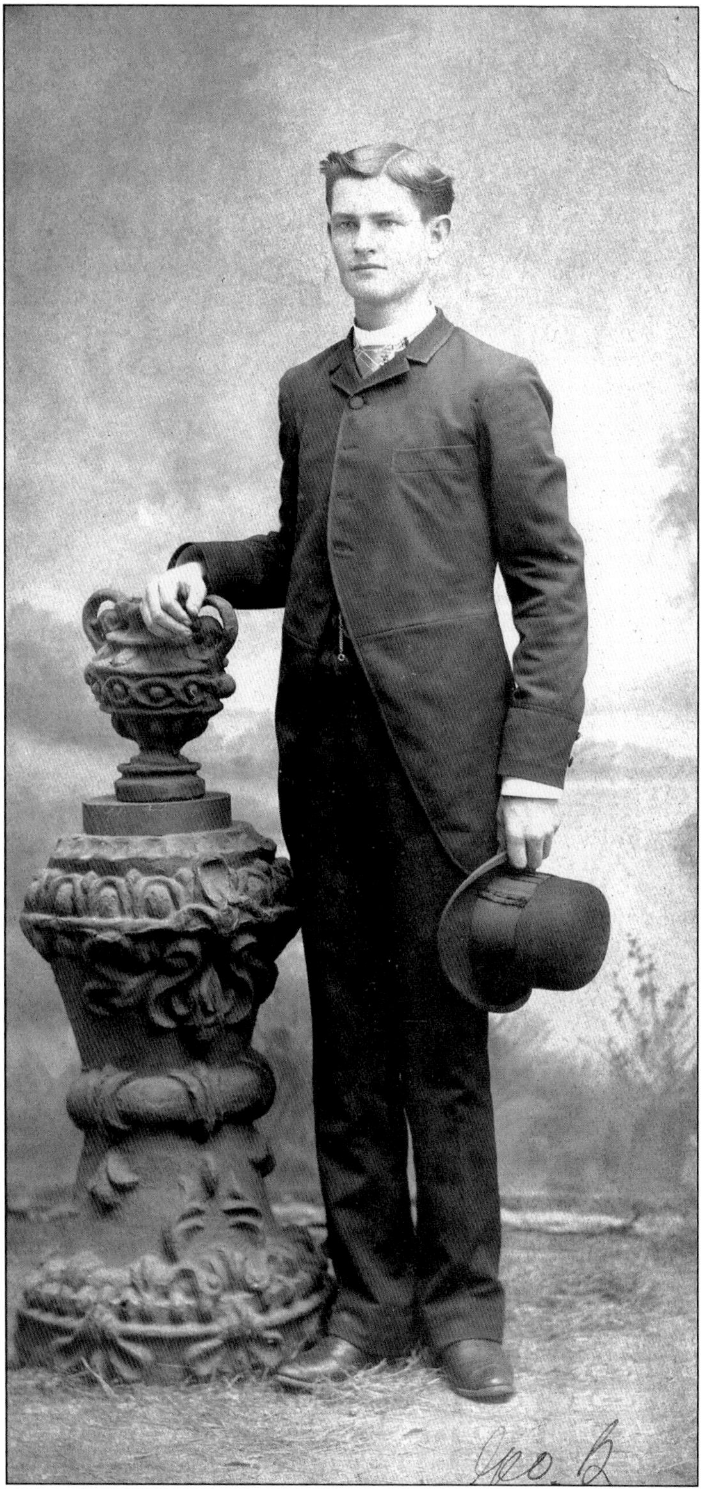

George Blanton was 19 years old and a student at Wake Forest College when this 1890 photograph was taken.

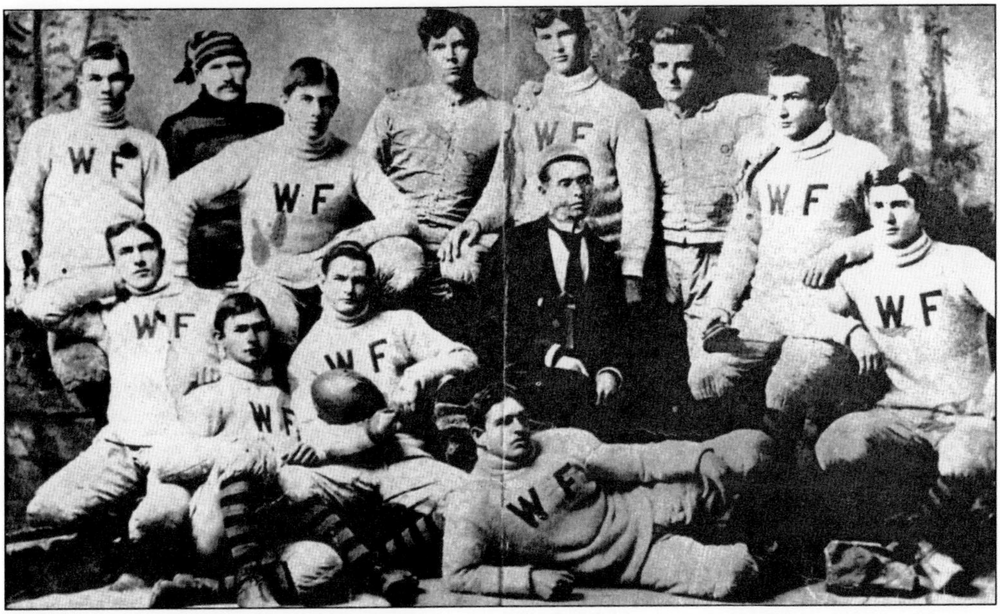

The 1892 Wake Forest College football team was captured in this photograph. George Blanton was the captain of the team. Pictured from left to right are the following: (front row) Tom Crudup; (middle row) Claud Wilson, Carl Pridgen, George Blanton (holding the football), David Prince (manager), and Tom Justice; (back row) Jack Howard, Walter Sikes, Raleigh Daniels, Rufus Fry, Sam Britton, Tom Hill, and Will Jones.

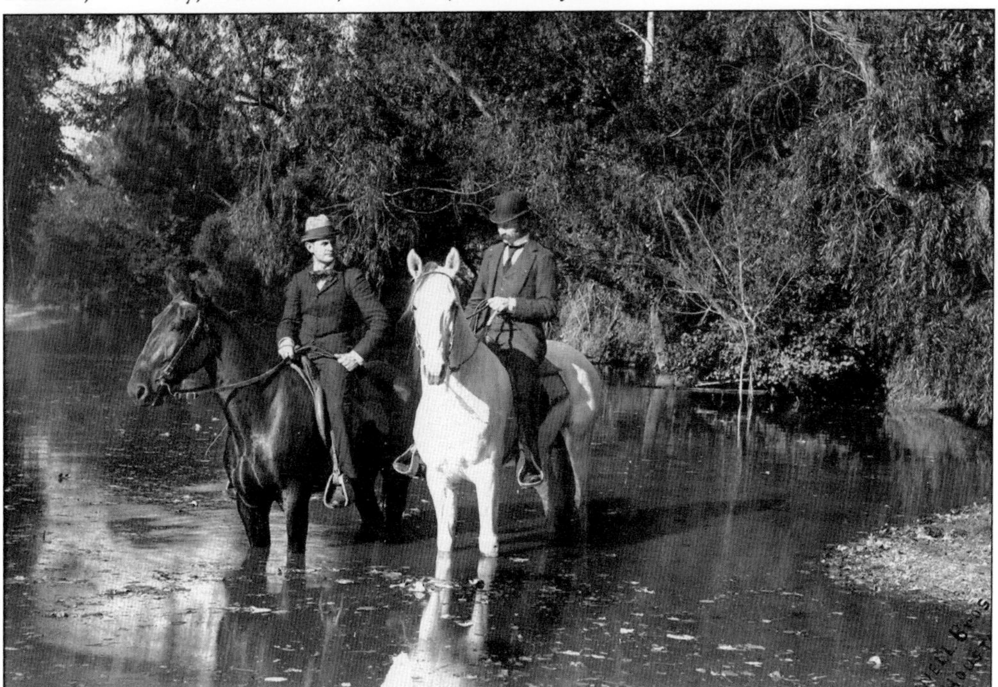

In the summer of 1893, George Blanton (left) visited his brother Charles in Meridian, Texas. They are pictured here together on horseback in the Bosque River. Two years later, they joined their father in Shelby to form B. Blanton & Company, Bankers.

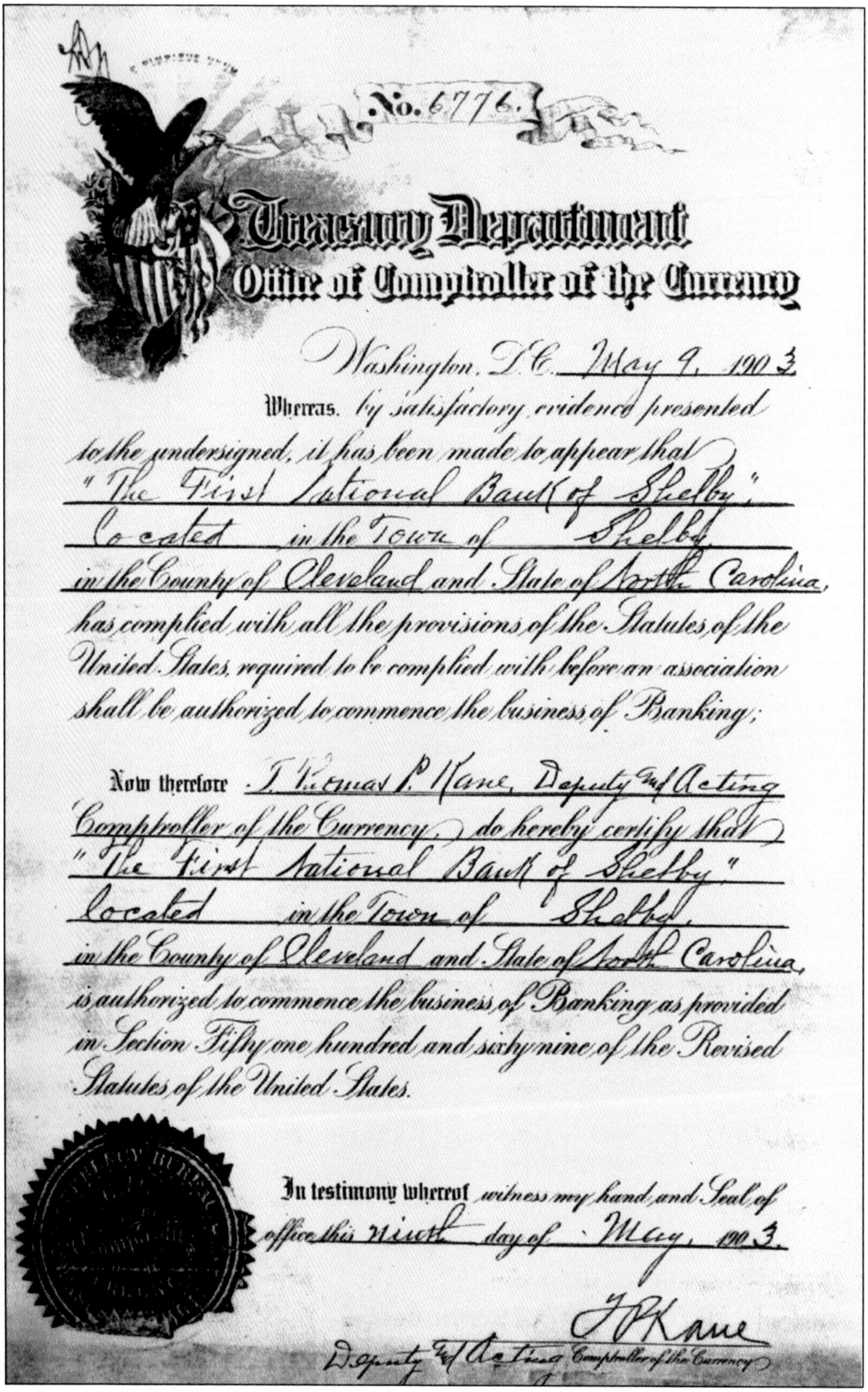

No. 6776.

Treasury Department
Office of Comptroller of the Currency

Washington, D.C. May 9, 1903

Whereas, by satisfactory evidence presented to the undersigned, it has been made to appear that "The First National Bank of Shelby", located in the Town of Shelby in the County of Cleveland and State of North Carolina, has complied with all the provisions of the Statutes of the United States, required to be complied with before an association shall be authorized to commence the business of Banking;

Now therefore I, Thomas P. Kane, Deputy and Acting Comptroller of the Currency, do hereby certify that "The First National Bank of Shelby" located in the Town of Shelby, in the County of Cleveland and State of North Carolina, is authorized to commence the business of Banking as provided in Section Fifty one hundred and sixty nine of the Revised Statutes of the United States.

In testimony whereof witness my hand and Seal of office this ninth day of May, 1903.

T P Kane
Deputy and Acting Comptroller of the Currency

B. Blanton & Company, Bankers received their national charter on May 9, 1903, becoming First National Bank of Shelby, North Carolina.

The date is unknown for this early First National Bank advertising calendar. It is likely from the 1920s.

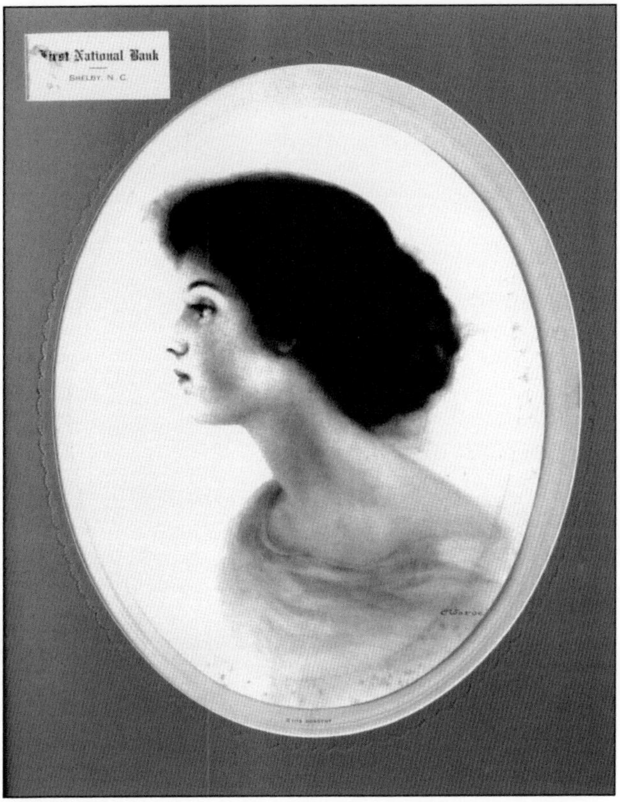

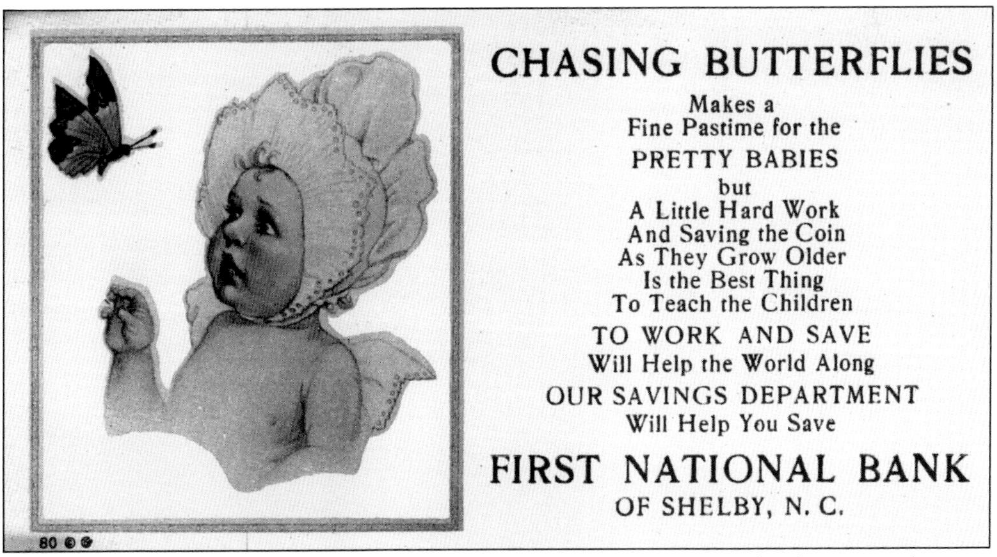

Here is an advertising ink blotter, probably from the 1920s. (Courtesy of Mike Royster.)

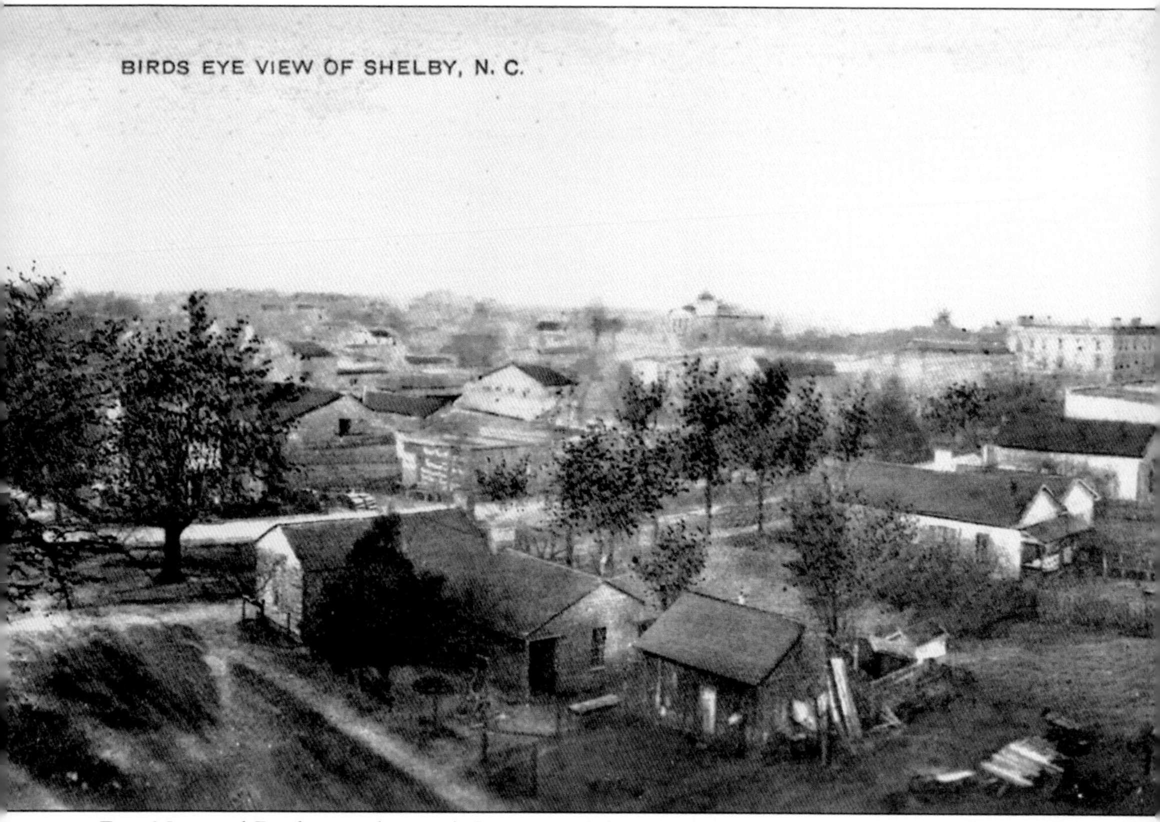

First National Bank is to the top left center of this c. 1905 postcard titled "Birds Eye View of Shelby." In 1903, Shelby was the center of an economically booming county. The *Cleveland Star* reported there were "in the city seven general stores, three hardware stores, 12 grocery stores, three millinery stores, one wholesale grocer, one commission merchant, three stove and tin-ware stores, two furniture dealers, a harness manufacturer, a tailor, two jewelers, two opticians, three drug stores, one piano-organ store, a marble yard and two undertakers.

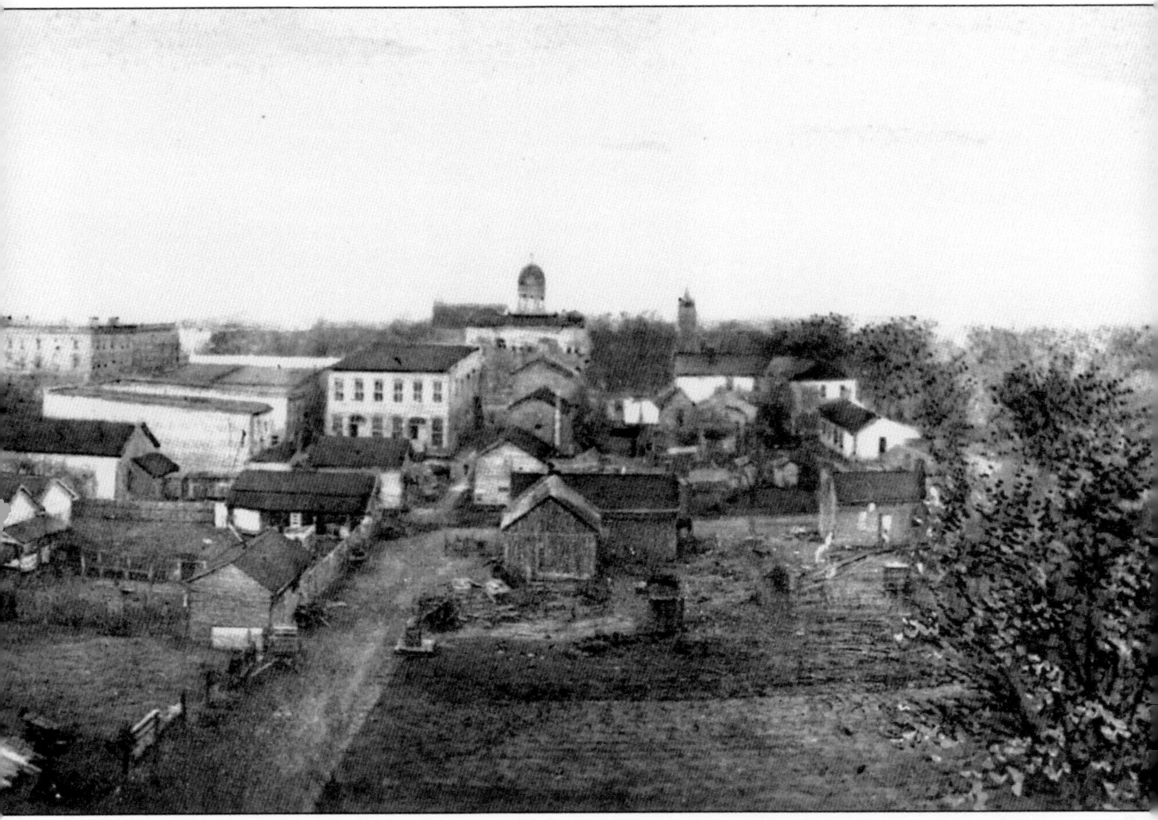

Additionally Shelby had five hotels including the 185-person Cleveland Springs Hotel, two cotton mills, a cotton seed oil mill, three cotton gins, a grist mill, a foundry and machine works, two lumber plants, a brick plant, two sash and blind firms, a steam laundry and four blacksmiths. . . . The county itself grew 15,000 bales of cotton, worked 275,000 acres of crops and had 13 cotton factories, 44 flour mills, 60 cotton gins, 33 lumber plants and a host of small businesses."

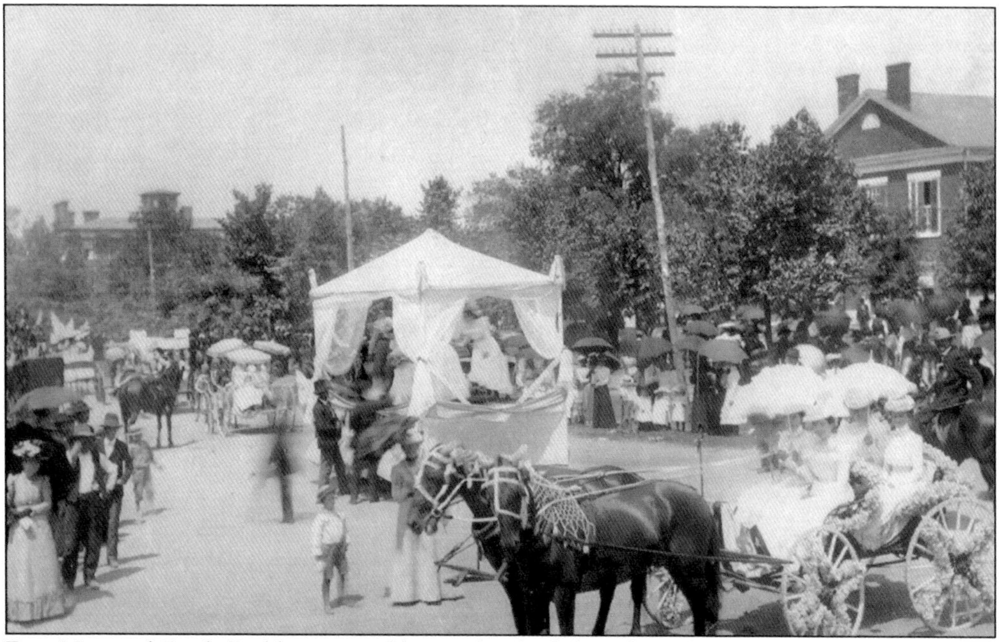

First National Bank Building is visible on the far left with its lookout tower on top of the building during the early 1890s. To the right is the old courthouse on the Warren Street side of the court square.

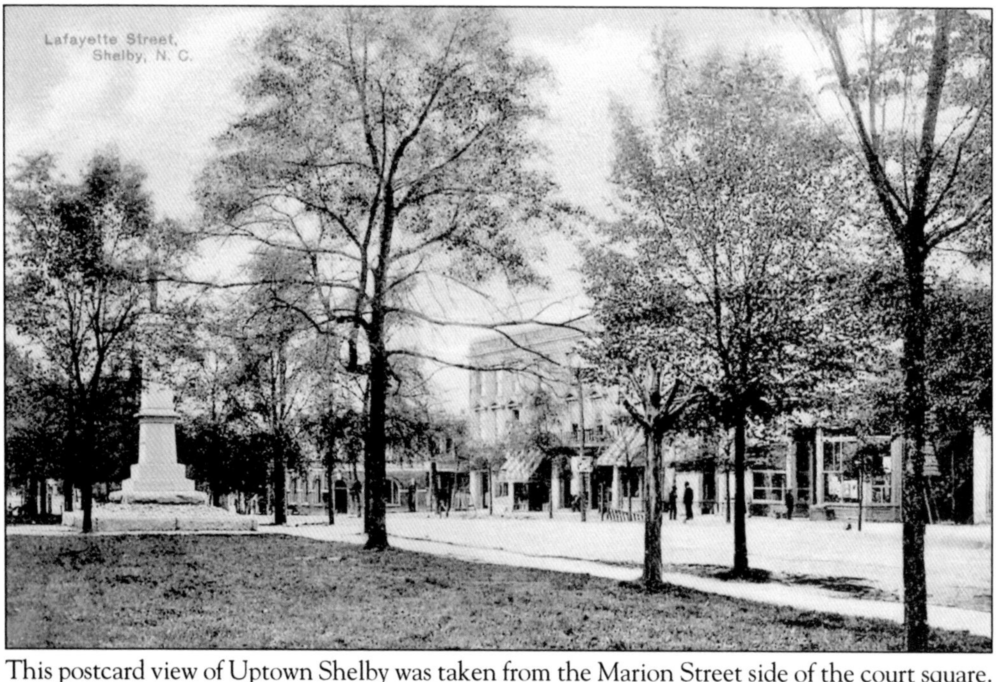

This postcard view of Uptown Shelby was taken from the Marion Street side of the court square. The Blanton Building is at the right and the bank building at the center of this *c.* 1910 image.

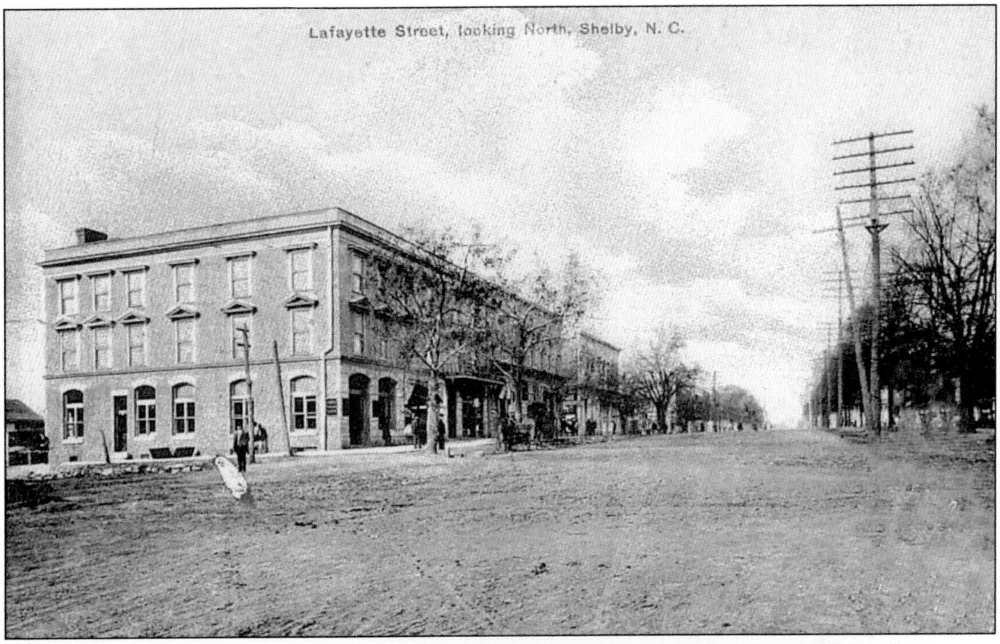

This postcard view shows Lafayette Street looking north with First National Bank on the corner. James Love, William Forbes, and Forbes's wife, Elizabeth, donated the land on which the city of Shelby was founded. James Love had visited Washington, D.C., and was so impressed with the width of the streets that upon his return to Shelby, he recommended that city planners adapt the same pattern for the new county seat.

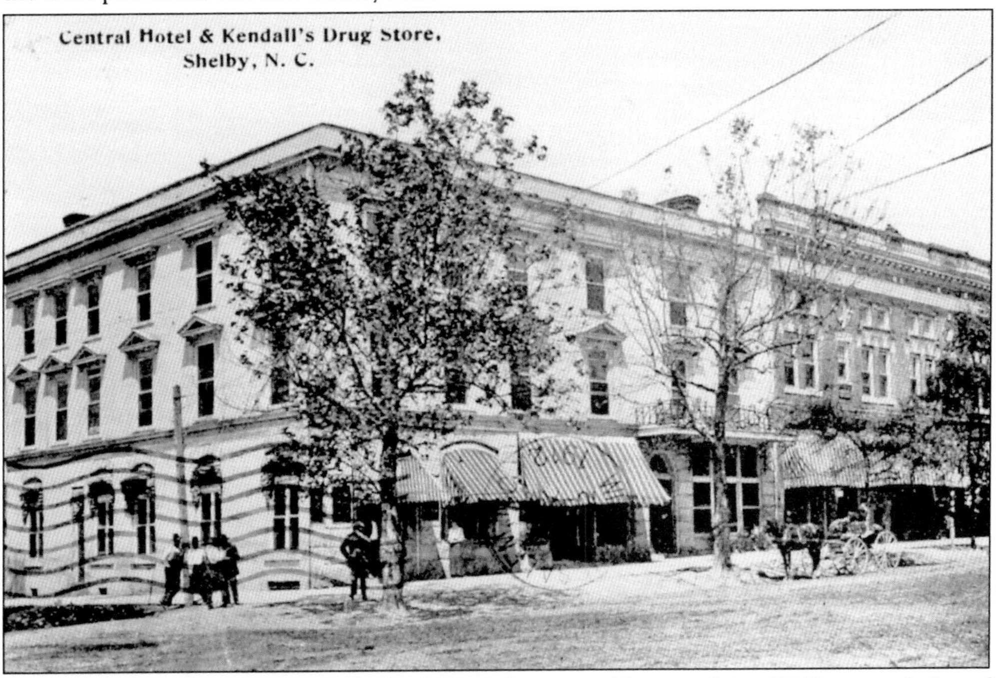

Awnings protect the entrance to the bank from the sun and heat in this c. 1910 postcard view of the bank and hotel. This picture shows the 1911 renovation of the adjoining Blanton Building with its decorative style. (Courtesy of Boyd Hendrick.)

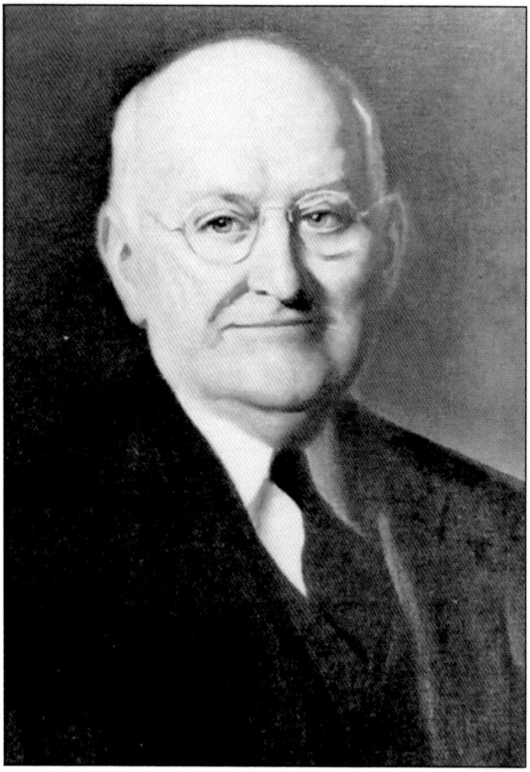

Charles Coleman Blanton was born on January 31, 1858. In 1884, Mr. Charlie married Ora Brewster of Sweetwater, Tennessee. She had moved to Shelby to teach music at the Shelby Female Academy. She died only six years after their marriage, leaving no children, and he never remarried. Everyone knew him as "Mr. Charlie" or "Uncle Charlie." He had a great enthusiasm for people and for the industrial boom that Cleveland County experienced in the early 1900s. His name became synonymous with the development of many industrial plants and businesses, including Cleveland Cloth Mill, Shelby Cotton Mills, Eagle Roller Mill, Ora Mill, Dover Mill, Lily Mills, Cleveland Mill and Power Company, and Shelby Building and Loan Association. He was also instrumental in seeing that Union Trust Company (now a part of BB&T) reopened after the bank moratorium. He was serving as president of Union Trust Company at the time of his death.

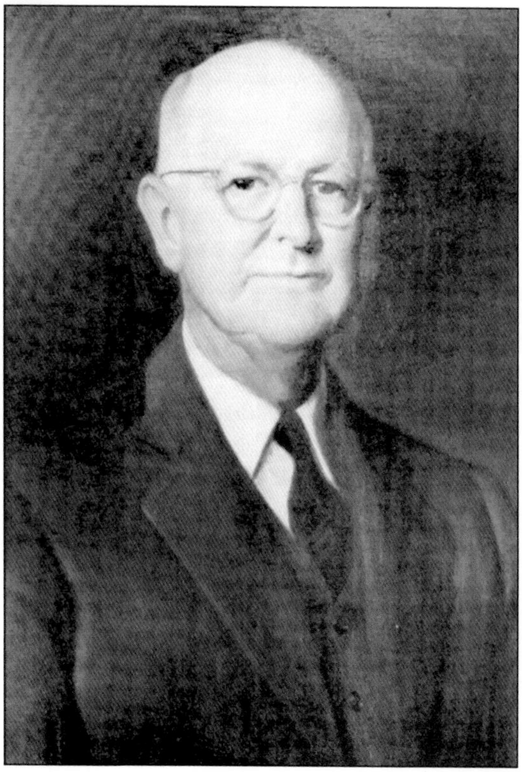

George Blanton Sr. was born on October 26, 1871. He married Ida Estelle Wood of Gaffney, South Carolina, on January 17, 1900. George Sr. followed his brother, Charles, as president and chairman of First National in 1937. He was succeeded as bank president by his son, George Jr., in 1947. Known for his gentle manner, George Sr. loved football and horseback riding. He and his brother, Charles, regularly embarked on morning horseback excursions. George Sr. had a fondness for football and believed in the importance of a good education for all children in Cleveland County. He served for several terms on the Shelby City School Board. For these reasons, the football stadium at Shelby High School was named in his memory. He served as president of Shelby Loan and Mortgage Company and Eagle Roller Mill. He also served as director on many of the boards for Cleveland County industries.

Maj. Henry Franklin Schenck served as the first vice president of First National Bank. He served on the bank's board of directors from 1903 until his death in 1915. Schenck was a pioneer in the industrial development of Cleveland County. He founded Cleveland Mill and Power Company and the Lawndale Railway and Industrial Company. (Courtesy of *Lawndale Railway and Industrial Company*.)

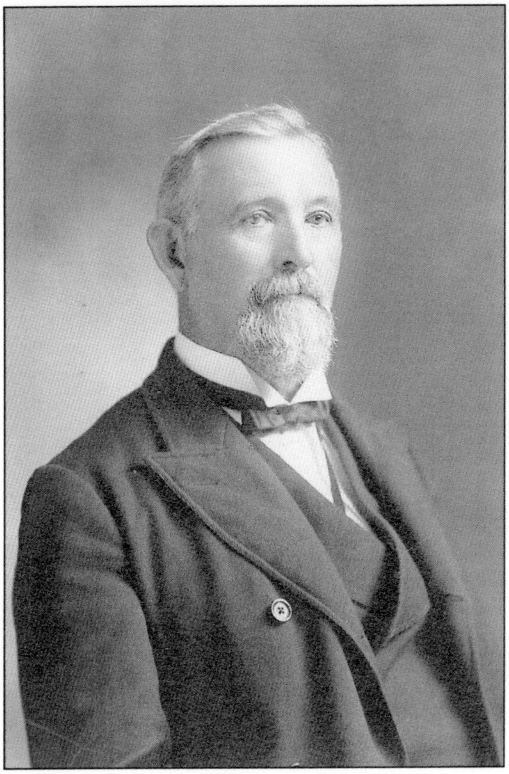

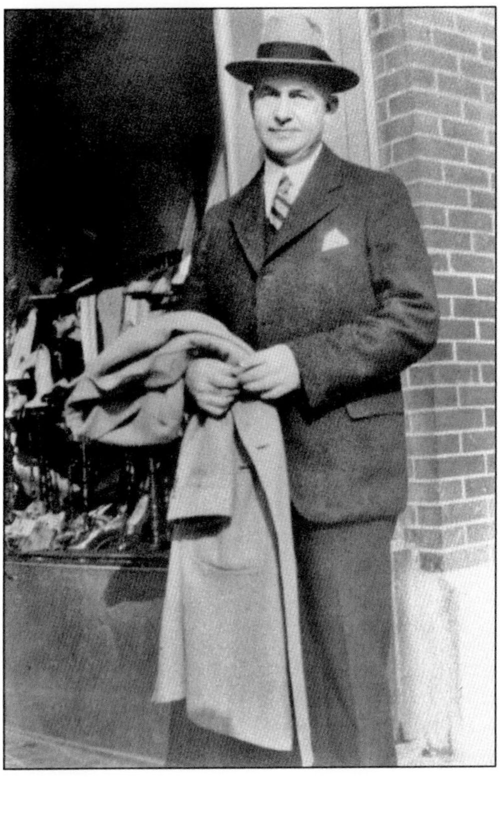

Forrest Eskridge was the son of Richard and Mary Judith Blanton Eskridge. The nephew of Charles and George Blanton, Forrest Eskridge served first as an assistant cashier and later as a cashier of First National Bank. Eskridge was instrumental in successfully lobbying Washington, D.C., to have First National Bank reopen after President Roosevelt's bank moratorium in 1933. He served as president of the North Carolina Bankers Association in 1933 and 1934, a difficult time following the bank moratorium. He is the only bank officer from First National to date to have been president of the association.

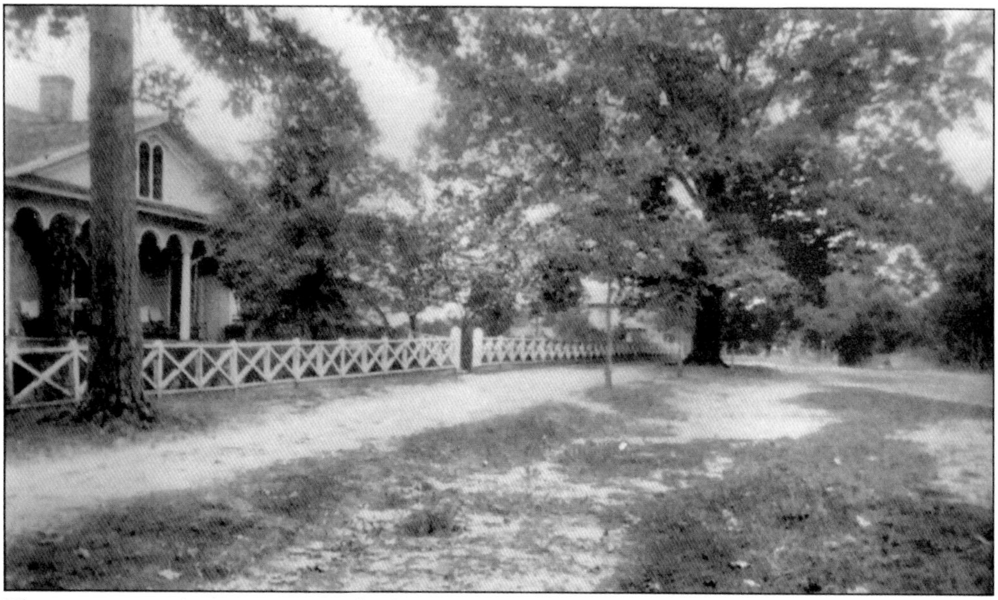

This one-story white cottage was built prior to 1870 on West Marion Street by the first bank president, Jesse Jenkins, and his wife, Hattie Beam Jenkins. This early 1900s photograph looks west. The home featured a large front porch with Victorian trim and tapered columns. H.D. Lee, the second president of the bank, and his wife, Sara Damron, also lived in the house. George Blanton Sr. purchased the house in 1900 for himself and his bride, Ida Wood Blanton.

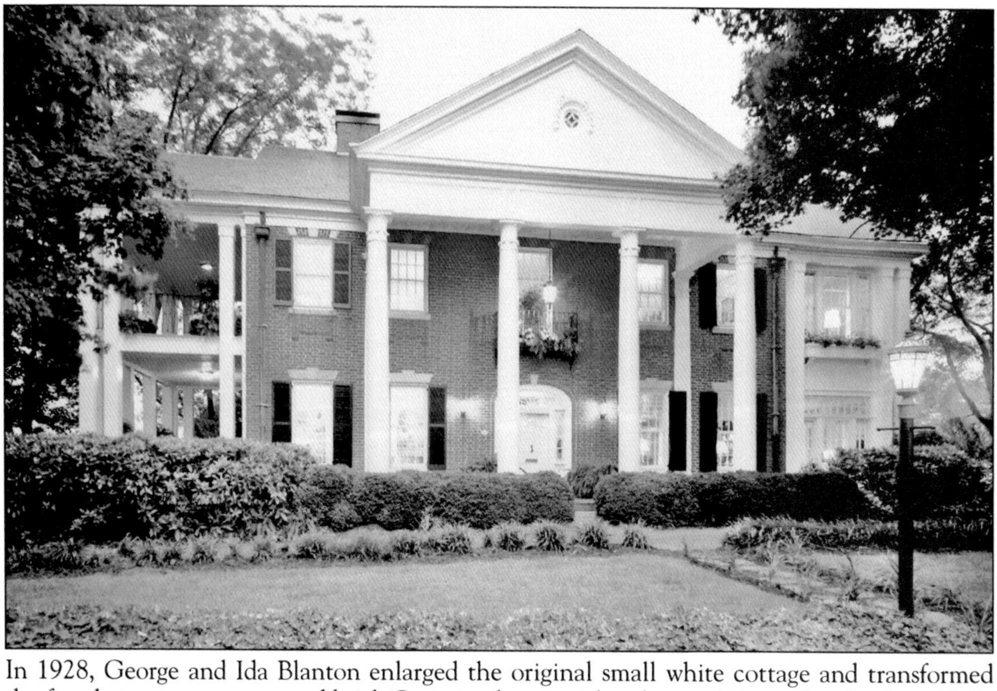

In 1928, George and Ida Blanton enlarged the original small white cottage and transformed the facade into a two-story, red brick Georgian home with columns. Prior to his death in 1944, Charles Blanton resided in the home with George and Ida Blanton Sr. George Blanton Jr. grew up in the house, making this home to five bank presidents. In the late 1970s, the house was given to Gardner-Webb University by the Blanton family.

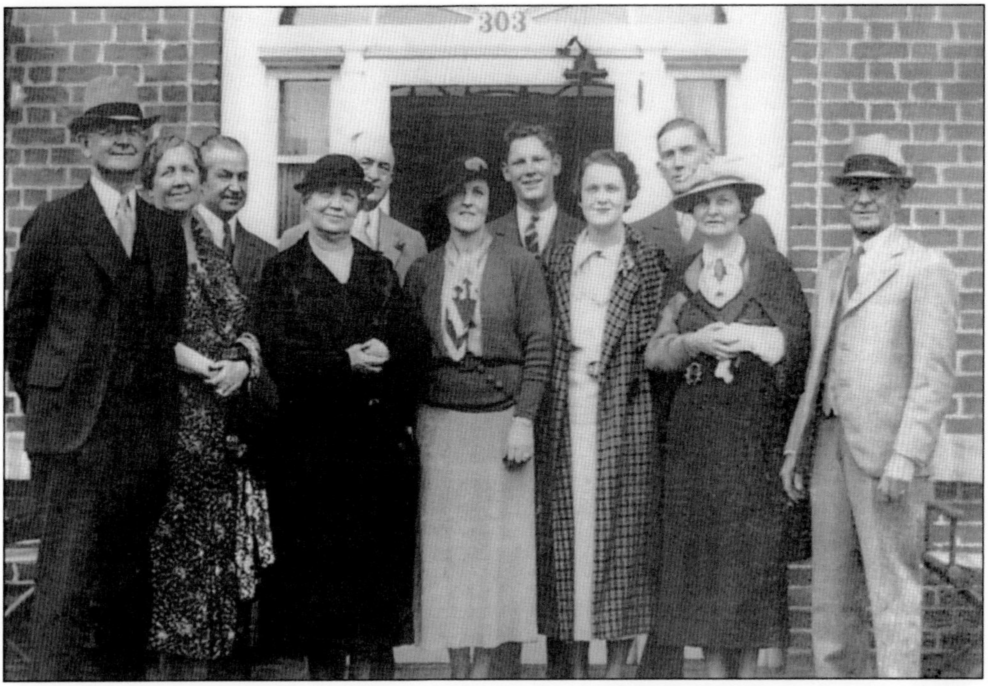

Pictured in Shelby at the home of George Blanton Sr. on West Marion Street are, from left to right, (first row) George Blanton Sr., Ida Blanton, Frances Roberts, Julia May Webb, Minnie Eddins Roberts (Carpenter), Lalege Oates Rorison, and Edgar Blanton; (second row) Fred Oates, Forrest Eskridge, George Blanton Jr., and Charles Webb.

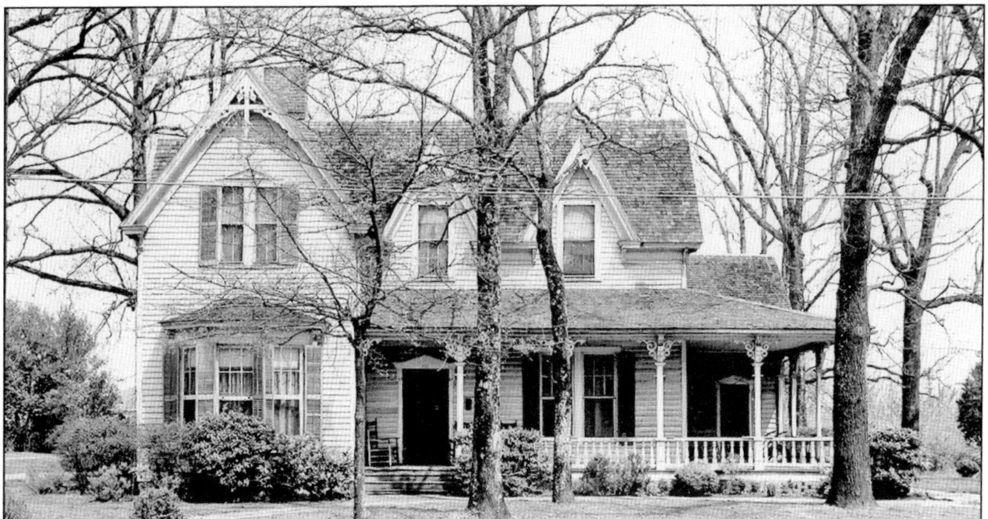

This house, located at 522 West Marion Street, was built for Burwell and Frances Blanton in 1884, as they desired to be closer to town. When Mr. Blanton later purchased the home of H.D. Lee on North Lafayette, he gave the Marion Street home to his oldest daughter, Mary Judith, and her husband, Richard Eskridge. They lived there with their son, Forrest Eskridge, until their deaths, and Forrest continued to live there until his death in 1943. This 1950 photograph reflects how the Victorian home looked before it was moved to 515 West Sumter Street by Charles and Mary Adelaide Austell.

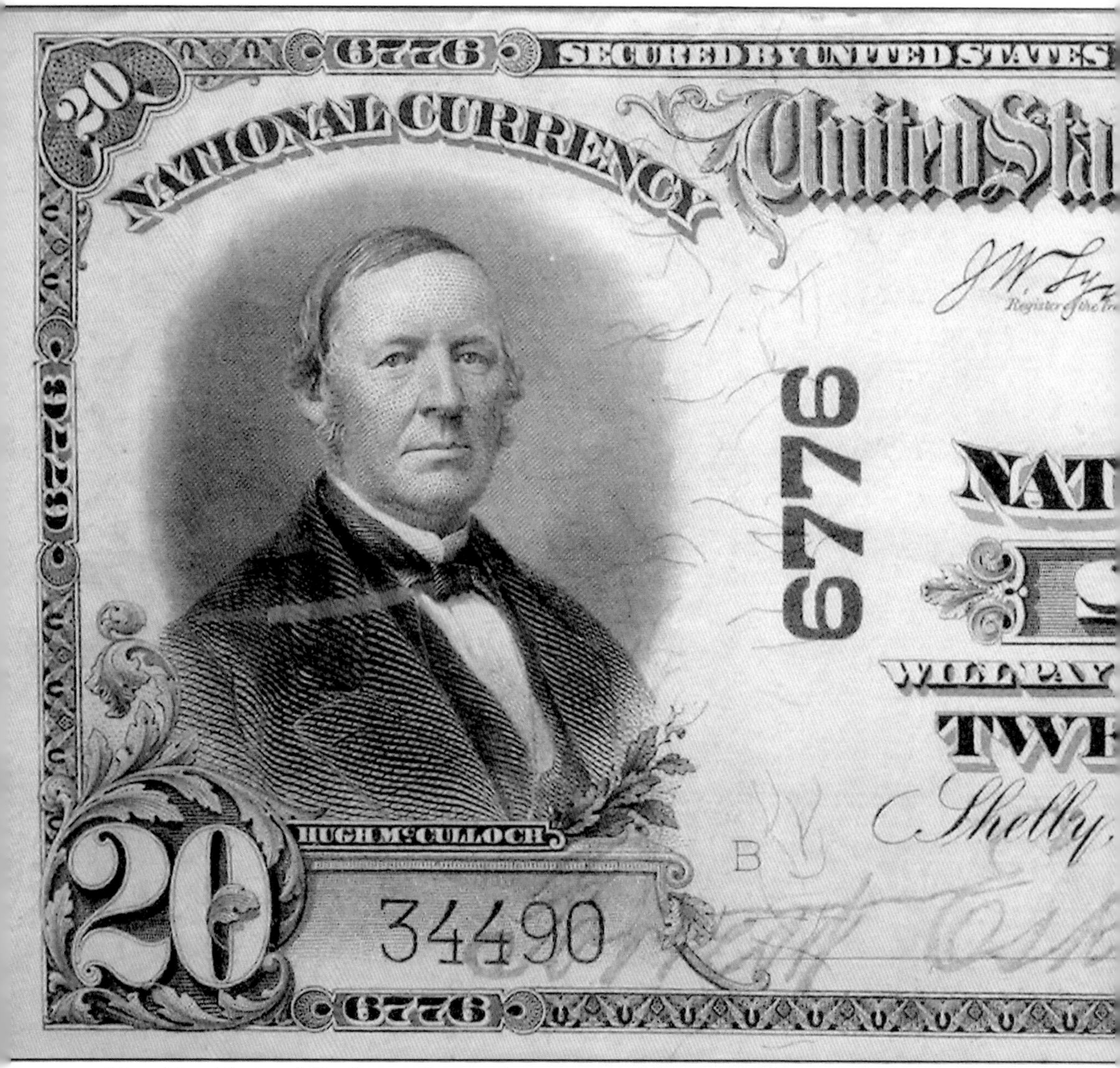

After First National Bank was chartered as a national bank in 1903, it was permitted to have the United States Treasury print national currency on its behalf. The first currency, dated April 3, 1909, was printed and shipped to the bank in denominations of $20, $10, and $5 in sheets of

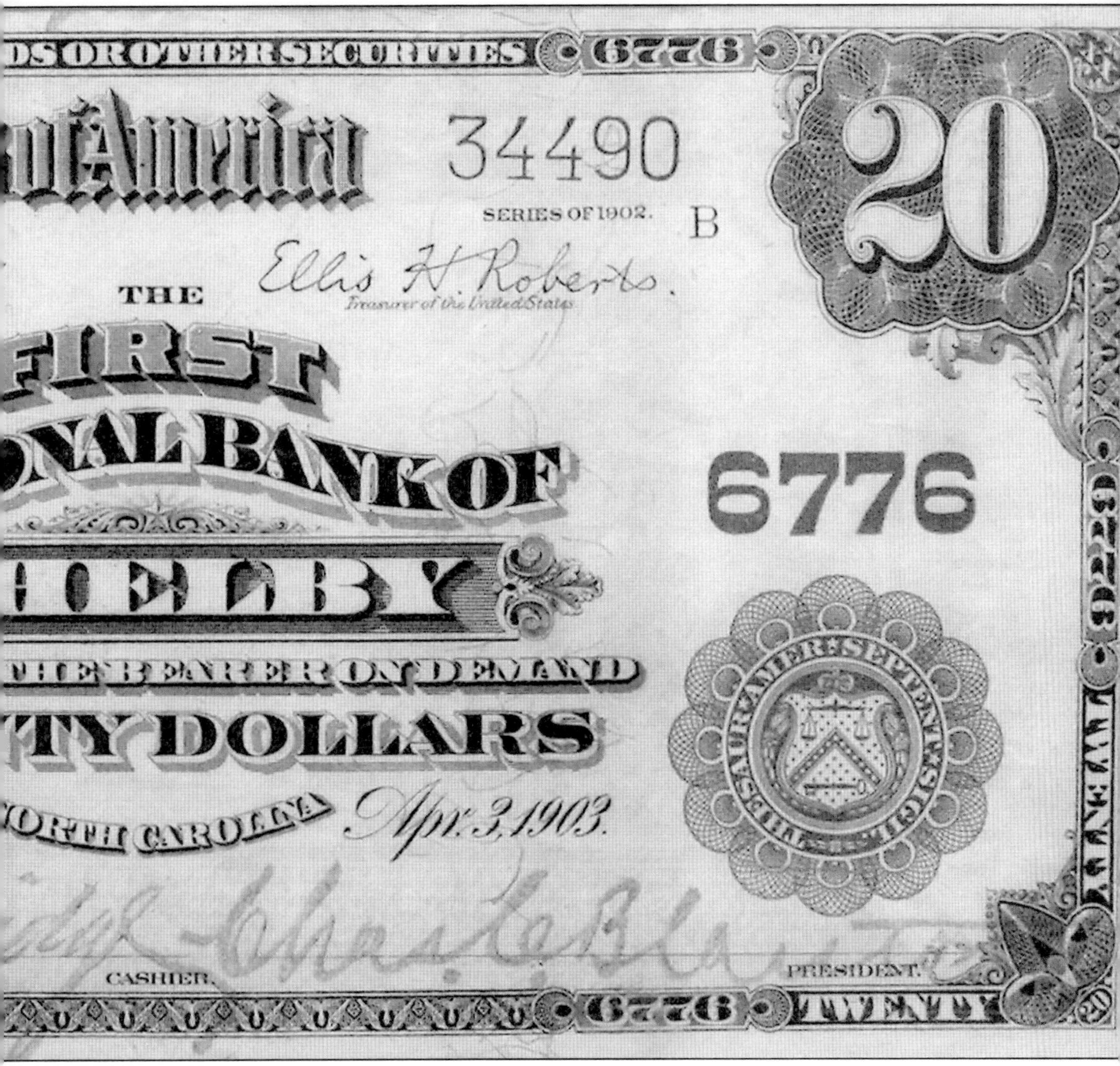

five notes per sheet. The notes were then hand-signed by Charles C. Blanton as president and Forrest Eskridge as cashier and cut into individual notes.

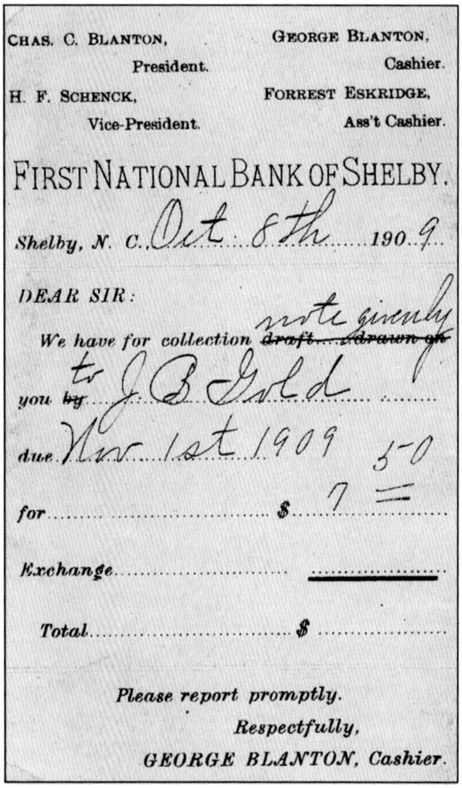

CHAS. C. BLANTON, President. GEORGE BLANTON, Cashier.
H. F. SCHENCK, Vice-President. FORREST ESKRIDGE, Ass't Cashier.

FIRST NATIONAL BANK OF SHELBY.

Shelby, N. C. Oct 8th 1909

DEAR SIR:

We have for collection note given by ~~draft drawn on~~

you to ~~by~~ J B Gold

due Nov 1st 1909 5-0

for $ 7 =

Exchange

Total $

Please report promptly.

Respectfully,

GEORGE BLANTON, Cashier.

Here is a postcard view of a First National Bank transaction dated October 8, 1909, that listed Charles Blanton, H.F. Schenck, George Blanton, and Forrest Eskridge as bank officers.

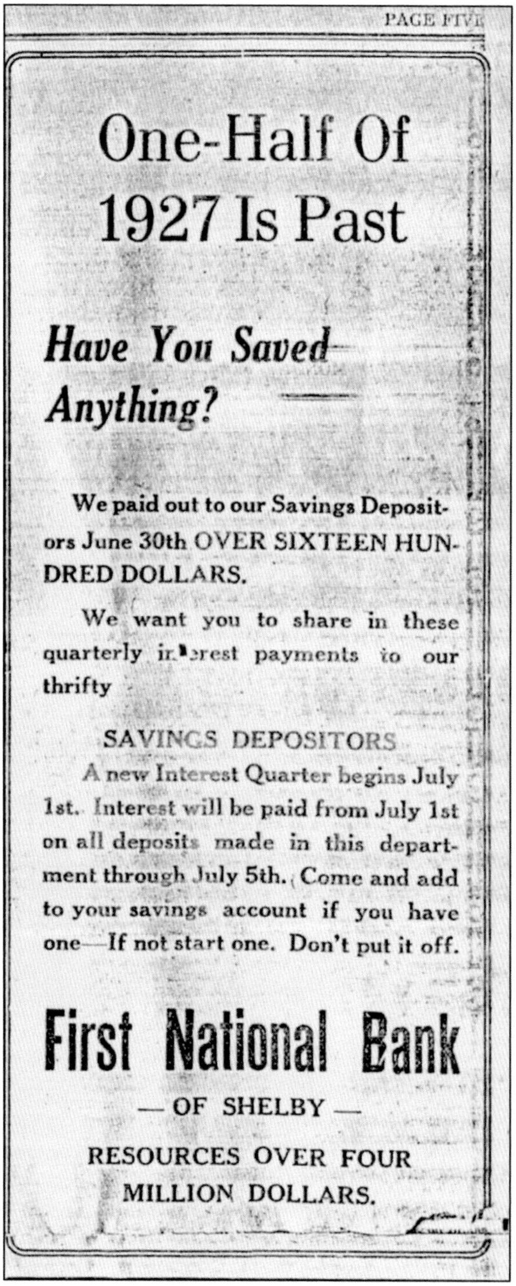

Shown here is an advertisement from the July 4, 1929 issue of the *Shelby Daily Star* encouraging patrons to save.

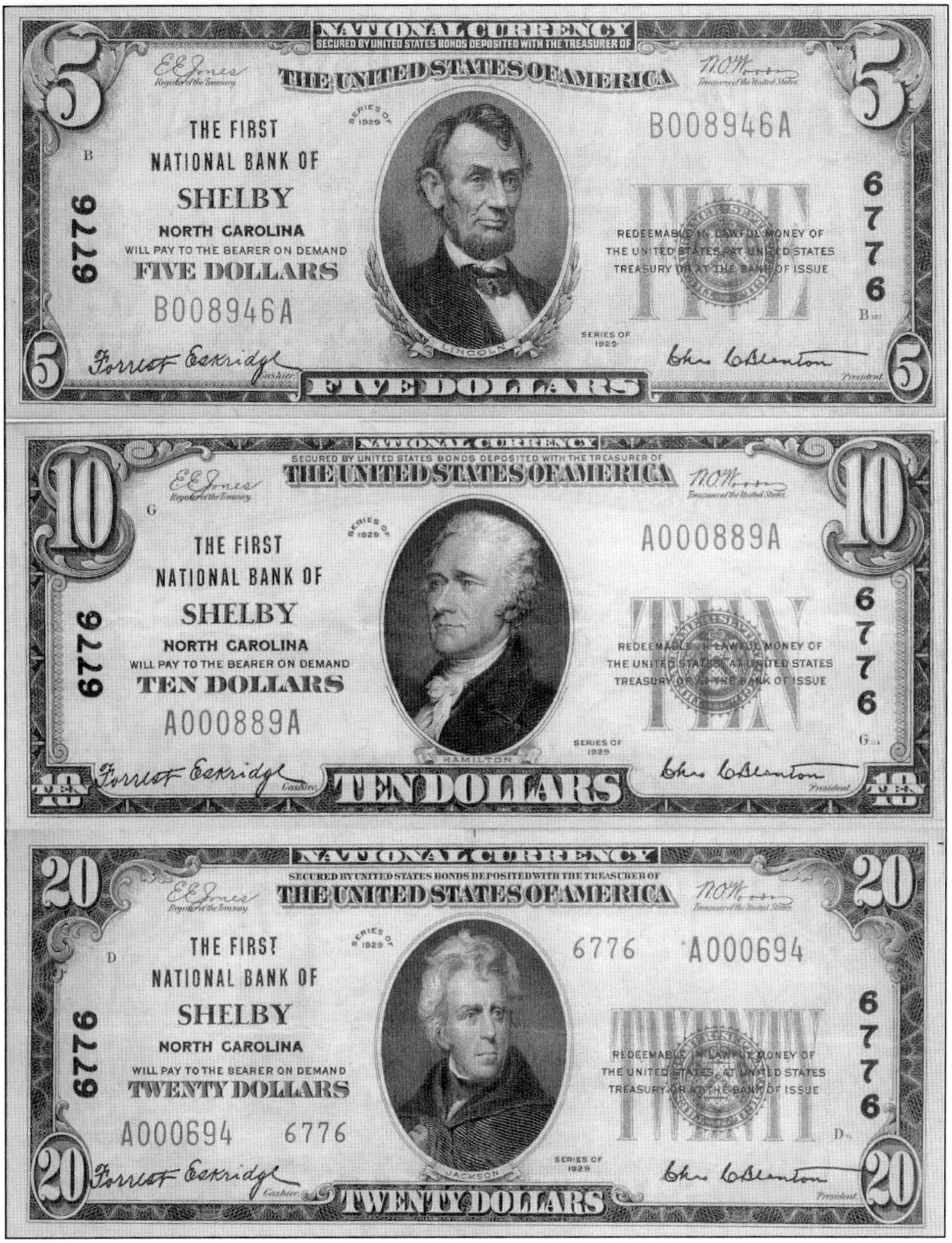

In 1929, the United States Treasury began printing current-size notes with signatures imprinted before shipping to the bank. First National continued to issue notes in denominations of $5, $10, and $20 with the preprinted signatures of Charles Blanton and Forrest Eskridge until 1935. First National Bank notes were negotiable all over the United States and its territories and payable at par. Before March of 1933, gold, silver, or bonds had backed all United States currency. After the moratorium on banks, the nation changed from the gold standard to the Federal Reserve Insurance backing up to $10,000 in deposits. In July of 1935, the national currency was declared obsolete and was supposed to be redeemed for regular currency. The total national currency printed for First National Bank of Shelby was $3,668,160. Outstanding in July 1935 was $242,700; there was $9,335 in large currency notes out.

The Cleveland Star

Extra

VOL. XXXV, No. 23 THE CLEVELAND STAR SHELBY, N. C. THURSDAY, FEB. 23, 1928 Published Monday, Wednesday, and Friday Afternoons.

3 DIE IN FIRE HERE

Central Hotel Burns; H. Kerr Gives Life

NAMES OF HOTEL GUESTS CARRIED ON THE REGISTER

Two Of Burned Men Gave Thier Lives For Others

Early Morning Blaze In Central Hotel Takes Heavy Property Toll And Three Lives. Dr. J. R. Henderson, Henry Kerr, and H. H. Carmichael Dead. Henderson And Kerr Die After Removal From Burning Building. Fire Halted At Noon.

KERR CONSCIOUS TO END; STAGG TELLS OF JUMP

Central Hotel Burns

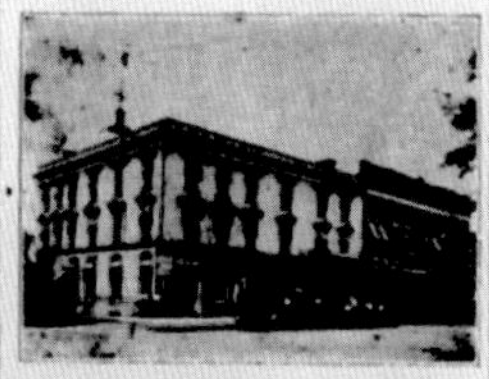

HENRY KERR GIVES LIFE FOR GUESTS IN HEROIC STYLE

Well Known Hotel Clerk Walks Burning Hallways And Knocks On Door Of Guests, Warning Them—Then Dies Of Burns In Hospital.

Two Youths Hold Hands And Escape--Unknown Hero

Waterman And Burroughs, Last Out, Tell Of Terrible Ordeal Groping In Hallway. Unknown Warned Them And Firemen Save Them.

BUSINESS FIRMS IN NEW PLACES, WILL CARRY ON

RURAL CARRIERS RENDER SERVICE

THREE EXTRAS PUT OUT BY THE STAR

$300,000 Property Loss

FIRE STARTED IN LINEN ROOM

Cage Tourney On At "Can" Tonight

Henderson Expected Death

Heart Rending Stories

Shown here is the front page of the February 23, 1928 issue of *The Cleveland Star* reporting the loss of life in the Central Hotel fire. The bank moved across Warren Street to a temporary location while the fire damage to the bank was repaired.

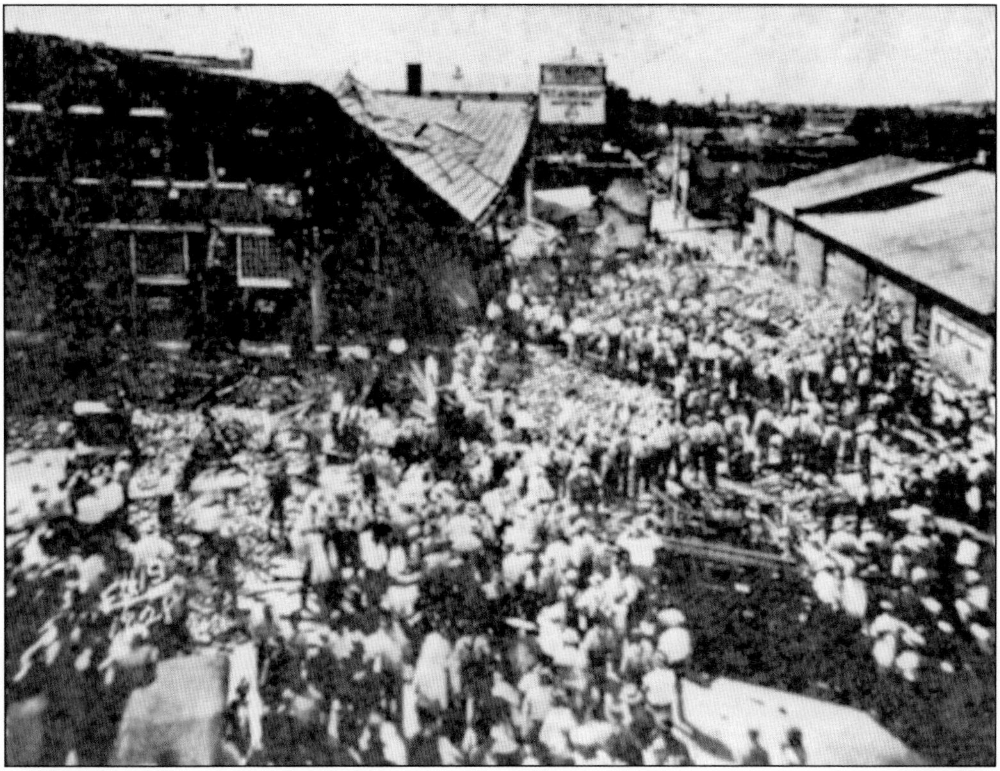

Nineteen twenty-eight was not the best of years for First National. Six months after the Central Hotel fire, the temporary housing for the bank collapsed from excavation work being made on an adjoining building. Six people were killed in the accident: customers Clyde Carpenter, Zeb Blanton, and Carl Blanton and bank employees Miss Ora Eskridge, Guy Green, and Alex Hoyle. The bank reopened two days later. Bank president Charlie Blanton declared, "the bank will reopen Friday morning for business in the storeroom formerly occupied by Stephenson's Drug Store and the monthly statements will go out on time."

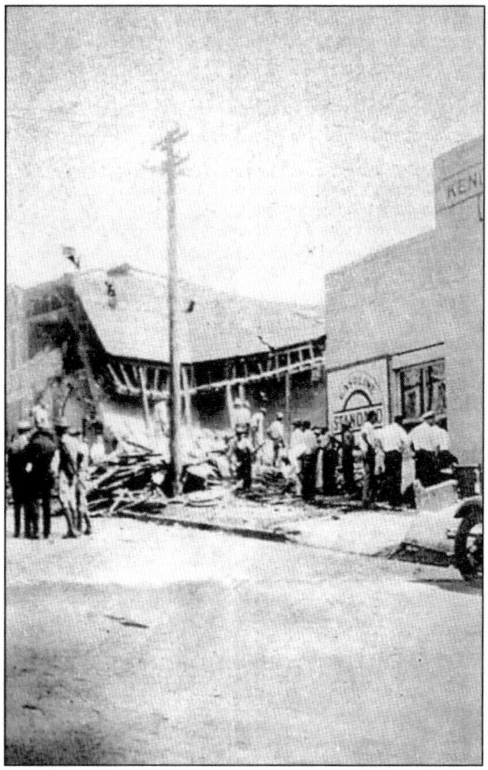

George Blanton Jr. was 14 years old when he took this photograph of the 1928 bank collapse using his Brownie camera.

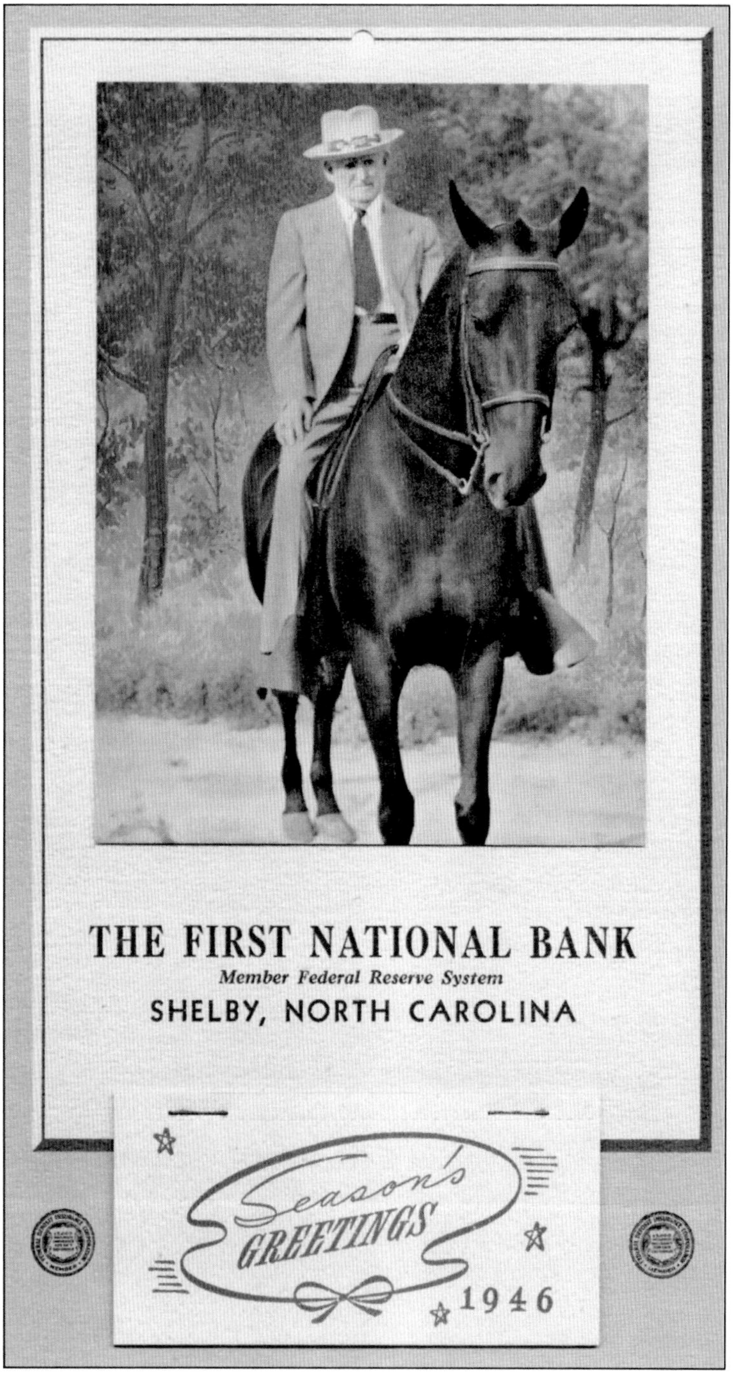

In 1946, First National Bank printed a calendar with the very familiar image of Mr. Charlie on horseback. Mr. Charlie passed away on November 24, 1944, and the calendar was produced in his memory. At Charles Blanton's funeral, Dr. Zeno Wall said, "In the passing of Charlie Blanton, we feel like saying one of the tallest trees in our forests has fallen: a tree which has for so many years offered protection, shade, and fruit for so many hearts, homes, churches, and places of business."

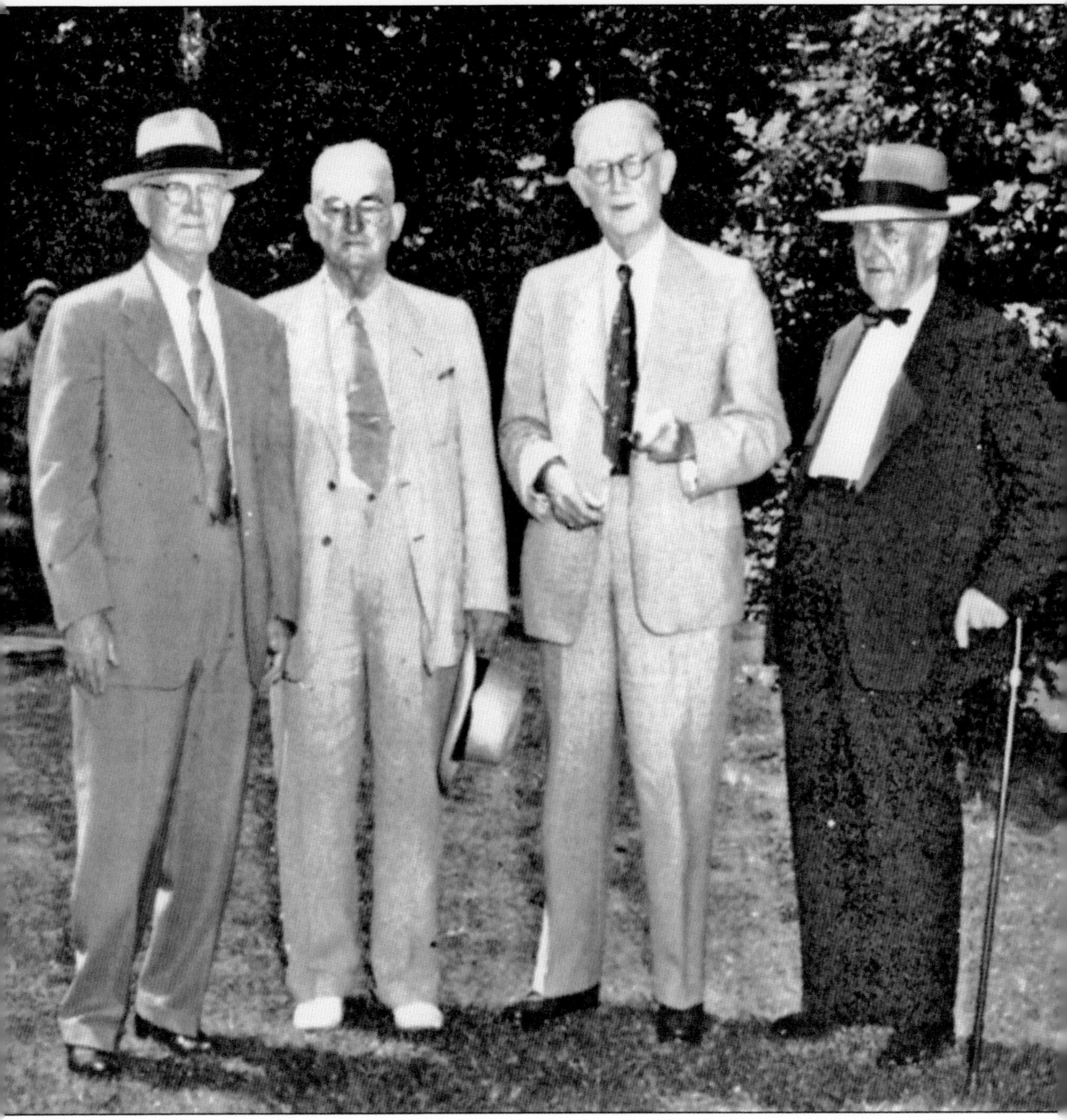

In his 1956 book, *The Living Past of Cleveland County*, Lee B. Weather wrote of the first college graduates from Cleveland County. Known as the "Four Horsemen," they are, from left to right, "George Blanton, banker and industrialist, Rev. Charles Durham, distinguished Baptist minister, E.Y. Webb, Congressman and Federal Judge, and Dr. E.B. Lattimore, physician who has ministered to the ills of Clevelanders for more than 60 years. Each of these men has lived and served full four score years; careers that are proof of the value of higher education."

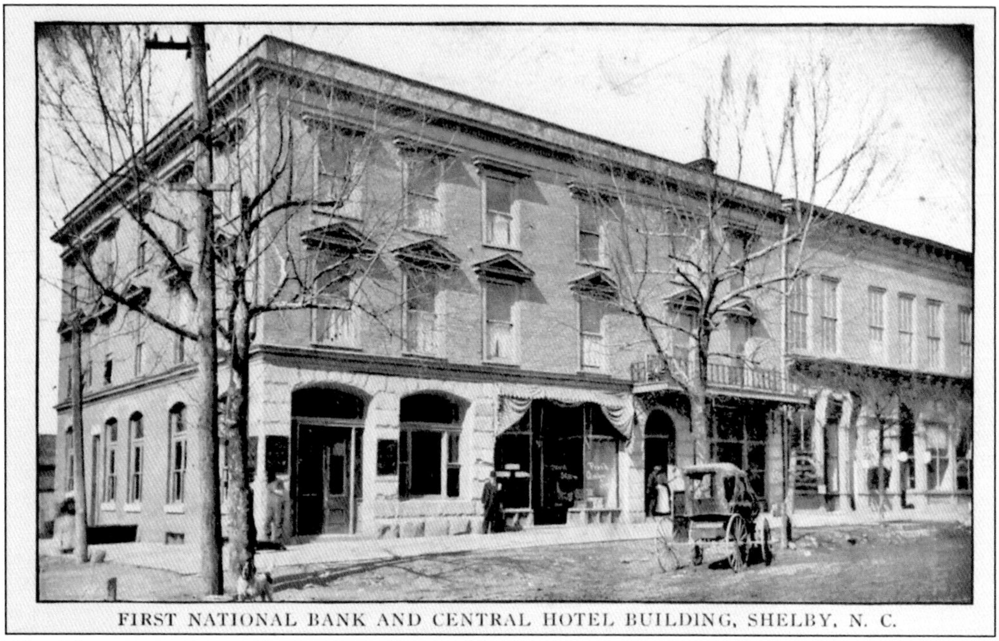

The Blantons renovated the Central Hotel building in 1905 and moved the bank from an inside office to the corner of the block. With time, the building would become known as the bank building.

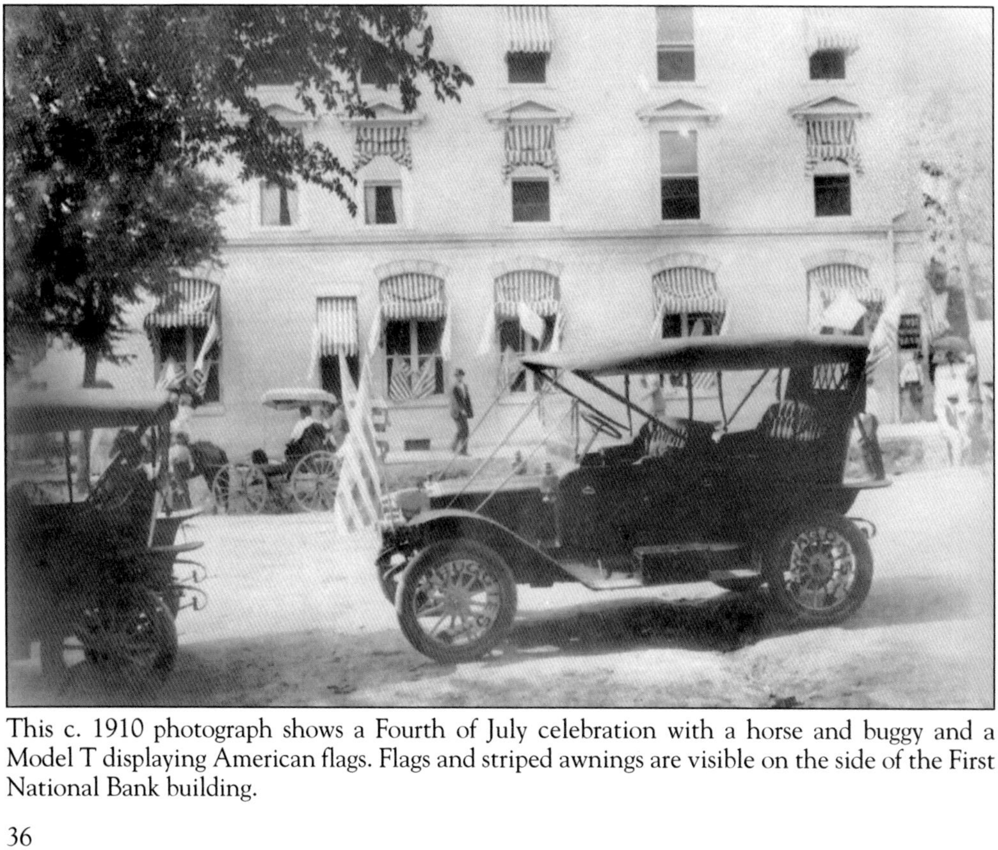

This c. 1910 photograph shows a Fourth of July celebration with a horse and buggy and a Model T displaying American flags. Flags and striped awnings are visible on the side of the First National Bank building.

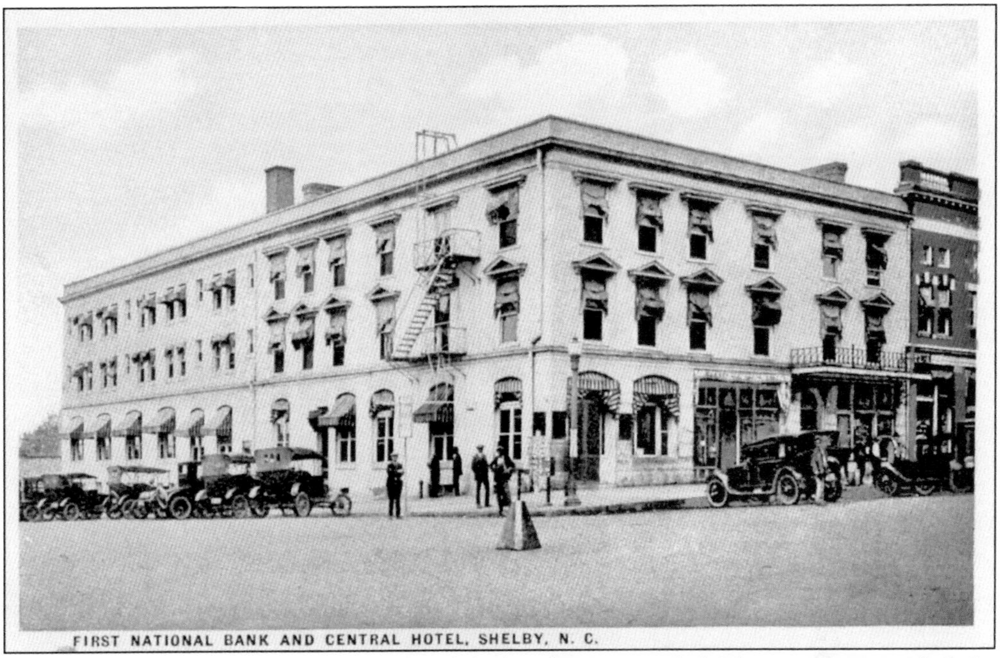

In 1911, both buildings were renovated and the hotel was expanded. The renovation included a new facade and cornice to the Blanton Building, which can be seen in this *c.* 1920 postcard.

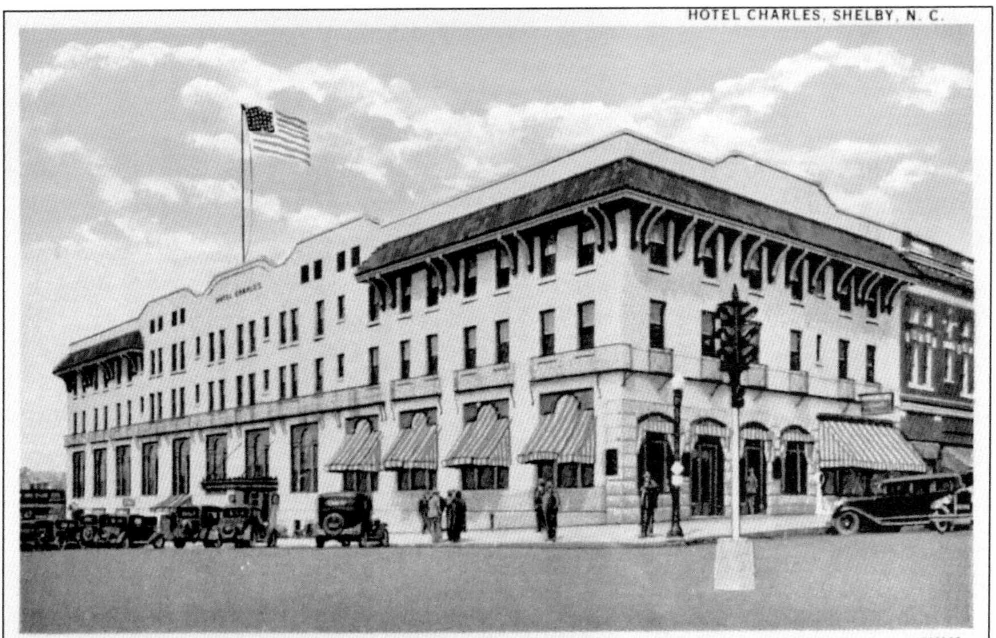

After the hotel fire in 1928, the building was once again rebuilt and the hotel renamed the Hotel Charles in honor of Charles Blanton. This 1930s view shows the latest addition to the expanded bank building.

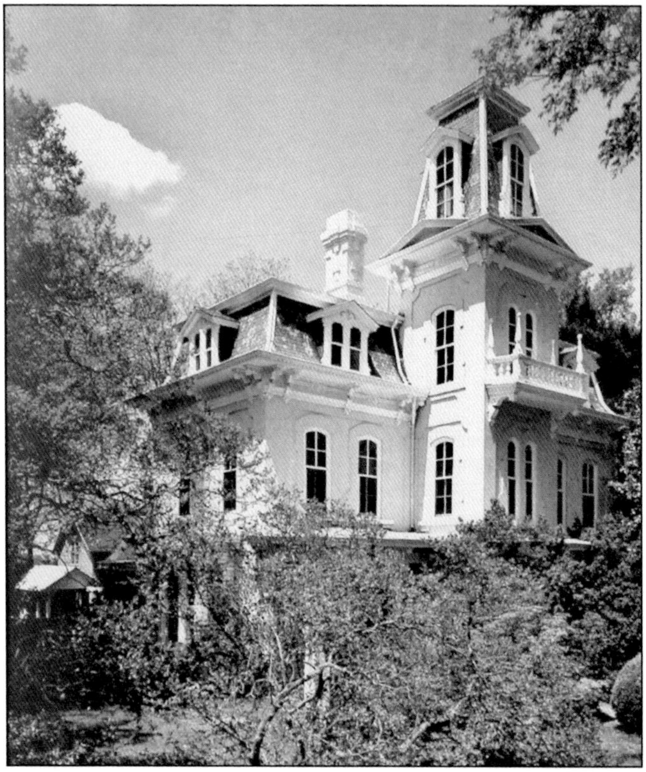

The Bankers House at 319 North Lafayette Street is easily the most recognizable home in Shelby. Jesse Jenkins built the Second Empire–design house in 1876. Jenkins later sold the home to H.D. Lee, who subsequently sold it to Burwell Blanton, who lived there with his second wife, Pattie Ramsey, and his two sons, Charles and George Sr. From 1937, George Blanton Jr. and his wife, Nancy Dicks Blanton, lived there. It is still the home of Mrs. Blanton. This means that all six presidents of First National, from Jessie Jenkins to George Blanton Jr., have lived in this house. To the left of the house you can see the horse barn and well house. (Courtesy of Mrs. George Blanton Jr., *Architectural Perspectives of Cleveland County, North Carolina.*)

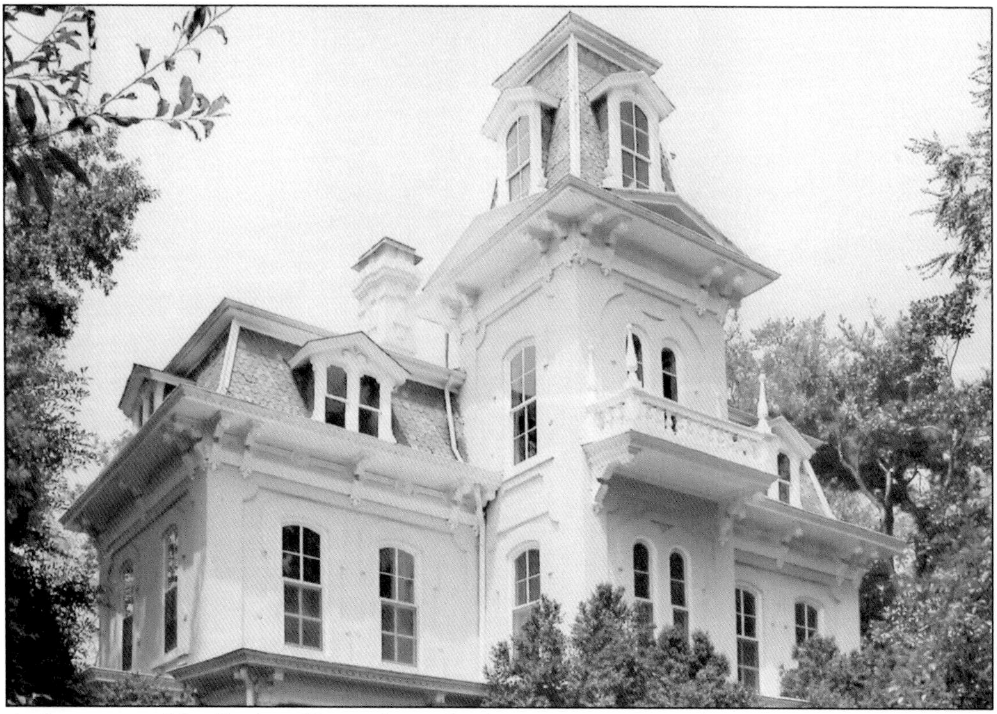

A closer view of the Bankers House shows the three-story tower on the front center of the house. (Courtesy of Tommy Forney, *Architectural Perspectives of Cleveland County, North Carolina.*)

A close-up view shows the intricate detail in the woodworking of the Bankers House. (Courtesy of George Blanton Chapell, *Architectural Perspectives of Cleveland County, North Carolina.*)

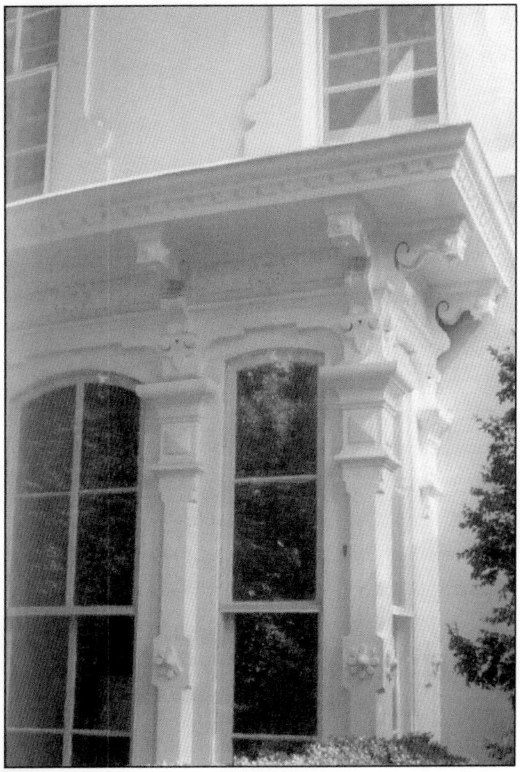

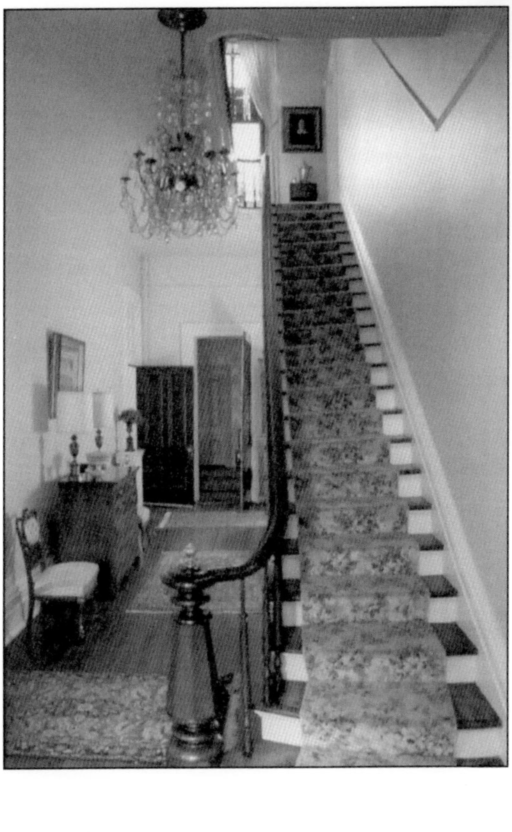

This interior view shows the majestic stairway in the front entrance to the Bankers House. (Courtesy of George Blanton Chapell, *Architectural Perspectives of Cleveland County, North Carolina.*)

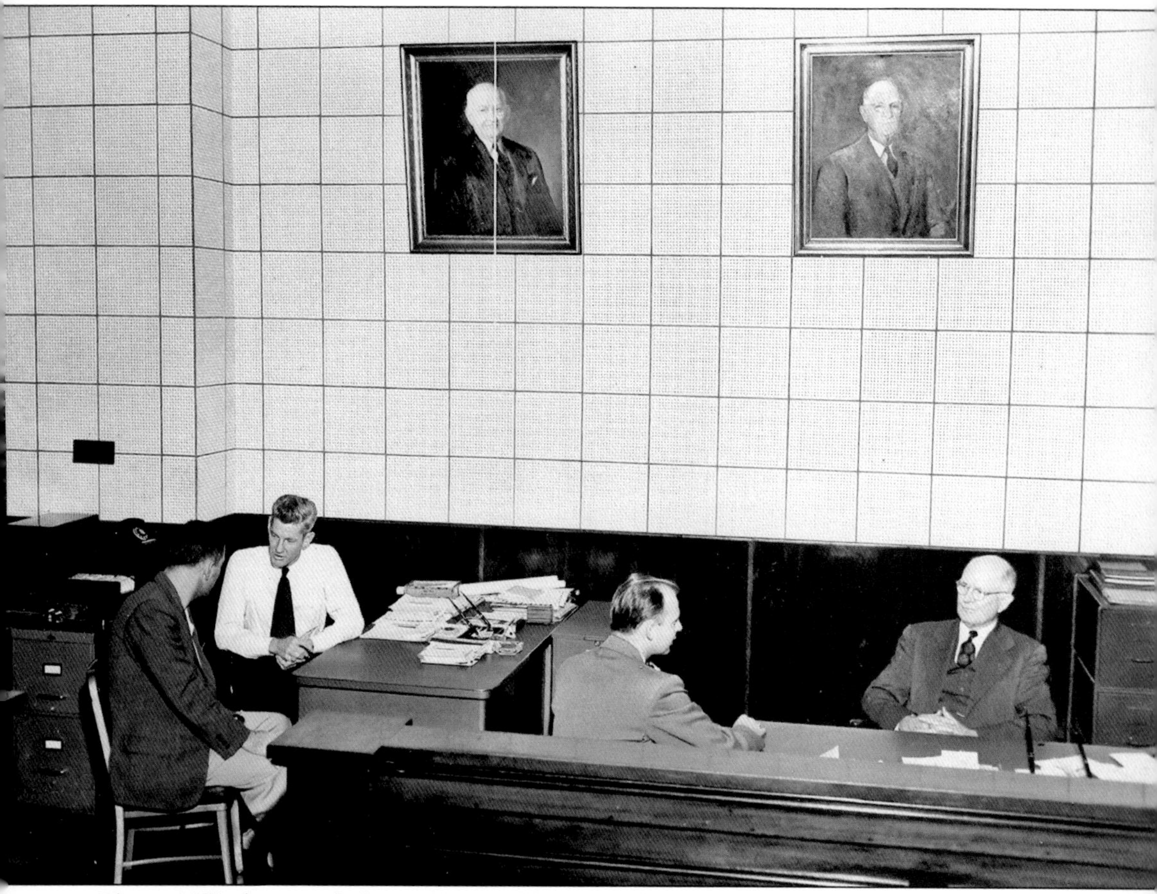

This c. 1950 photograph depicts George Blanton Jr. (second from left) meeting with a customer alongside his father, George Sr. (right) in their open office space in the bank lobby. The two gentleman bankers served a combined 128 years in the banking industry, spanning from 1895 to 2000. On the wall above are portraits of Charles Blanton and George Blanton Sr.

Two

BANK HISTORY *1947–2004*

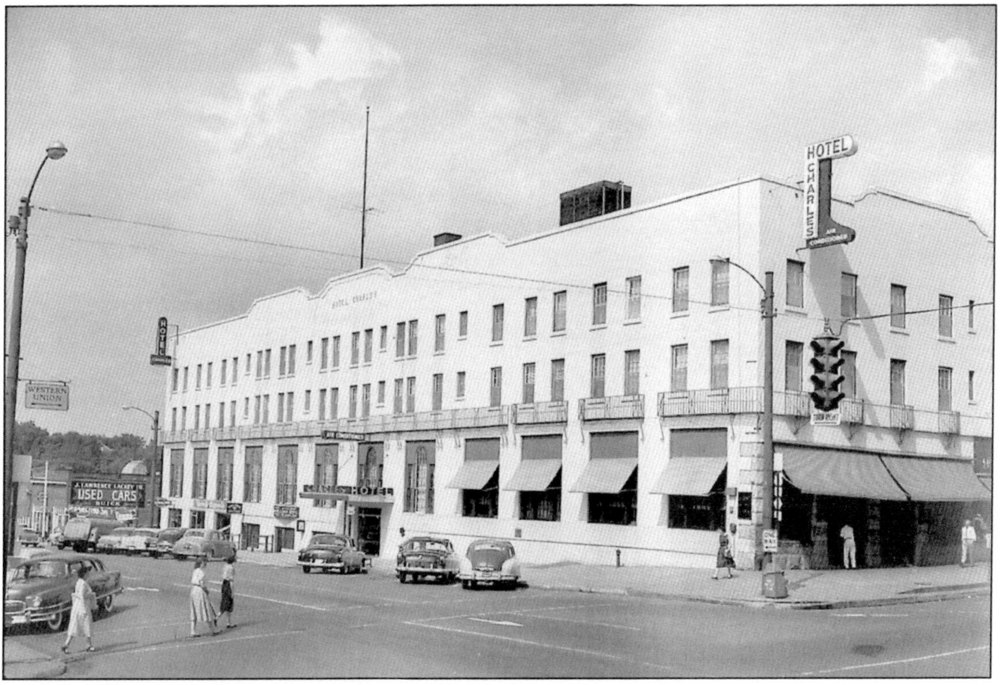

As World War II ended in 1945, the world and towns like Shelby were entering a new era. First National Bank emerged from the World War II era as Shelby's predominant financial institution. This c. 1950 photo shows the bank and the Hotel Charles as they appeared at the time. The awnings covering the bank's windows were characteristic of the time. (Courtesy of *Architectural Perspectives of Cleveland County, North Carolina* and the Lloyd Hamrick Collection.)

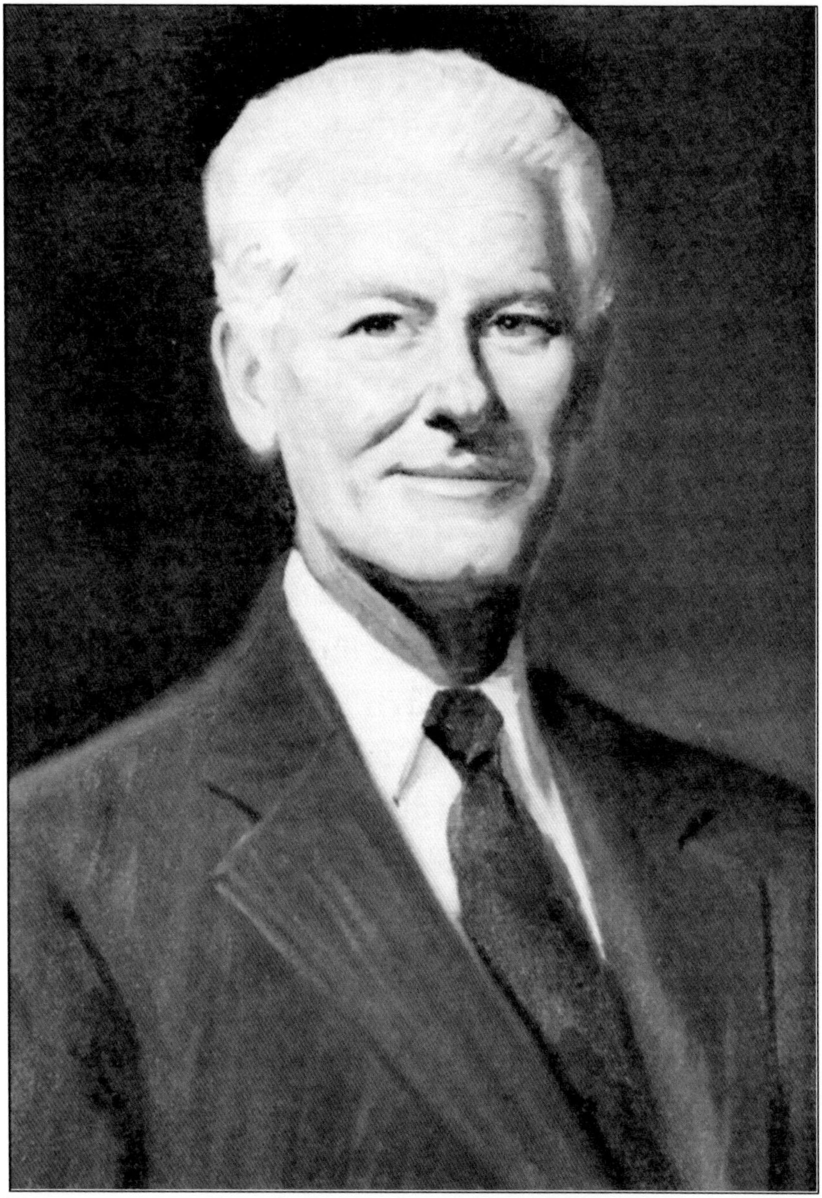

George Blanton Sr. was ready to turn over part of the leadership reins to his only son, George Blanton Jr. In 1947, George Jr. became president of the bank at age 32. He was said to be the youngest president of a national bank in the United States at that time. As the bank continued to grow in assets and deposits and in services provided to the people of Cleveland County, its need for space resulted in expansion into new areas of the building, which would continue for several decades. In the mid-1940s, the bookkeeping department was moved under the bank lobby where there had been a boardroom. Vaults were added in bookkeeping under the two vaults in the main lobby. A ladies' lounge was also added. In 1946, the bank had established the first separate Consumer Loan Department in the state of North Carolina, with Flay Gardner as its head. The new department and a new boardroom were located under the hotel lobby in an area that had been built for a barbershop and that was later used for a savings and loan. Even with these additions, First National had no more than 35 employees in 1950.

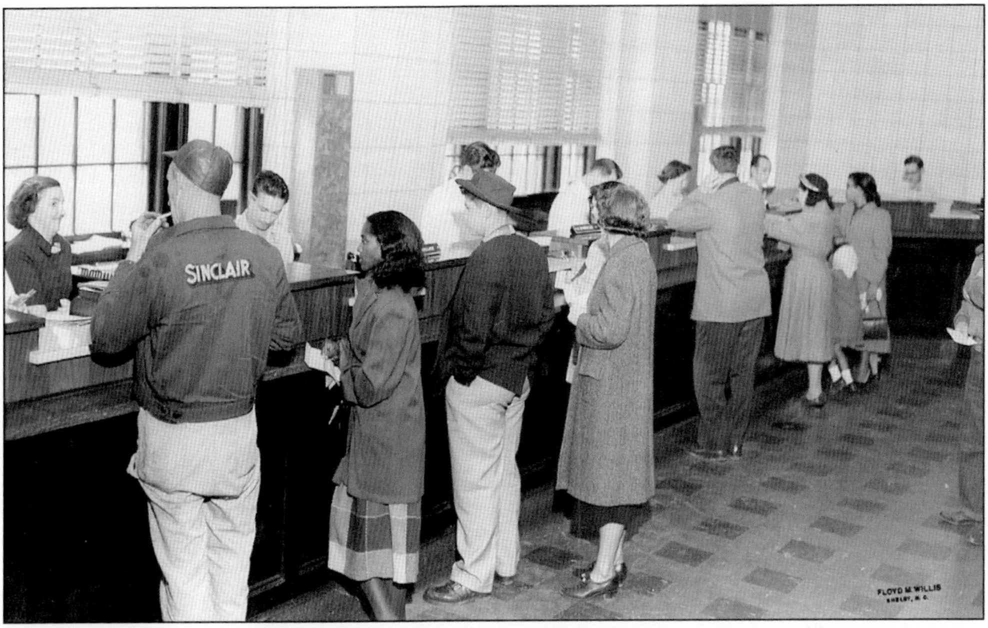

This Floyd Willis photo of the teller line, *c.* 1950, is the first of several that give us a look at the people of First National. From left to right behind the counter are Virginia White (bookkeeper), Max Wallace, Ralph Roberts, Hardin Lee, Evelyn Ingle Hopper, Graham Greene, and Fred Morehead (tellers).

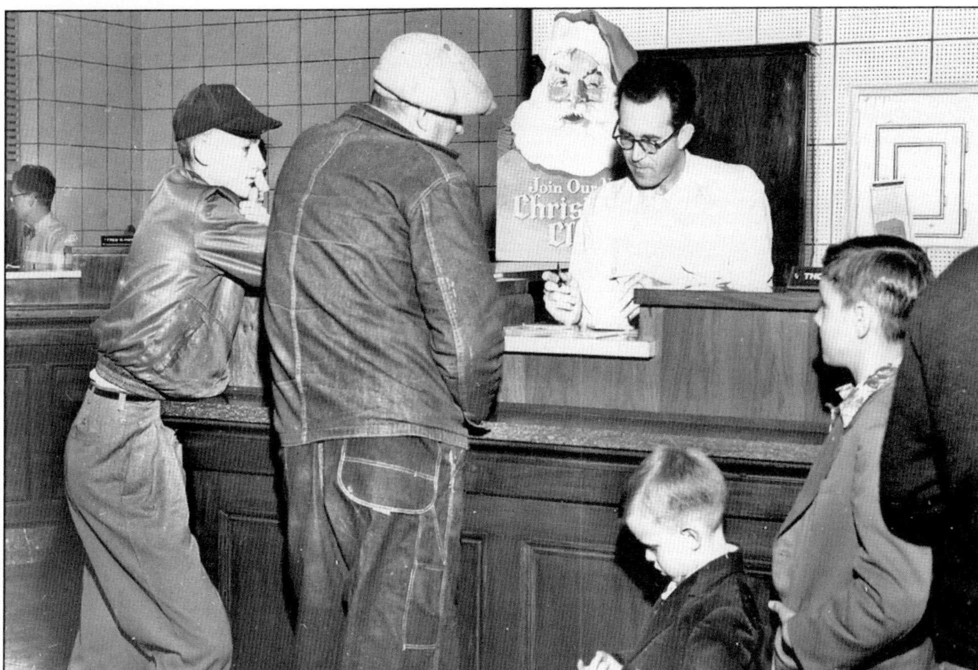

The bank had a program for years known as the Christmas Club. Customers could deposit a set amount each week and get their coupon book stamped. In November, Christmas Club members would receive a check in time for Christmas shopping. Children could deposit as little as 25¢ or 50¢ per week. Here, Tom Porter helps a customer.

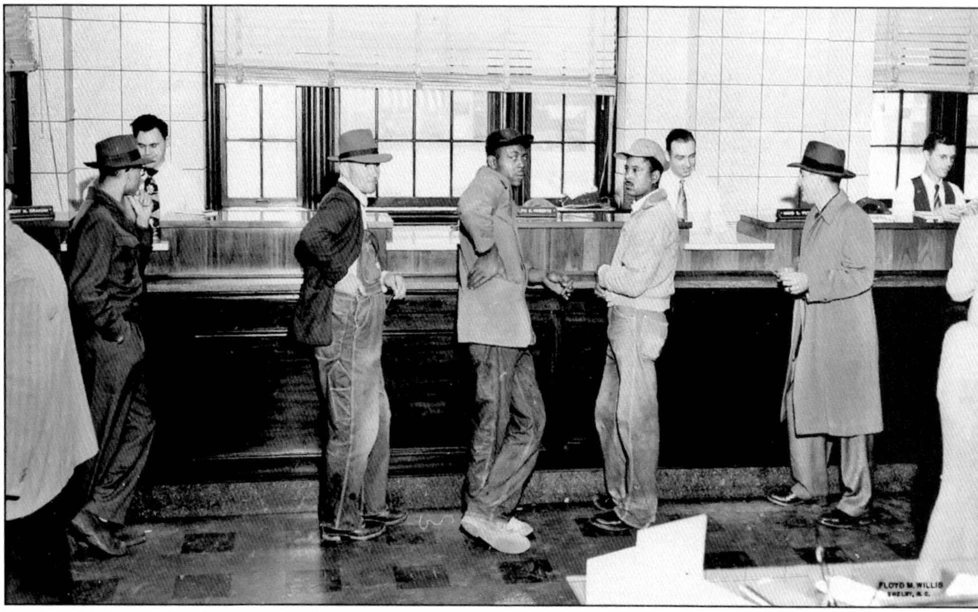

Tellers Robert Graham, David Putnam, and Vaughn Whitaker, pictured here from left to right behind the counter, serve a group of typical working men. Based on the social customs of that day, men were more frequent than women as customers. To the far right, the customer in the top coat in Ben E. Hendricks. The windows to Warren Street are still open. They would be covered from the 1960 renovation until they were reopened in the 1998 remodeling.

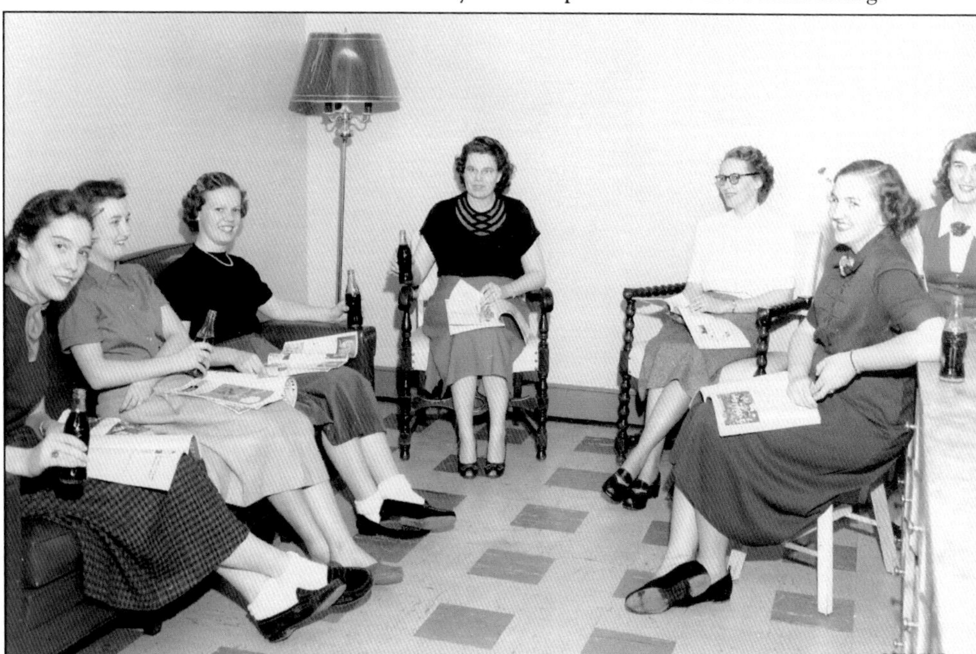

The newly added ladies' lounge seemed to be a popular place for a coke. Seen here, from left to right, are Barbara Tiddy Elliott, Iva Blankenship, Mary Ann Teele Hendrick, Mabel Jones Elliott, Sue Blanton, Virginia White, and Libby Watson. Mabel Elliott is still working at First National in 2004.

One service that was already in place by 1950 was the night depository. Pictured here is First National customer Gerald Morgan. Morgan is representative of the businessmen who depended on his hometown bank. Mr. Morgan operated the Shelby Supply Co. on North Lafayette and the Shelby Farmers Minor League Baseball team.

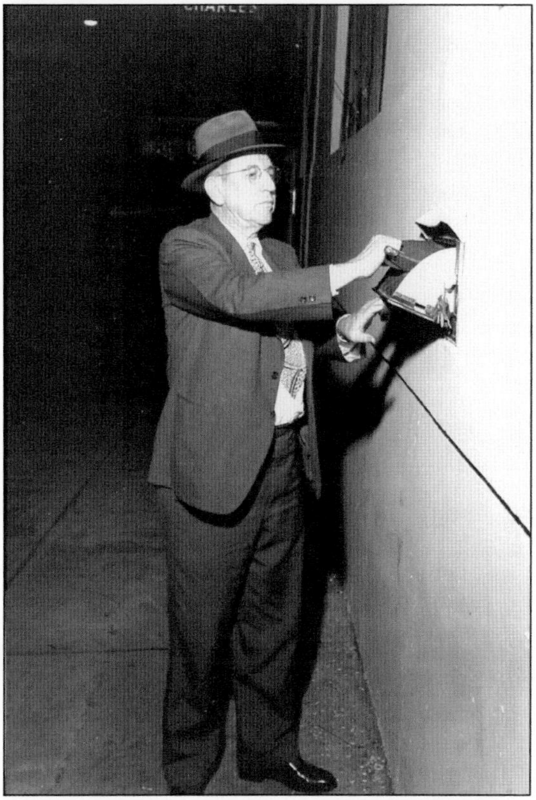

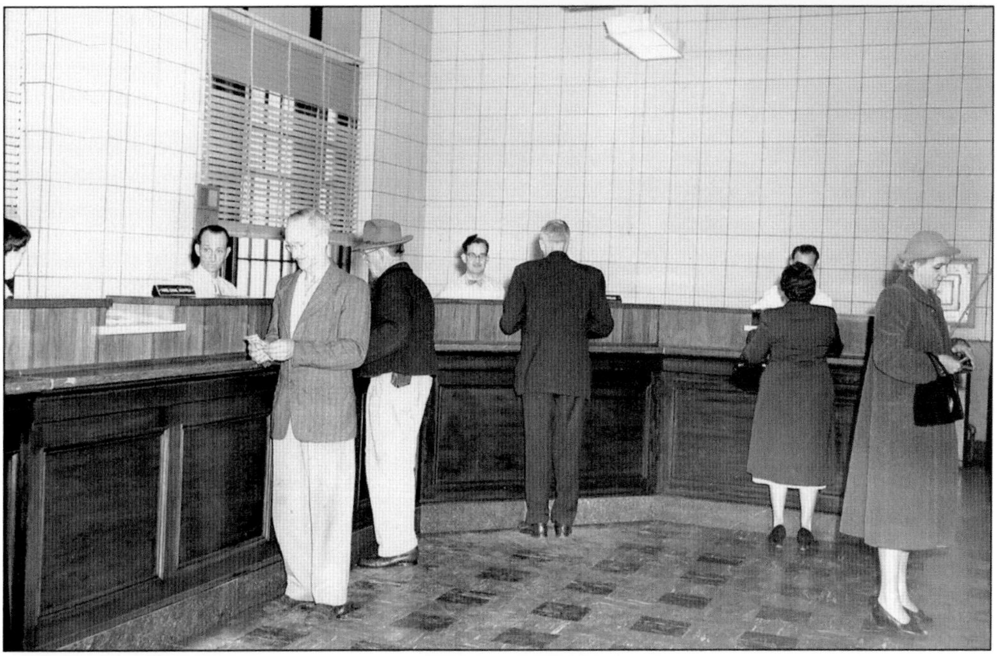

This view of the teller line shows, from left to right behind the counter, tellers Evelyn Ingle Hopper, Graham Greene, Fred Morehead, and Tom Porter (hidden). In a day when most transactions were done at the bank, an abundance of tellers was needed.

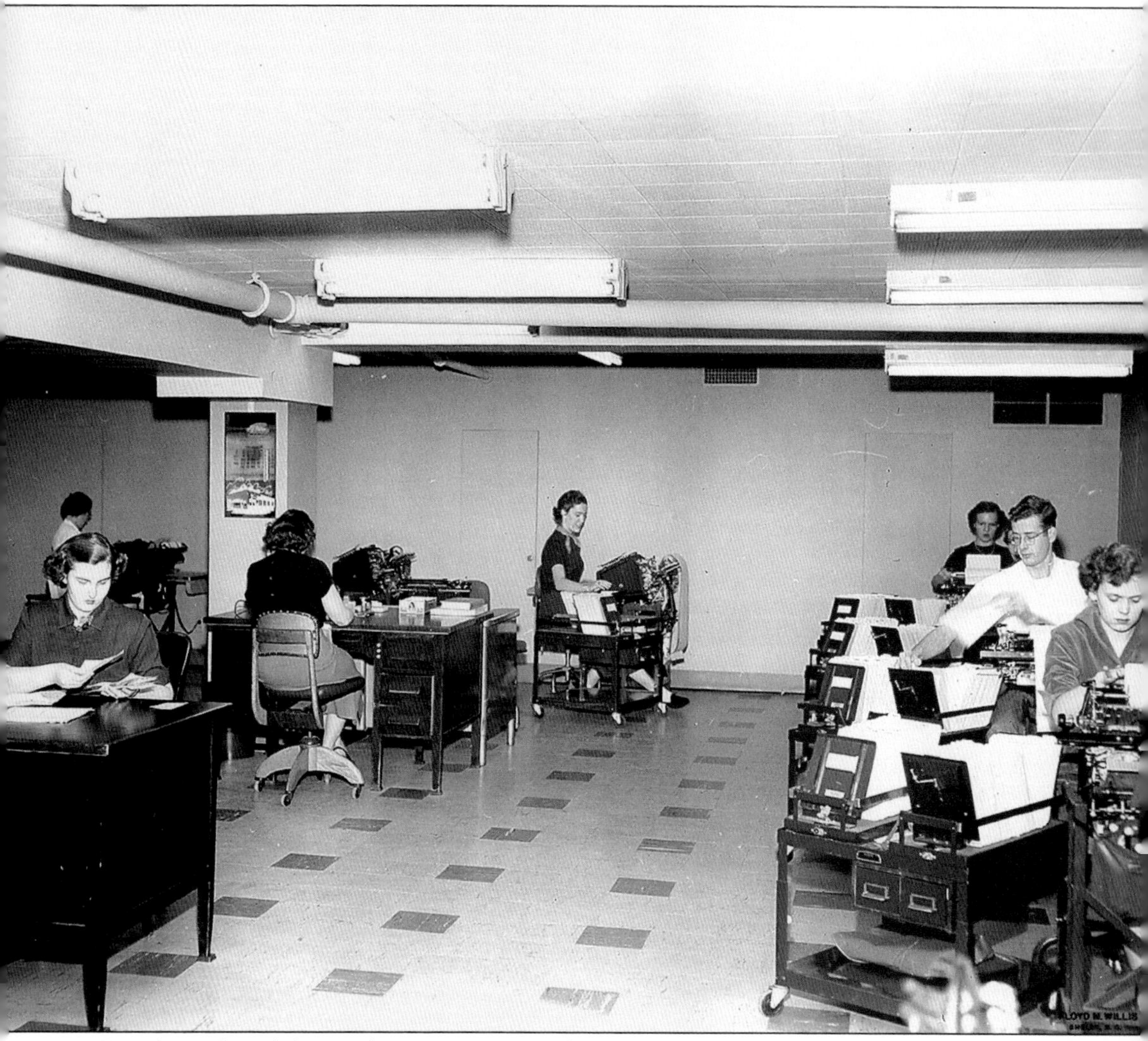

Seen here, from left to right, are Virginia White, Martha Lee Clark (in background), Mabel Jones Elliott, Barbara Tiddy Elliott, Mary Ann Teele Hendricks, Jim Crowder, and Jo Propst in the operations area of the bank. The technology of over a half-century ago can be seen in this photo. Senior Vice Pres. Bobby G. Smith, who began his career at First National in 1952, stated that the greatest change during his tenure has been technology. He and Mabel Jones Elliott, whose service dates from the 1940s, describe a system in which checks were examined individually, entered on ledgers, and ultimately printed on monthly statements. People used counter checks. The bank called regular customers who did not have funds to cover a check. Mr. Smith points out that although computers have replaced old machines and ledgers, people's needs have not really changed. Customers' feelings are still important. Calling people by name is important. Bank employees still need to give a personal touch and be interested in the customers and their needs.

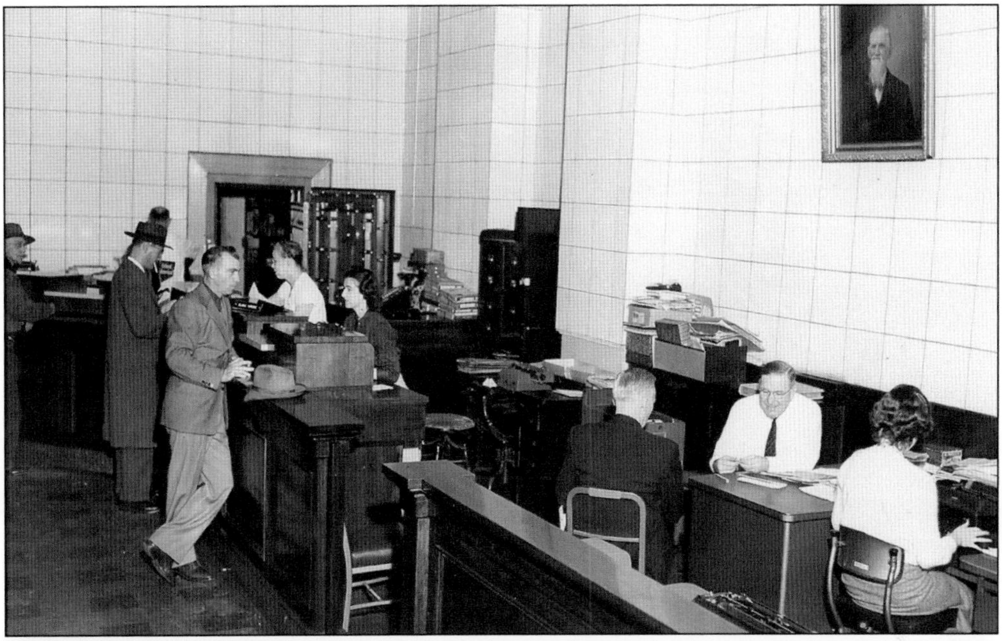

This c. 1950 photo shows longtime bank employee Clarence Mull seated at his desk helping a customer. Mr. Mull was in the bank in 1928 when the building collapsed. He was pulled from the rubble, assumed to be dead, and put on a flatbed truck to be taken to Palmer Mortuary. On the journey, he moved, and the medics realized that he was actually alive. Longtime teller Clara Greene is seen talking with a customer.

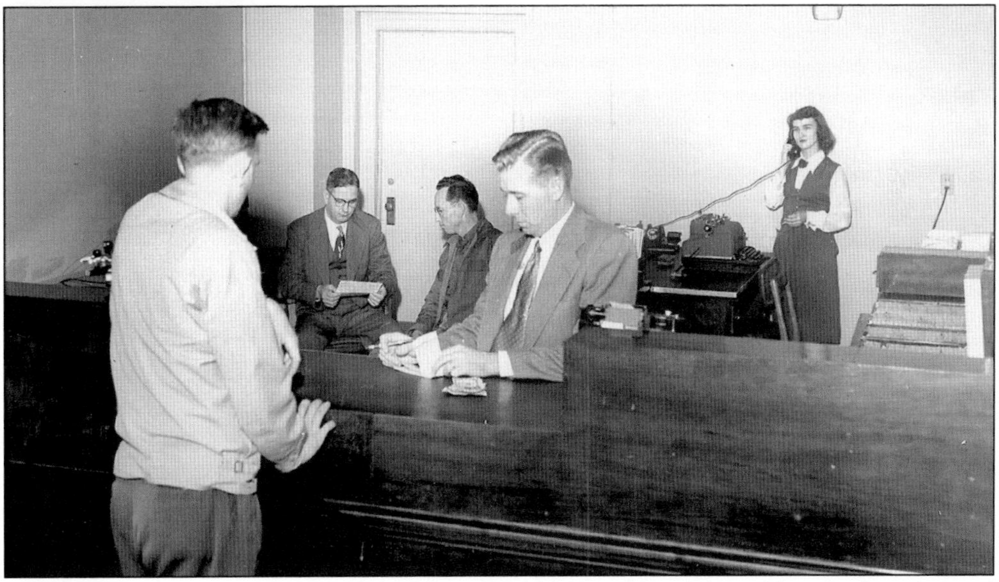

This picture from the same era shows three First National employees. Flay Gardner (second from left) is talking to a customer. Emmett Matthews is on the teller line (second from right), and Libby Watson (far right) is in the background. One must remember that the teller line and all the desks with bank officials were all in the area that is today the lower level or lobby. The "platform" area to the right of the main entrance was added to the bank around 1960 when the Cleveland Drug Co. relocated across the street on West Warren.

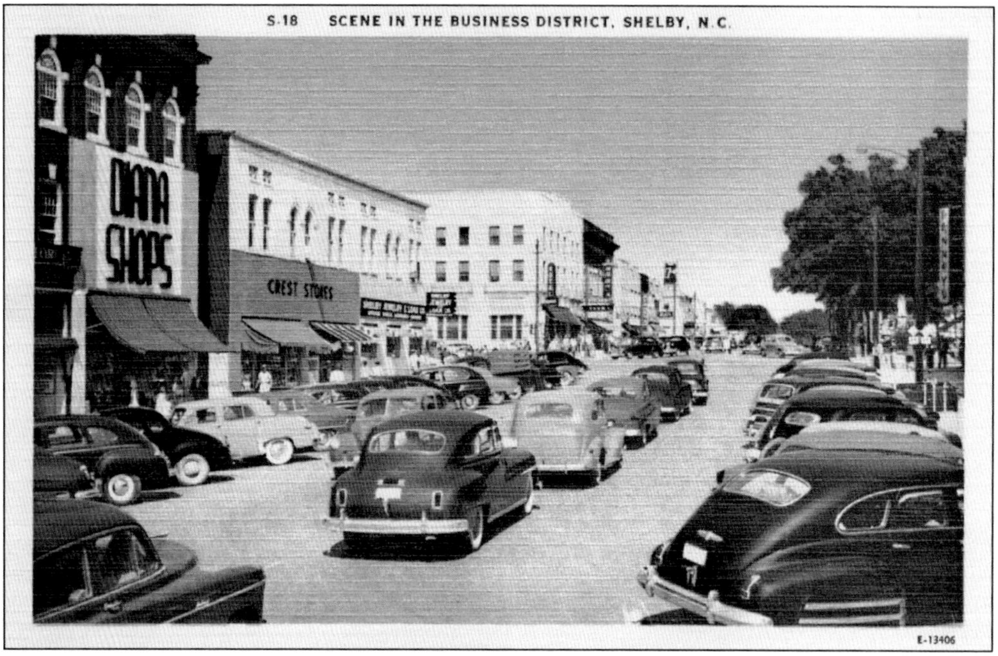

These two photos show the external environment of the 1950s. This Asheville Post Card Co. postcard shows Lafayette Street looking north, *c.* 1950. The bank building, with its awnings and Hotel Charles sign, can be seen. In the middle of the card, the people, the traffic, and the parked cars show the busy nature of Uptown Shelby in those days.

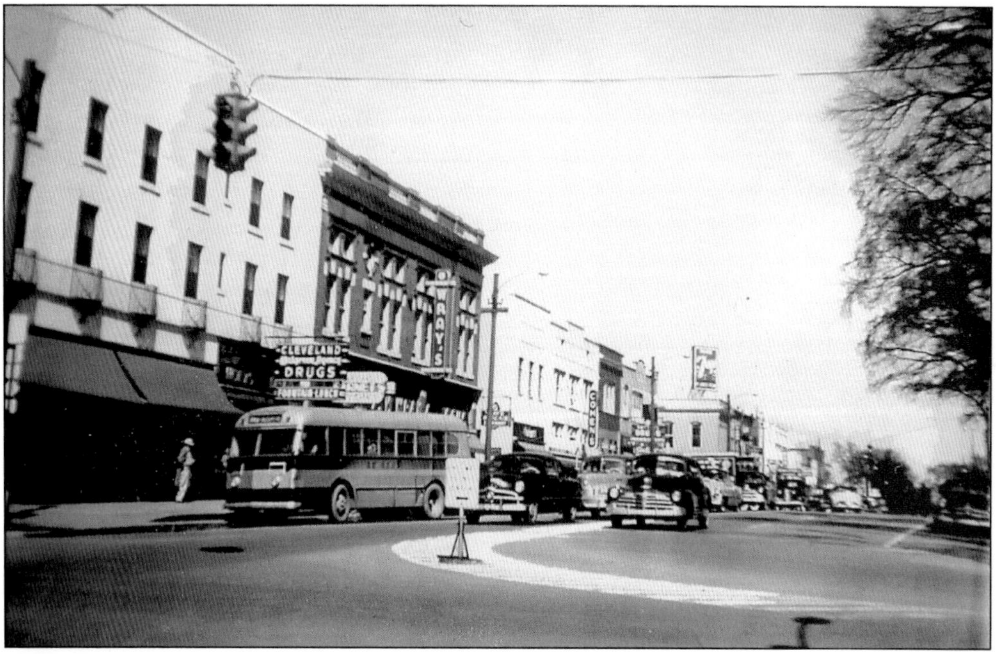

This clear front view of the bank reveals the two building that First National occupies today. Only part of the white (Charles) building was occupied by the bank. The photo shows the one-way traffic around the old courthouse that lasted for several years. The bus was a part of a long-gone bus system that transported County residents to Shelby to shop.

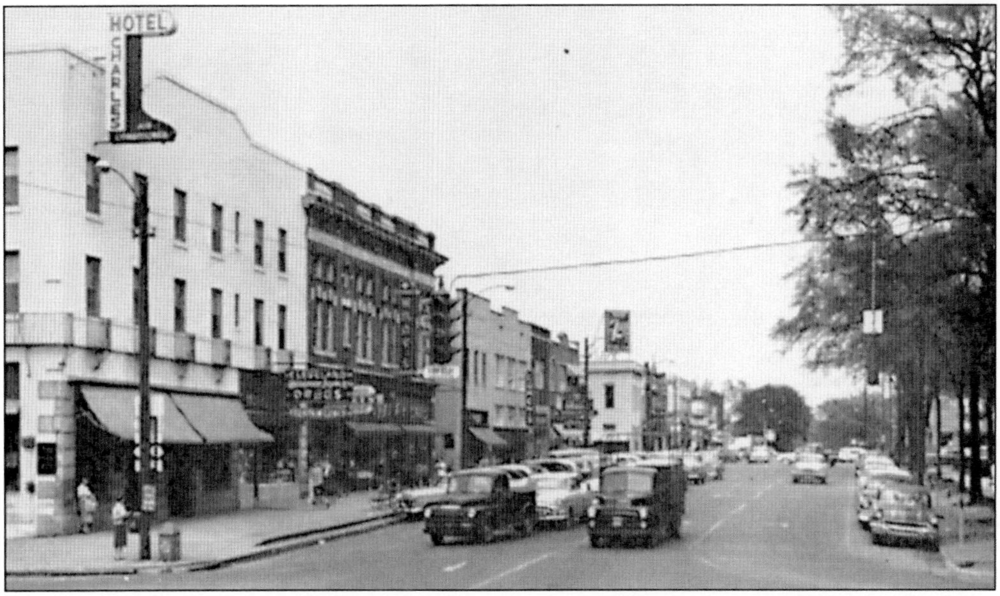

This 1956 picture from Lee B. Weathers's history of Cleveland County clearly shows the whole block that the bank occupies today. The darker building (the Blanton Building) was occupied by A.V. Wray and Six Sons, which for decades was one of Shelby's leading uptown department stores. Between Wray's and the bank, there was a jewelry store and the Cleveland Drug Co., long a gathering place for political discussion.

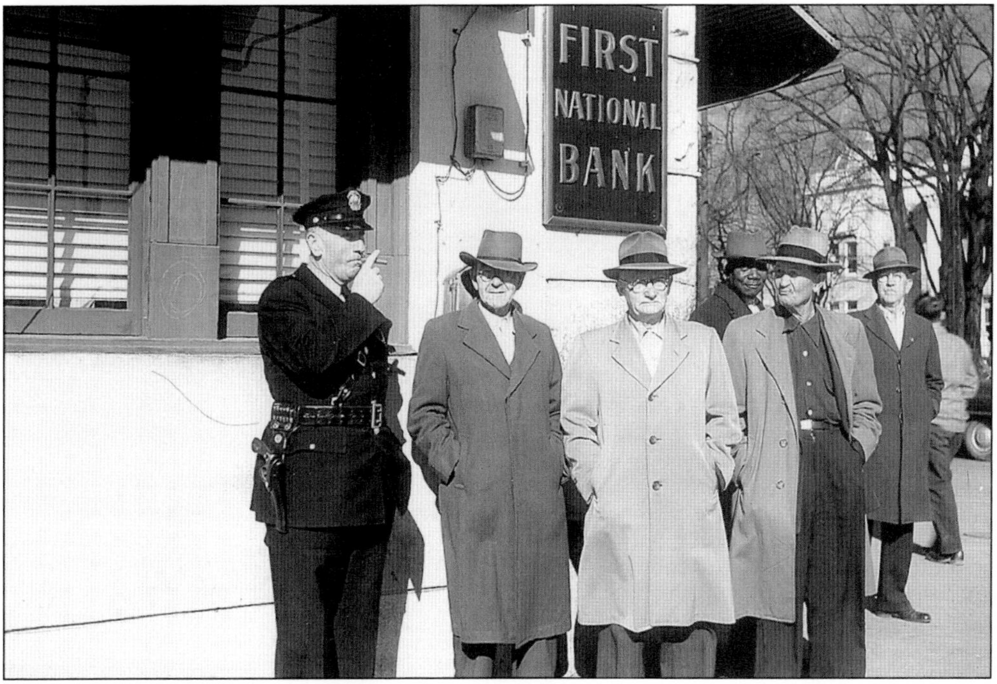

This photo shows a common sight in the 1950s. The bank corner at Lafayette and Warren was a gathering place for men. Officer Paul Stamey was an institution in the Shelby Police Department. On the wall of the bank was a telephone that connected officers on the corner to the police department at city hall.

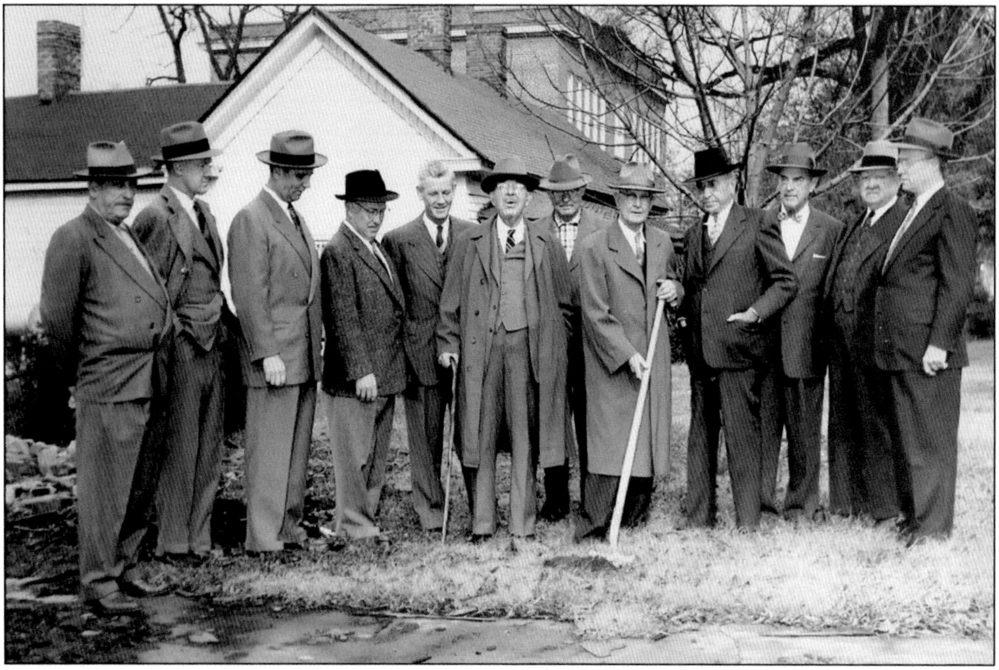

For three-quarters of a century, First National Bank had one location—the corner of Lafayette and Warren. Now that branch banking was allowed, First National Bank was proud to open its first teller service branch, South Branch, in 1956. The new location was at 526 South Lafayette Street. This ground-breaking picture from December 1955 shows a "who's who" of Shelby and Cleveland County. (One might note that no women were pictured in that different era.) The men, shown from left to right, are A.A. Ramsey (contractor); L. Pegram Holland (architect); directors Don Carpenter and C.S. Mull; bank president George Blanton Jr.; directors J.F. Roberts, Tom Cornwell, and George Blanton Sr. (also chairman of the board); R.T. LeGrand Sr.; Lee B. Weathers; O.M. Mull; and J.R. Dover Jr. The tall building behind the house is the Lafayette Elementary School, which has since been demolished.

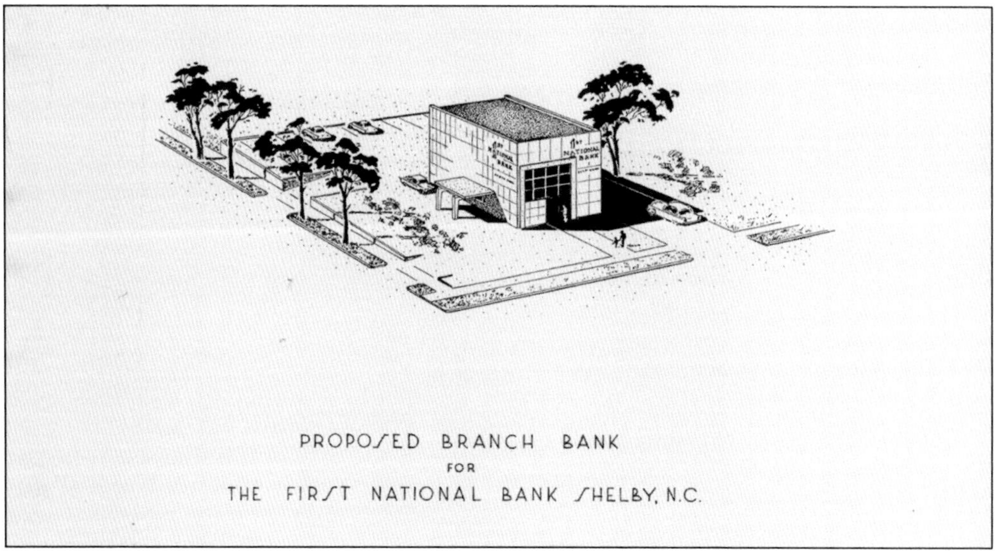

The architect's drawing of the new branch shows a new feature, a drive-up window.

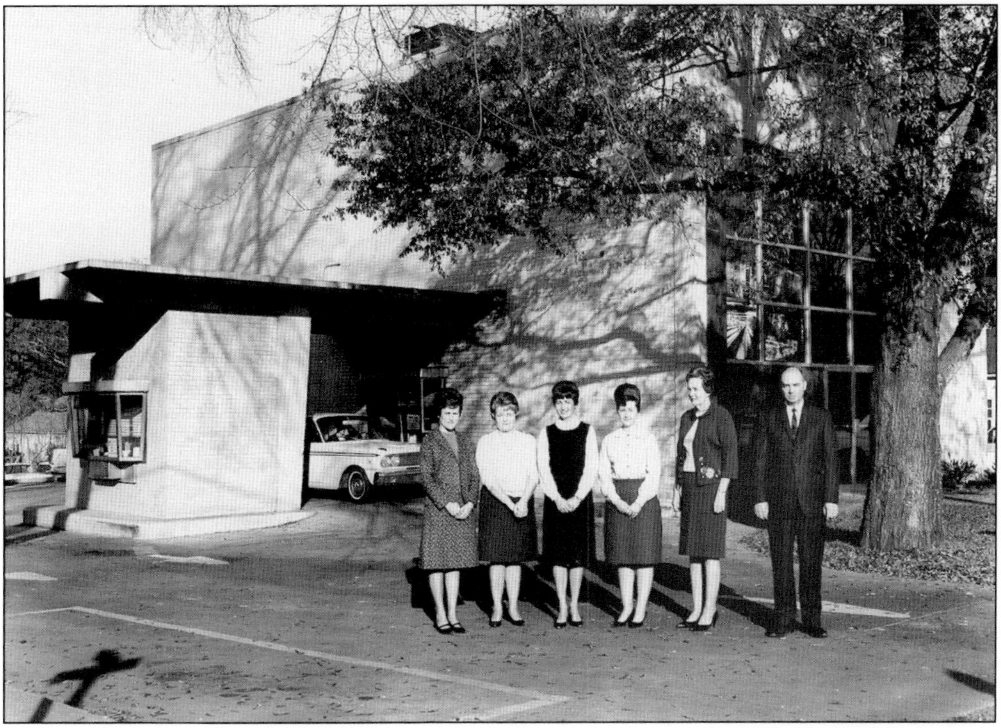

Several years after the South Lafayette Street branch was opened, the staff poses in front of the bank. Pictured from left to right are Pat Webster, Lib McSwain, Ada Ruth Hamrick, Mary Rudisill, Louise McBrayer, and David Putnam. Later, a six-car modern automatic teller system was added on the north side of the building.

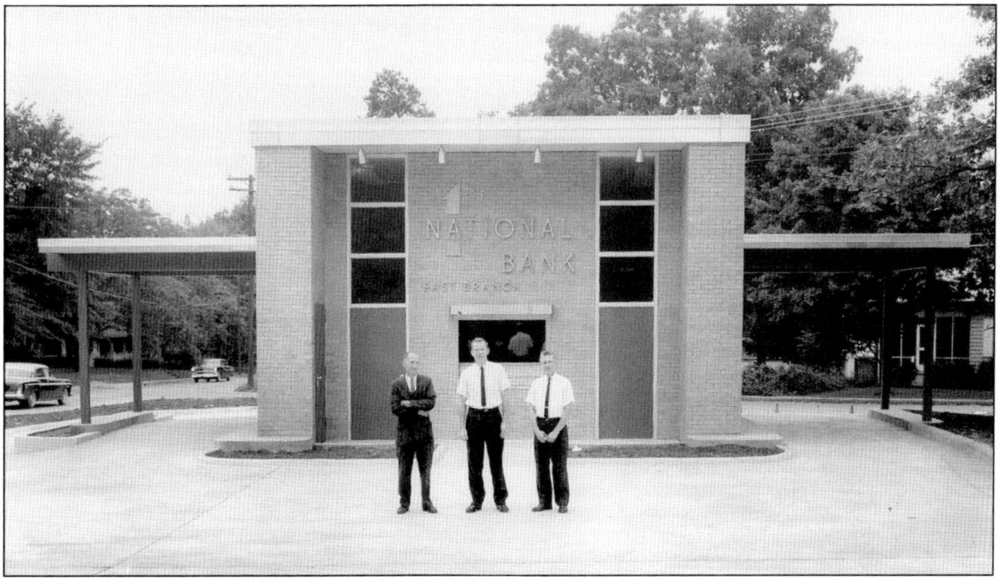

With the success of the South Lafayette branch, First National decided, in 1961, to build a branch at East Marion Street and Lineberger Street. The East Branch is still in operation today. This early photo of the East Branch shows three bank employees. They are, from left to right, Graham Greene, Bobby Guffey, and Max Wallace.

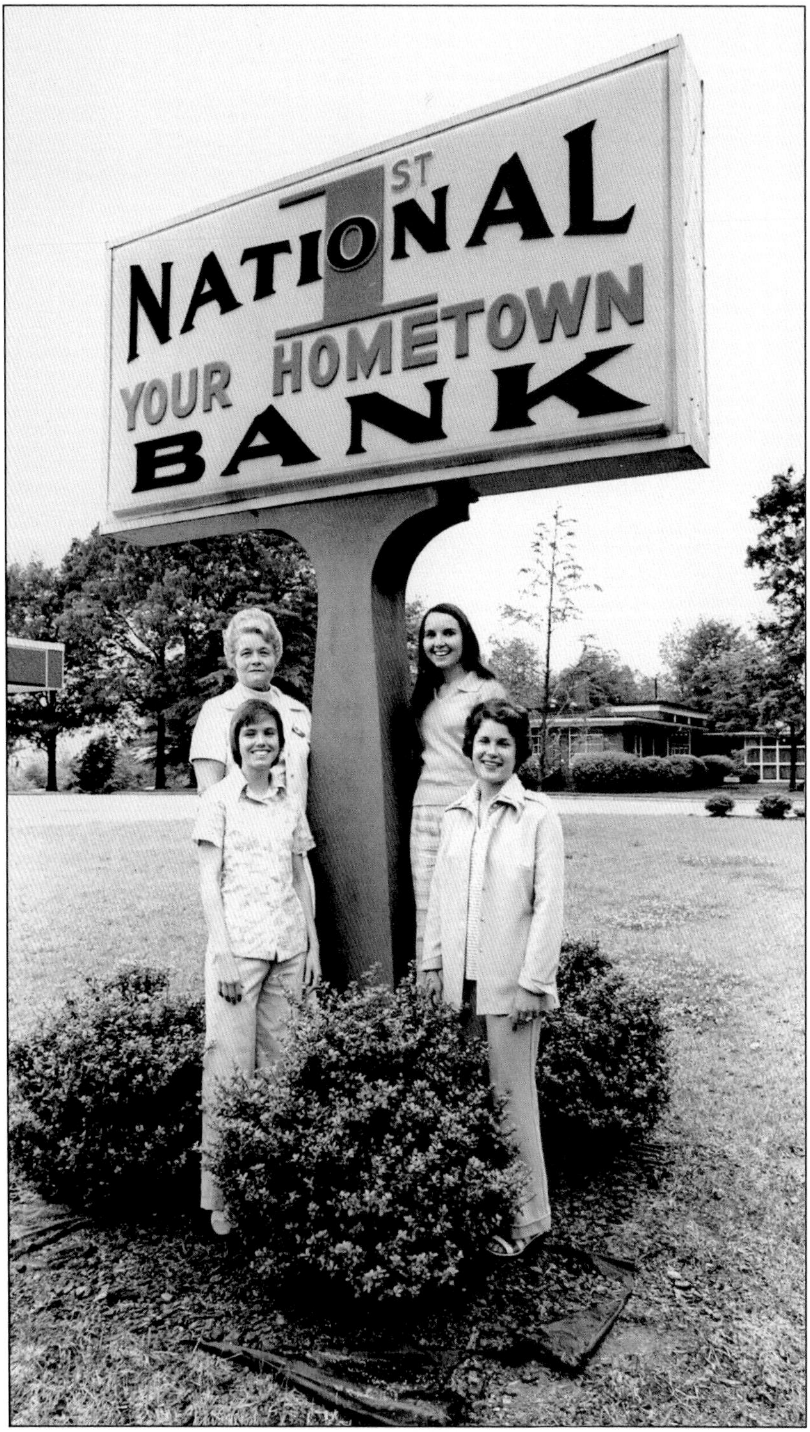

In the early 1970s, North Branch was added for drive-through customers at Lafayette and Lee Streets. This photo shows four women who worked there in the early years. They are, from left to right, (top row) Lib McSwain and Barbara Conner (Fitch), who is today the manager of the South Branch; (bottom row) Jeanie Davis and Lydia Blanton, the daughter of George Blanton Jr.

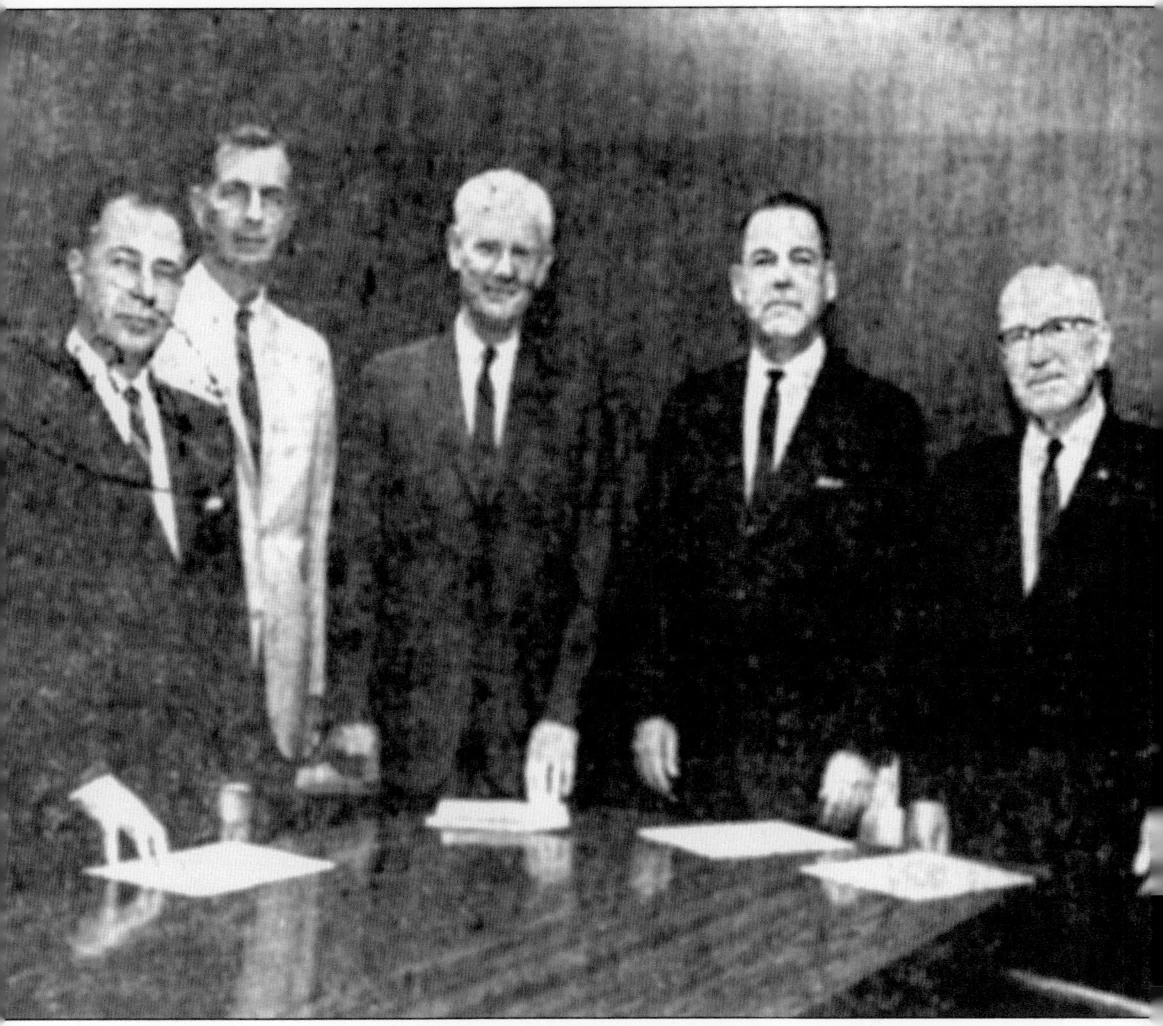

This 1966 advertisement in the *Shelby Daily Star* shows five men who were leaders in the developments described here. They are, from left to right, William E. Pearce, Ed Hamilton, George Blanton Jr., Horace Carter, and Clarence Mull. In the 1950s, the bank began making plans for a trust department. By 1953, the Federal Reserve System granted the bank trust powers. Horace Carter, formerly an Office of the Comptroller of the Currency (OCC) bank examiner and a vice president and a commercial loan officer at the bank, accepted the responsibility of developing a trust department. The first account for the new department was the George Blanton Sr. and Ida Wood Blanton Trust. In 1954, the board of directors established a profit-sharing plan for the bank's employees, thus establishing the second account. As the trust department grew, Dorothy Pearson became Mr. Carter's assistant in 1970. As Mr. Carter planned for early retirement, Fritz Russell, a lawyer with previous trust experience, joined the bank as vice president and head of the department. Unfortunately, Mr. Russell died of cancer in 1983. He was replaced by William E. (Bill) Plowden Jr., an attorney who still directs the department. Today, with Vice Pres. David T. Thompson, employee benefit specialist Theresa Hamrick, trust operations officer Dot Pearson, and assistants, the department administers estates, personal trust accounts, managing agencies, custody accounts, and a full array of employee benefit accounts. The department also handles financial planning, discount brokerage, and full-service brokerage.

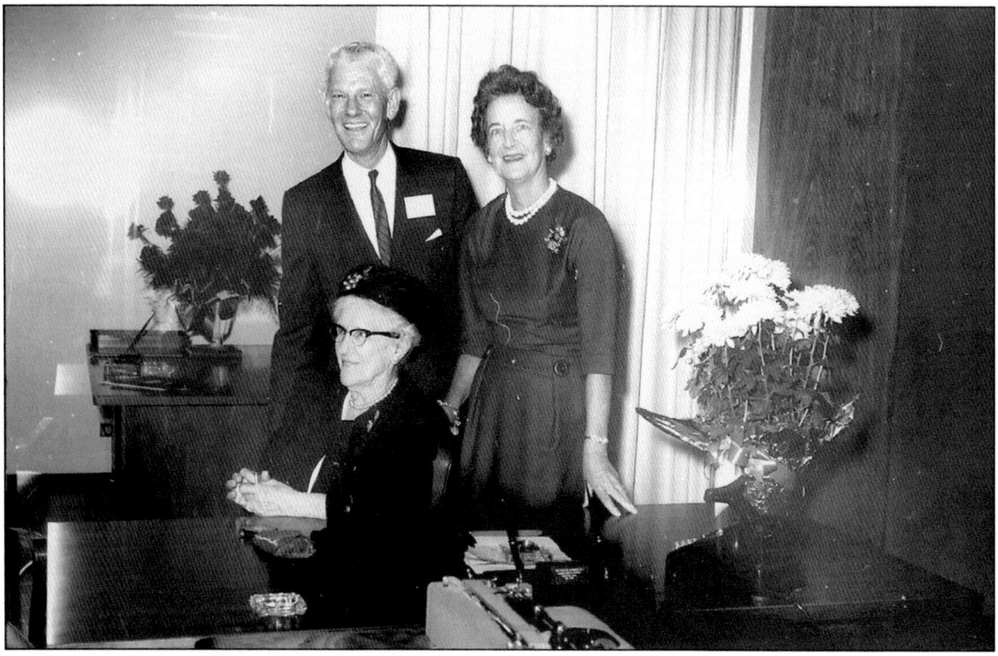

During the event showing the newly renovated lobby in 1960, Mrs. George Blanton Sr. (Ida Wood) sits at the desk while her son, George Jr., and daughter, Millicent Blanton Thompson, stand behind her.

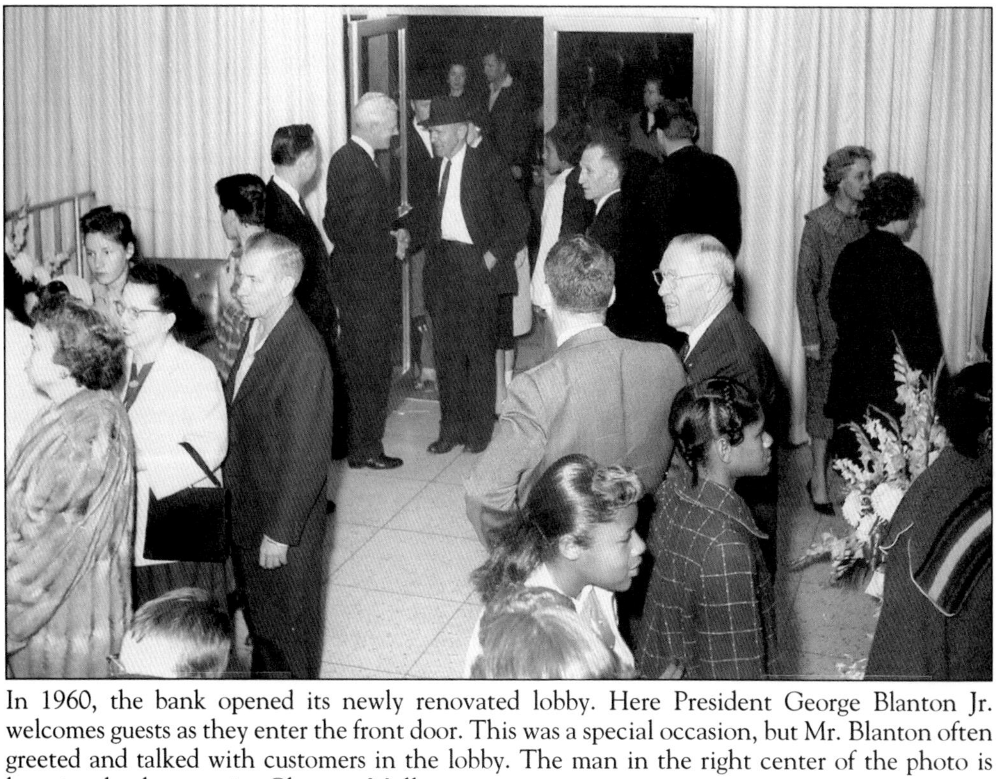

In 1960, the bank opened its newly renovated lobby. Here President George Blanton Jr. welcomes guests as they enter the front door. This was a special occasion, but Mr. Blanton often greeted and talked with customers in the lobby. The man in the right center of the photo is longtime bank executive Clarence Mull.

In 1961, First National hired another descendant of Burwell Blanton—Edgar Blanton Hamilton. Hamilton had a B.S. degree in industrial management from Georgia Tech. In time, Mr. Hamilton would replace George Blanton Jr. as president, CEO, and chairman of the board.

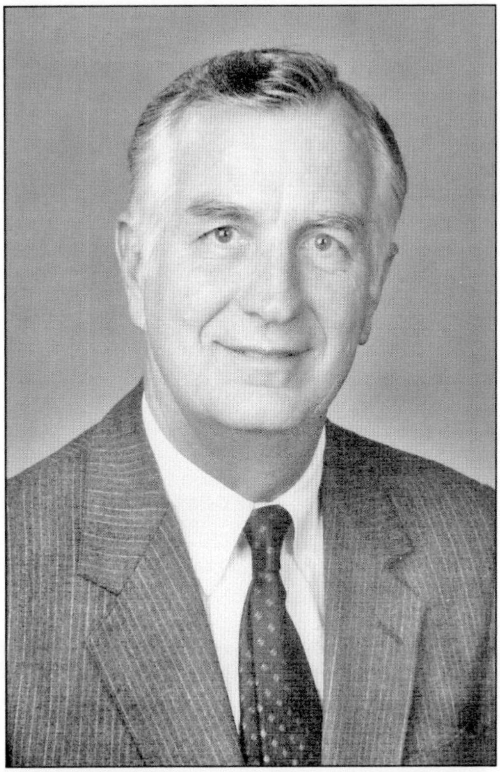

This photo shows Ed Hamilton as many friends and customers see him. In a most positive way, they call him "Easy Ed." He maintained an open-door policy while he led the bank. During his years of advancement at the bank, he also was very involved in the community. He filled leadership roles at the Episcopal Church of the Redeemer; served as treasurer of the Cleveland County Historical Society, director of the Salvation Army, president of the Shelby Rotary Club, chairman of the Cleveland County Cancer Society and Heart Fund, and chairman of the Economic Development Commission and of the Cleveland County Chamber; and chaired a campaign in support of the Cleveland Community College bond referendum.

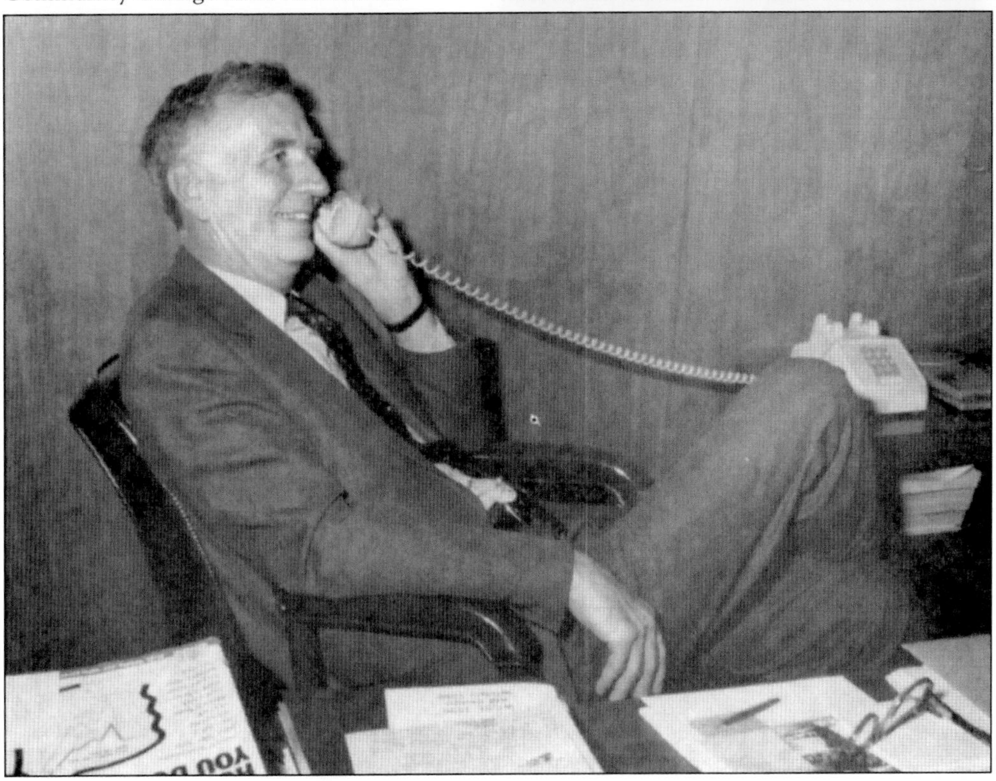

In the 1960s, bank management realized that there was a need for a more structured loan department. While the old jokes that said that the notes were kept in cigar boxes were not entirely true, management realized that making loans required more efficient and orderly handling. The board hired William E. (Bill) Pearce, who had been an OCC bank examiner and who had served for 25 years at North Carolina National Bank (now Bank of America). Mr. Pearce arrived in January 1966 and would give 15 more years of full-time service and an additional 10 years of part-time service to First National.

Mr. Pearce gained a distinction he probably could have done without. Early in his career, he became known as "the person whom the bank robber got." In the days of Saturday banking, in the fall of 1967, a nicely dressed man came into the bank and asked to see the president. Since Mr. Blanton was not in, the man asked to see the cashier of the bank. When they reached Mr. Pearce's office, the man drew a gun and asked for $50,000. Mr. Pearce told him he could only get $25,000 and went to teller Vaughn Whitaker and asked for the money. After vault custodian Fred Morehead had secured the money, Mr. Pearce ("cool as a cucumber"), trying to remember what he had learned about how not to panic in a robbery, walked out of the bank with the robber. After the man found his car (he left the keys in the ignition and it had been moved), they left town. The robber assured Mr. Pearce he would not harm him if he would cooperate. Mr. Pearce reported, "He was sort of interesting to talk to." He got two $20 bills and a $10 bill from Mr. Pearce and gave him one of the bank's $50 bills because the robber said there is "no point in your taking a loss." The robber dropped Mr. Pearce at the Carolina Theater in Charlotte where *Dr. Zhivago* was playing. After Mr. Pearce spent 30 minutes inside as instructed, he came out and arranged a ride back to Shelby. The robber and most of the money were found in Atlanta the next day. In the picture at right, Shelby Police Chief Knox Hardin stands in for the bank robber in a reenactment of the robbery.

Mr. Pearce made positive contributions to the loan operations of the bank. Also, he managed the bank's investment portfolio, which consisted of the United States Treasury bills and bonds and municipal bonds. He also gave sound advice to many, including Ed Hamilton, Bobby Smith, Brenda Page, Adelaide Craver, Helen Jeffords, and Bill Plowden.

Berube To Be Transferred To Cleveland County Jail

Allen James Berube, 29, charg- by the FBI with robbery of elby's First National Bank, is reported by unofficial sour- s late yesterday to be on his ay to Shelby under federal es- rt for transfer to Cleveland unty Jail.

Yesterday morning in Atlanta, . Berube waived the right to unsel and preliminary hearing. is reported to have agreed to transferral to Shelby and his nd was set at $50,000.

No official source in Shelby e yesterday would state when rube and his federal escorts uld arrive at the local jail. rlier, law enforcement officials re had told The Times that robbery case could come to al at any site in the U. S. der federal laws.

The young, dark-haired and, parently, talkative accused nk robber had been released m federal penitentiary in At- ta, Ga. just nine days prior Saturday when he is alleged have walked into First Nation- posing as a governmental of- ial, and at gunpoint forced

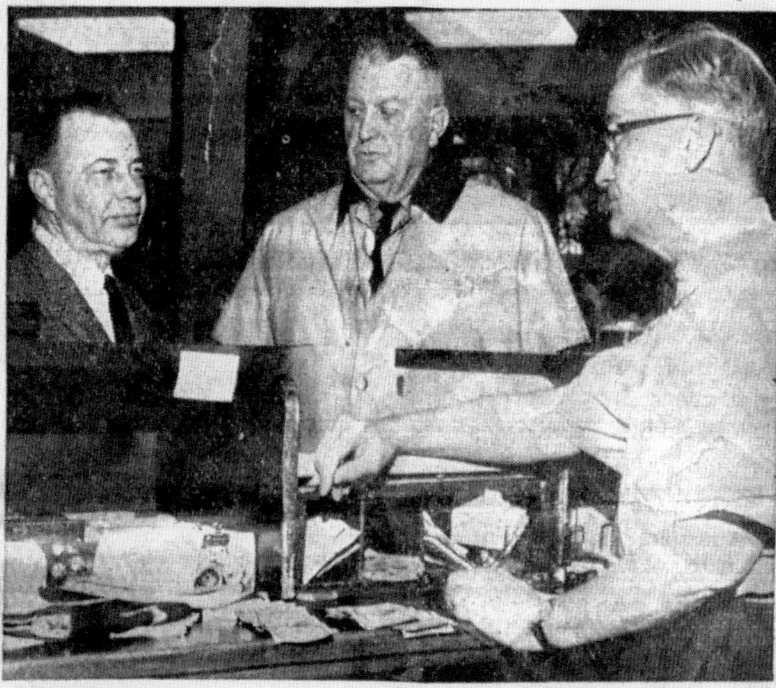

RE-ENACTMENT — William E. Pearce, First National vice-president, at left, assumes the same stance he occupied Saturday when he, at gunpoint, accompanied a bank robber to draw $25,000 in cash from Assistant Cashier Fred Moorhead, right. Shelby Police Chief Knox Hardin yesterday took the role and position that the young, well-dressed hold-up man occupied when Saturday's events transpired just before 1 p.m. bank closing time.

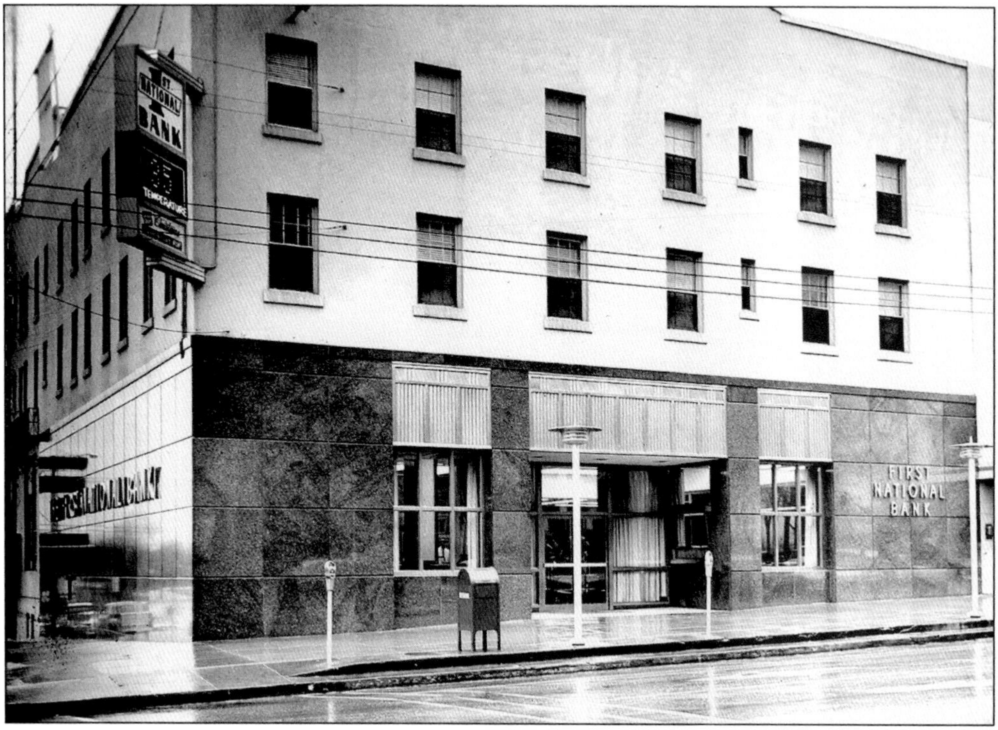

By the 1970s, the bank was occupying a large part of the Charles Building. The Hotel Charles had closed in 1967. The time and temperature sign had become a downtown trademark. The bank had grown from a one-room business to a modern, well-designed facility. However, there was still room to grow both financially and physically.

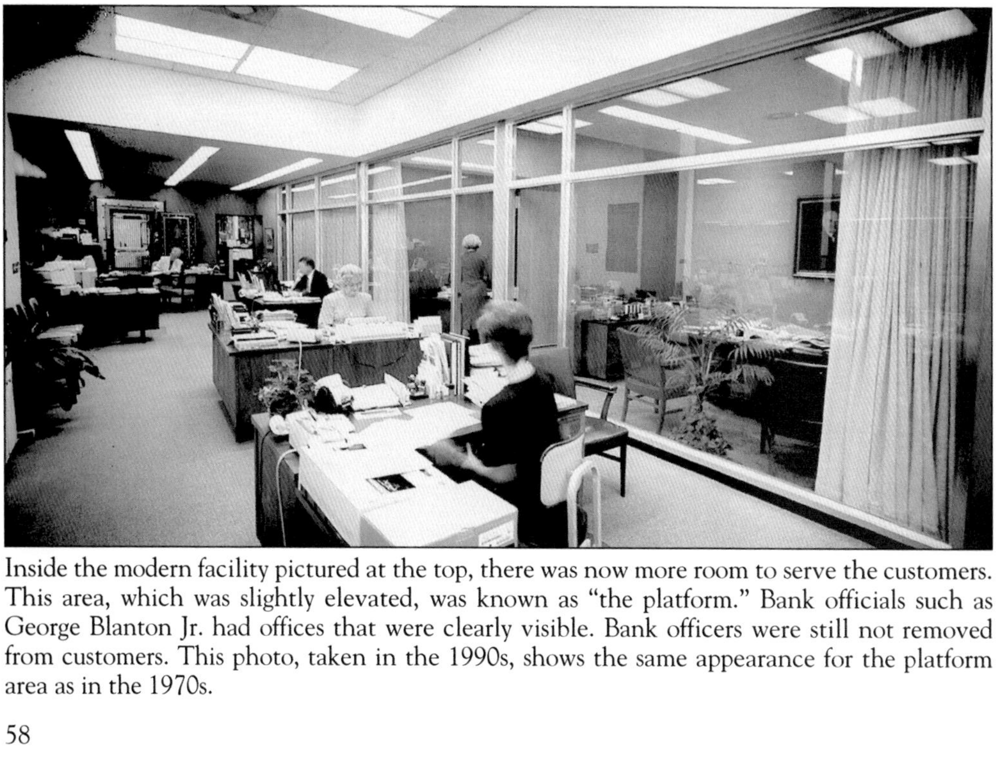

Inside the modern facility pictured at the top, there was now more room to serve the customers. This area, which was slightly elevated, was known as "the platform." Bank officials such as George Blanton Jr. had offices that were clearly visible. Bank officers were still not removed from customers. This photo, taken in the 1990s, shows the same appearance for the platform area as in the 1970s.

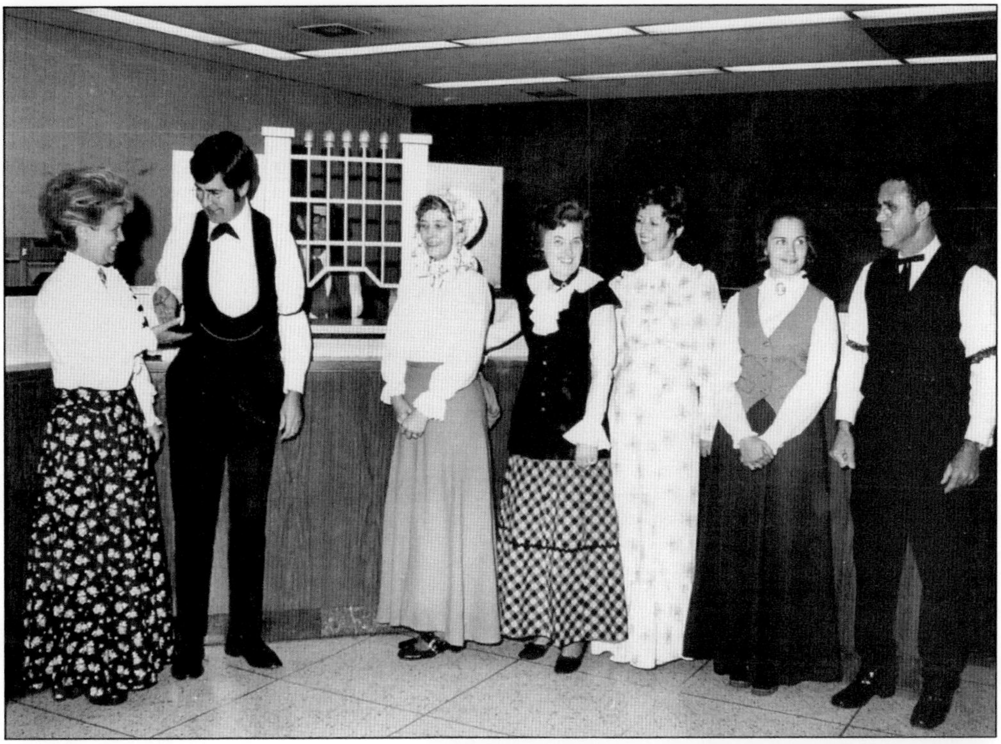

In 1974, First National celebrated its 100th birthday. Bank employees dressed in 19th-century costumes for the event. Pictured from left to right are Helen Bost, Bobby Smith, Estelle Ledford, Dorothy Shytle, Barbara Allen, Becky Jackson, and Calvin Blaylock.

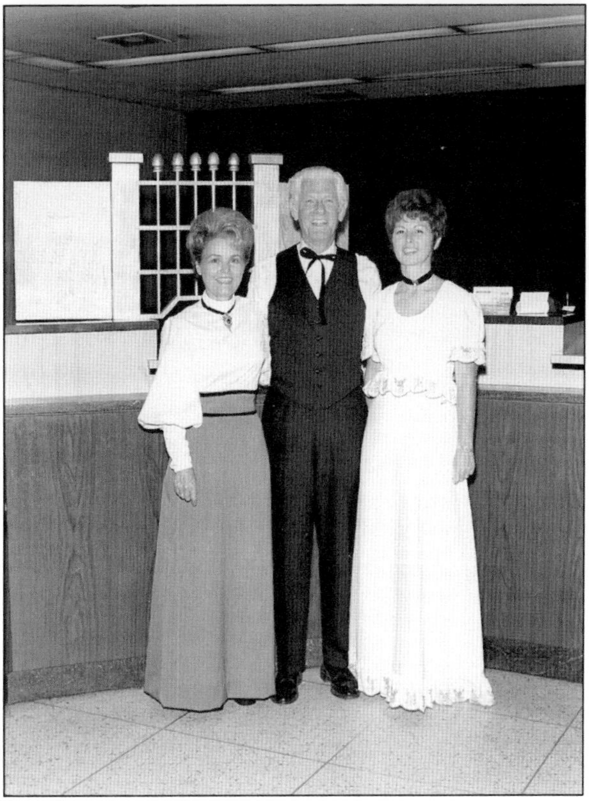

President George Blanton Jr. poses with Helen Bost (left) and Barbara Allen at the bank. A large celebration was also held at Shelby High School's George Blanton Stadium (named for George Blanton Sr.). Danny Davis and the Nashville Brass played for approximately 2,000 people who attended. George Blanton Jr. and others went up in a hot-air balloon.

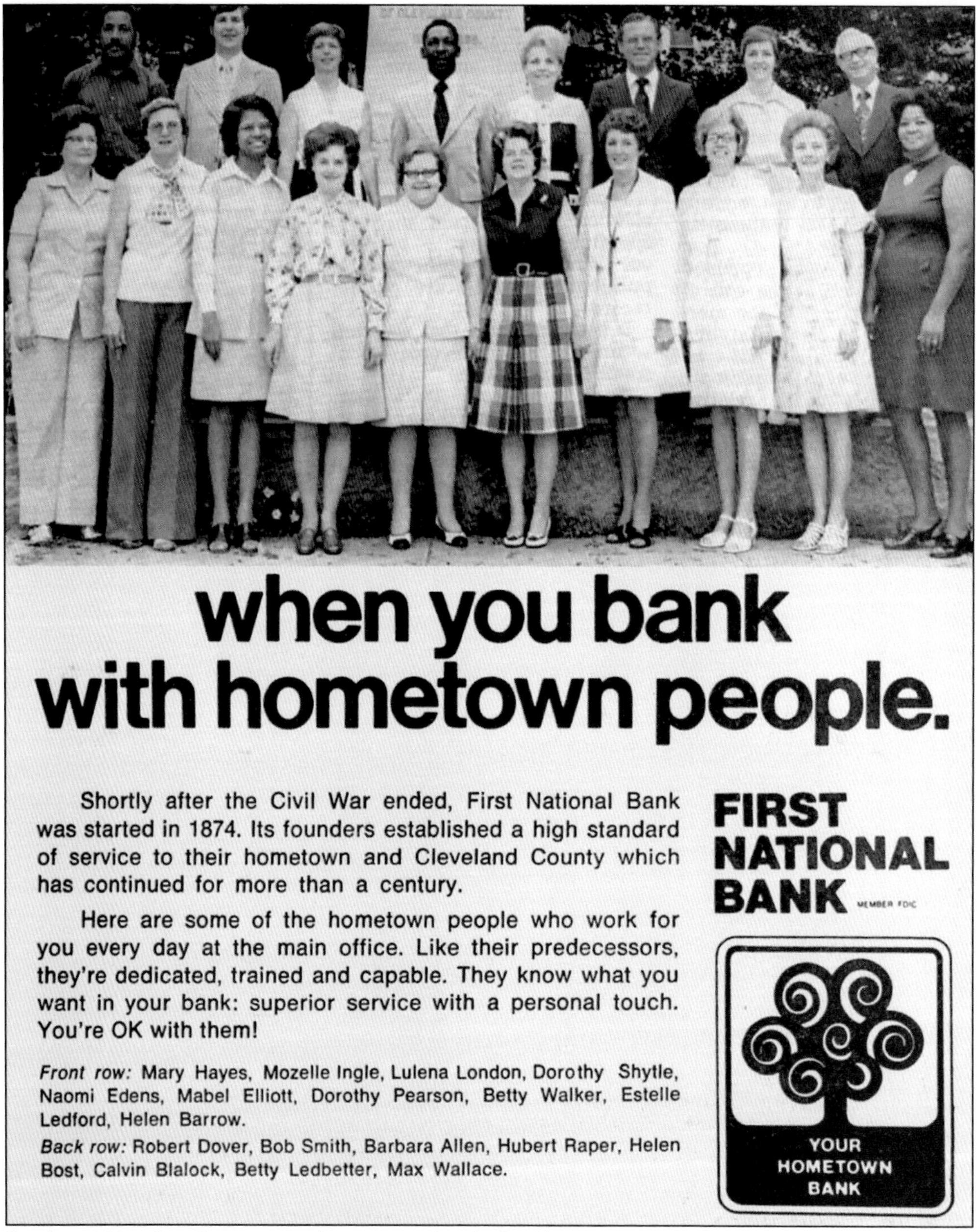

By the 1970s, the phrase "your hometown bank" had become common. The bank's copyrighted logo shows a tree whose roots represent strong, longtime involvement in banking, and the curved branches represent embracing the customers and the community it serves. These 18 employees were only a part of the work force.

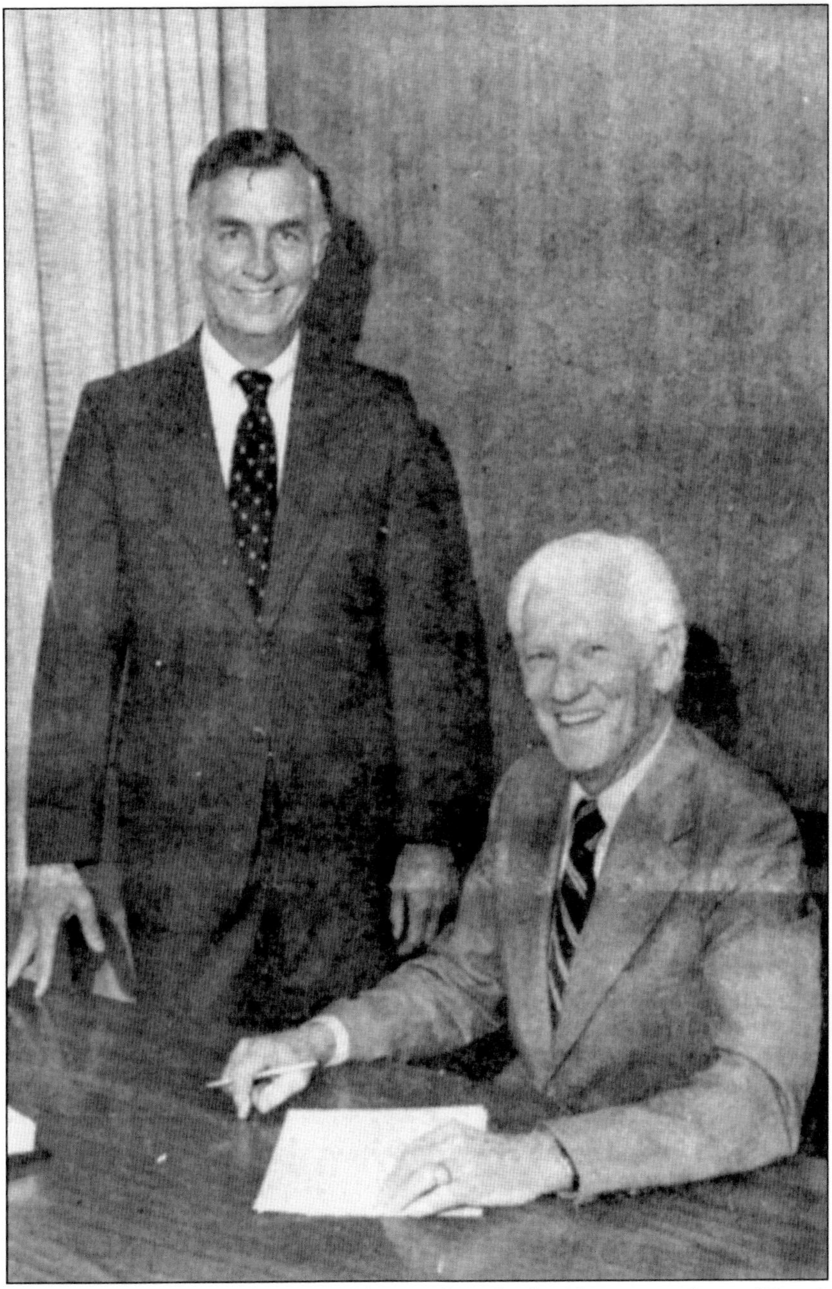

In 1979, the bank board named George Blanton Jr., who had been president of First National Bank for 32 years and chairman for 20 years, to the position of chairman of the board and CEO. Edgar Blanton Hamilton, another descendant of Burwell Blanton, was named president of the bank. Both Mr. Blanton and Mr. Hamilton had been very active in loan development, but at this time, Mr. Blanton transferred most of the loan development to Mr. Hamilton. Although Mr. Blanton was a regular in the bank for another 20 years, this began the transition to the bank's future leadership. Then, in 1989, while Mr. Blanton remained chairman of the board, Mr. Hamilton became CEO as well as president. In 1996, Mr. Blanton became chairman of the board emeritus, and Mr. Hamilton was named chairman of the board and CEO.

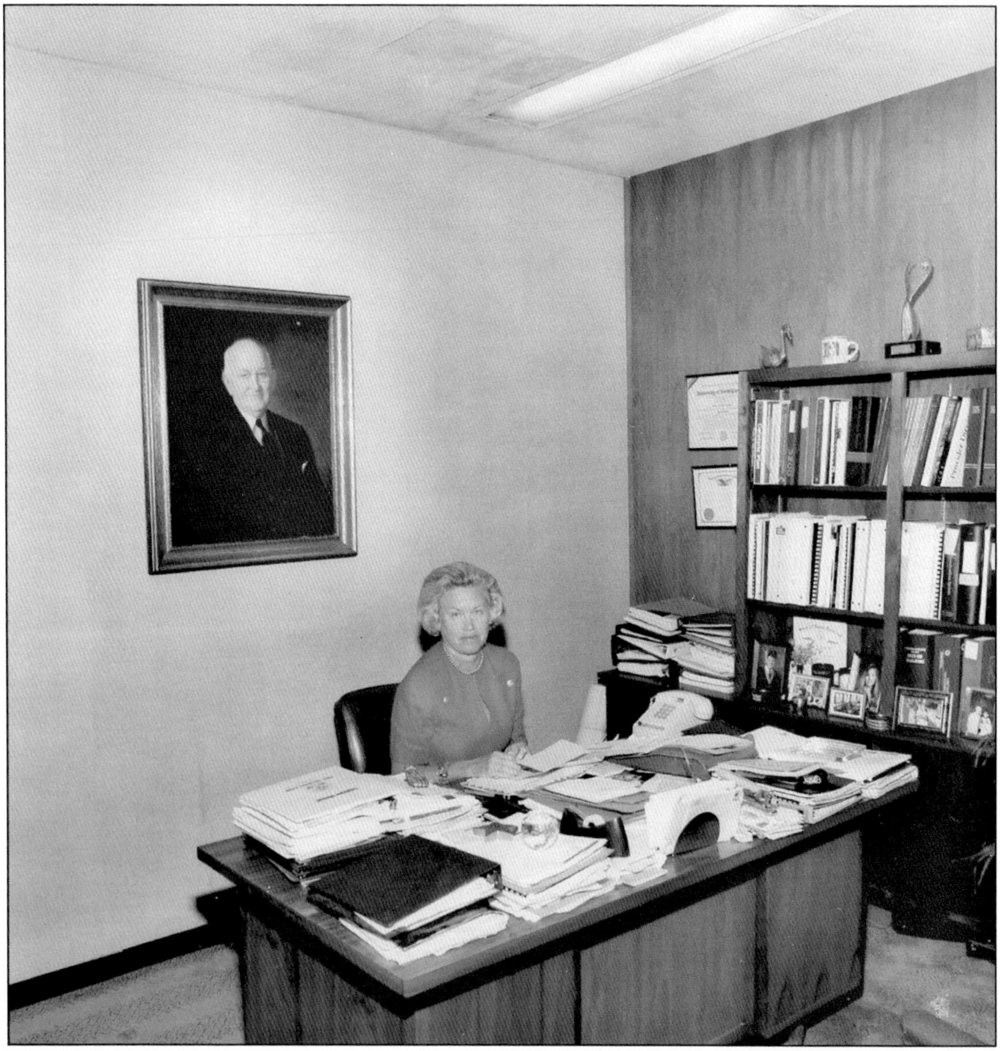

The 1980s brought the bank many changes. In 1981, George Blanton Jr. and Edgar B. Hamilton hired Adelaide Austell Craver, who was also a descendant of Burwell Blanton. She had graduated from Duke University with a B.A. in economics. She received a J.D. degree from UNC-Chapel Hill in 1967 and would become the first woman licensed to practice law in Cleveland County. She was named vice president and cashier. She was elected to the board in 1991 and became president and COO in 1996. In 1998, Ms. Craver became president and CEO.

The 1980s also brought the period of bank deregulation. In 1980, the Negotiable Order of Withdrawal (NOW) Account was approved for banks. Within certain limitations, the bank could now pay interest on checking, and the Insured Money Market Account (IMMA) was introduced. In the high interest period of the 1980s, banks paid 13 percent to 17 percent on IMMAs. By the late 1980s, most regulations on the interest banks could pay were removed, except for business checking. FNB, as did all banks, had to now be competitive on interest paid to depositors and interest charged to borrowers. This made what longtime commercial loan officer of the bank Clarence Mull had said, "you do what the traffic will bear," referring to interest charged on loans, appropriate also for interest paid on deposits.

In the photograph of Ms. Craver in her office, the portrait of Charles Blanton is seen on the wall.

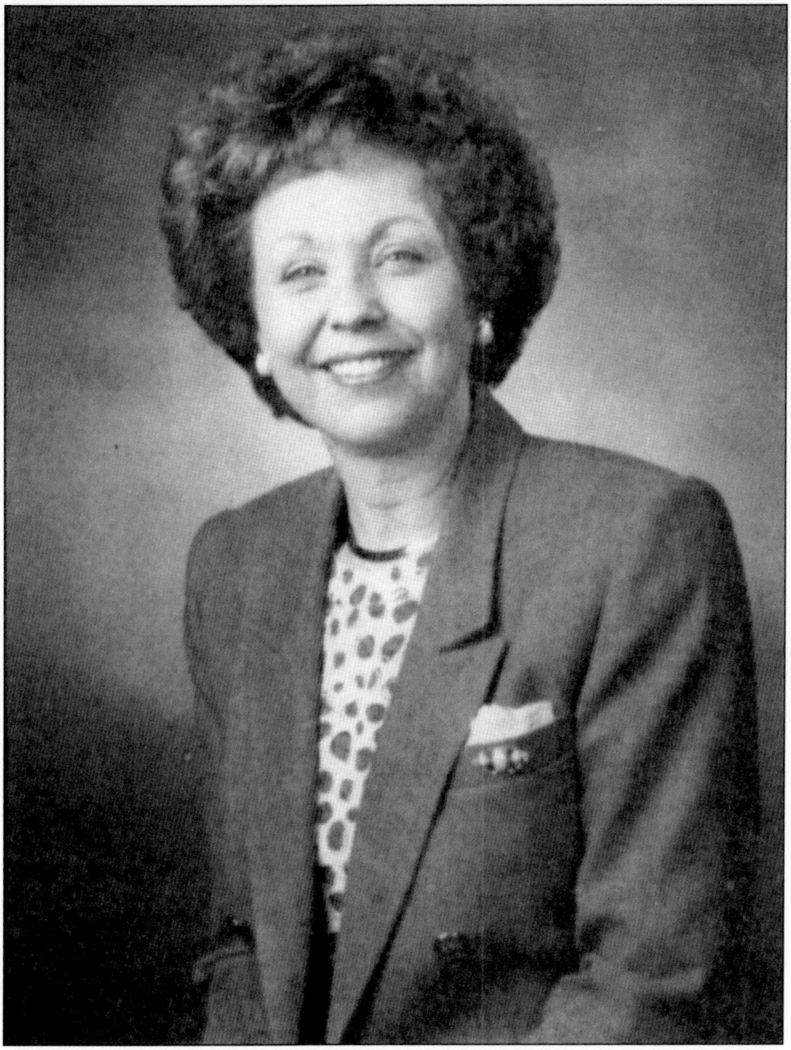

Ed Hamilton had done a good job overseeing the bank's advertisements, but the late 1980s brought the need for a full-fledged marketing officer. Brenda F. Page (shown here), who had worked her way to the head of the bookkeeping department, seemed the natural fit for this job. Brenda, who is now a bank senior vice president, had 30 years of banking experience and was active in many community organizations. Brenda's abilities as bank calling officer were instrumental in helping the bank establish new full-service offices in the late 1980s and into the 1990s. Chapter four will be dedicated to examining the bank's many activities in the community under Brenda's leadership.

Mr. Hamilton also added two people who are members of the board and of the bank's executive committee today. (Both are pictured in chapter three.) When Fritz Russell Jr. died, William E. Plowden Jr. joined the bank as vice president and trust officer. Also, the bank's need for a more highly trained specialist led to the hiring of Helen A. Jeffords in 1983 as vice president and comptroller.

Later, in 1999, the bank's management team was further enhanced by Peggy Paksoy's addition as vice president for public relations. She also handles training, strategic planning, and special projects. She brought 11 years experience as president of the Cleveland County Chamber of Commerce.

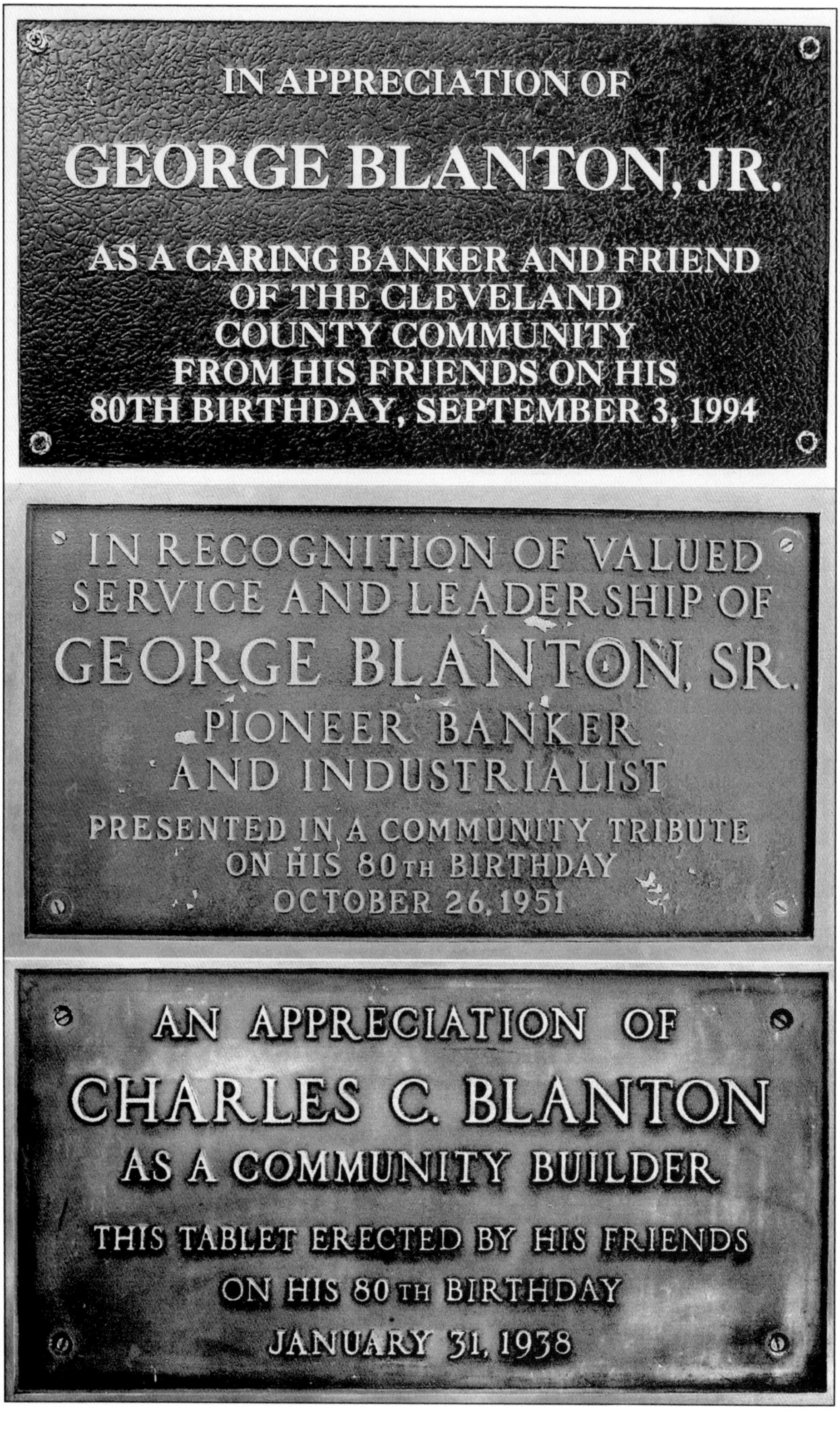
IN APPRECIATION OF
GEORGE BLANTON, JR.
AS A CARING BANKER AND FRIEND
OF THE CLEVELAND
COUNTY COMMUNITY
FROM HIS FRIENDS ON HIS
80TH BIRTHDAY, SEPTEMBER 3, 1994
IN RECOGNITION OF VALUED
SERVICE AND LEADERSHIP OF
GEORGE BLANTON, SR.
PIONEER BANKER
AND INDUSTRIALIST
PRESENTED IN A COMMUNITY TRIBUTE
ON HIS 80TH BIRTHDAY
OCTOBER 26, 1951
AN APPRECIATION OF
CHARLES C. BLANTON
AS A COMMUNITY BUILDER
THIS TABLET ERECTED BY HIS FRIENDS
ON HIS 80TH BIRTHDAY
JANUARY 31, 1938

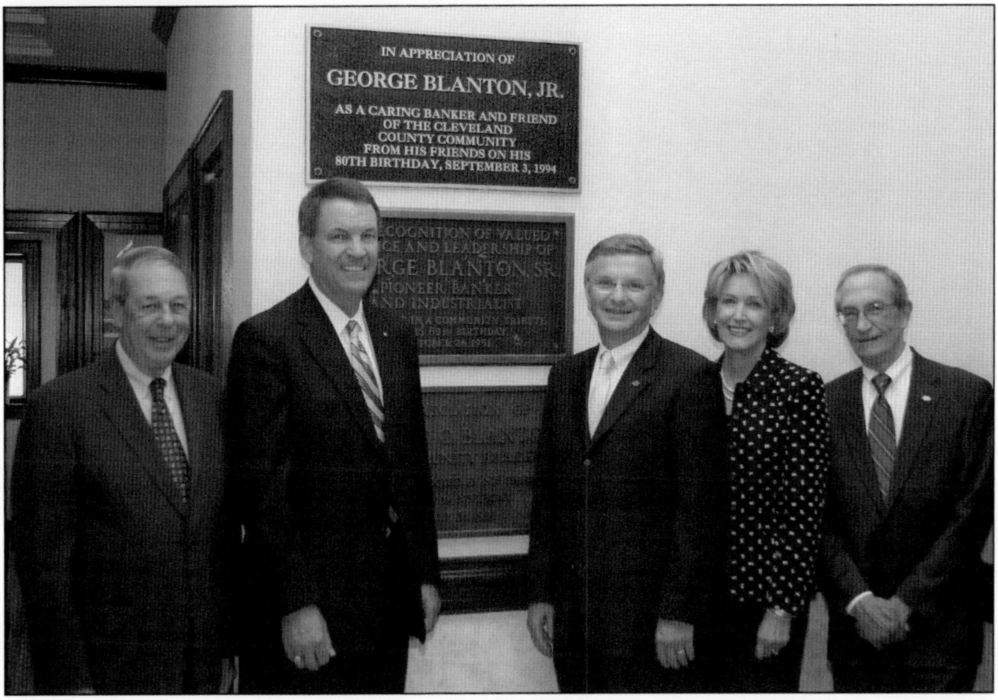

As the bank continued to adjust to a changing banking era, it was building on a strong foundation built by men such as the three men honored on their 80th birthdays by the plaques (left page), now displayed in the bank's lobby. Each of these men were still working at the bank on his 80th birthday. Flanking the plaques in the photo above are senior officers of the bank's management team, from left to right, are Tom Harris, Earl Lutz, Joe Henderson, Peggy Paksoy, and Bob Eakins.

In the 1990s, Mr. Hamilton led the bank through a period of change. New regulations were coming from the Federal Reserve, the FDIC, and the Office of the Comptroller of the Currency (OCC). New committees such as the Asset Liability Committee were created. Many department heads became involved in seeing that their department met regulations. When Richard Walker, the bank's first internal auditor, was ready to retire, FNB hired J. Thomas Harris in 1990. Mr. Harris had 15 years of auditing experience as well as other banking experience. He is now senior auditor and he is also over compliance, headed by Sharon Leigh, and bank security, headed by Phillip Witherspoon.

Mr. Hamilton also realized there was a need in the bank for a credit risk officer, and in 1995, Robert Eakins was hired. He had worked for two years at the Federal Reserve and 23 years as a bank examiner for the OCC. Today, in addition to being senior vice president and head of the credit committee, he is over loan administration, headed by Sandra Griffin, and collections, headed by Carl Adam and Lin Robinson.

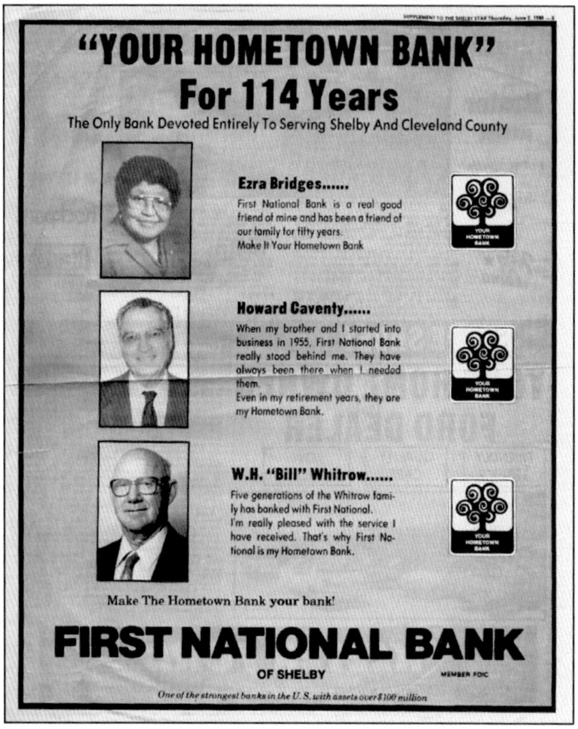

This ad of the late 1980s contained testimonials from three longtime customers. Ezra Bridges remembers a time when George Blanton Sr. told her she could sign her own loan while she was getting a college education. She returned to Shelby and became a longtime teacher and leader in the African-American community and the town at large.

In the 1990s, the bank's strategic planning committee worked to increase the loan market and take a more proactive stance to develop business. A policy of "Total Relationship Banking" meant fulfilling the customer's total banking needs. A home mortgage division, which is headed today by James Woods, was added. Veterans in commercial loans such as Mr. Hamilton and Mr. Smith were joined by experts such as Joseph B. Henderson Jr., senior vice president and head of the bank's loan division; Earl H. Lutz Jr., a senior vice president who is over several offices and lending programs; and Bruce G. Hodge, vice president and executive in Gaston County. These three bring a total of 80 years or more of banking experience to the bank. Retail lending is headed by Cecil D. Clark, vice president, and includes Vice Pres. Larry C. Beasley and Assistant Vice Pres. Dana Lundquist, who recently joined the bank. Loan production and service is very important at the full-service offices and people such as Vice Presidents W. Hill Hudson III at the Highland Office, Daniel L. Denton at the South Cleveland Office, Kenneth H. Miller at the Upper Cleveland Office, E. Allen Martin at the Bessemer City Office, and Jeffrey T. Triplett at the West Cleveland Office contribute greatly to loan development. (See chapter five for more information on bank offices and their staffs.)

In December 1998, First National contracted a cash purchase of First Carolina Federal Savings Bank of Kings Mountain, North Carolina. The sale was closed in April of 1999. This was the bank's first acquisition of another financial institution. With this acquisition, First National not only entered the Kings Mountain market, but also acquired a foothold in Gaston County. First Carolina's history can be traced to the incorporation of Kings Mountain Building and Loan Association in 1907. From this acquisition, First National acquired some valuable employees, such as Brenda Lovelace, now vice president, commercial loan officer, and the head of the Kings Mountain office, and Michael Weisman, now senior vice president and head of bank brokerage. Also, Dr. John McGill and Glee Bridges Jr. are now valuable directors of the bank.

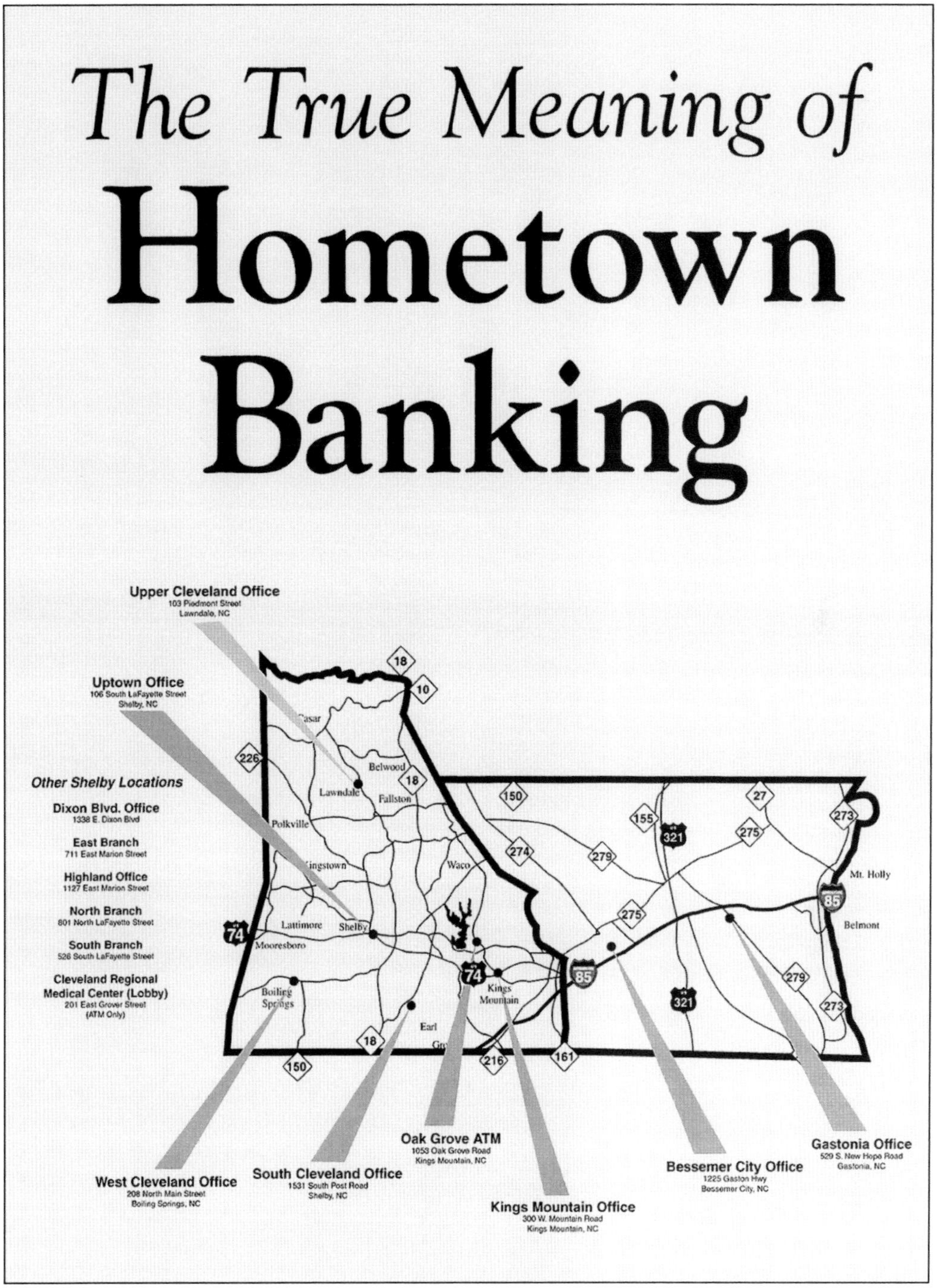

For the last 15 years, First National has been expanding its market area. The Upper Cleveland office was opened in 1989, the South Cleveland office in 1992, the West Cleveland office in 1994, and the Highlands office in 1996. In 1999, First National purchased First Carolina Federal, which had offices on East Dixon Boulevard in Shelby, in Kings Mountain, and in Gastonia. The Bessemer City office was built in 2000, and a third office is planned for Gaston County on Wilkinson Boulevard, which will serve the Cramerton and Belmont area.

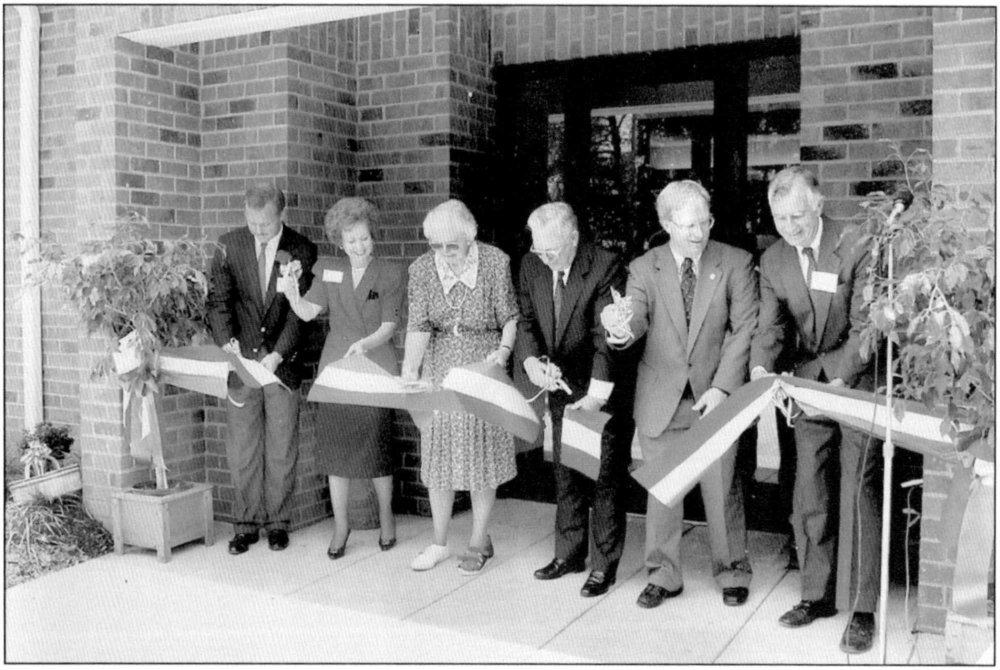

The South Cleveland office was opened in 1992 with a ribbon cutting. Seen from left to right are Cecil Clark, Brenda Page, Arrie Ellis (mayor of Earl), Hugh Dillingham Jr. (mayor of Patterson Springs), Scott Neisler (mayor of Kings Mountain), and Ed Hamilton.

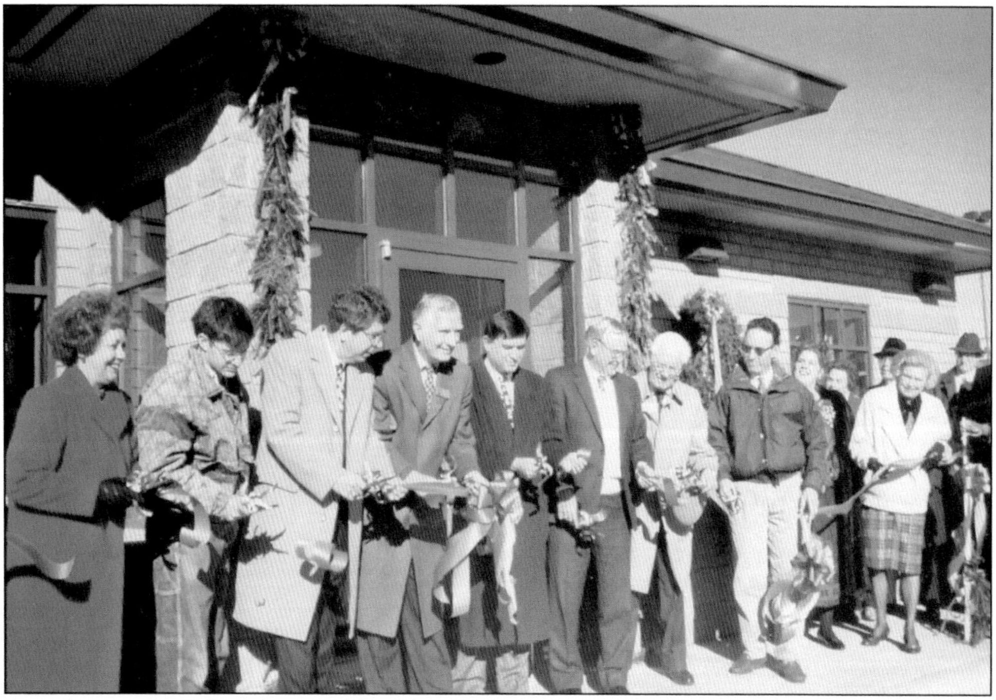

Branch manager Hill Hudson III (third from left) and Ed Hamilton (fourth from left) join Shelby Mayor Mike Philbeck (fifth from left), County Commissioner Jim Crawley (sixth from left), and others in the ribbon cutting at the new Highland branch on East Marion Street in Shelby.

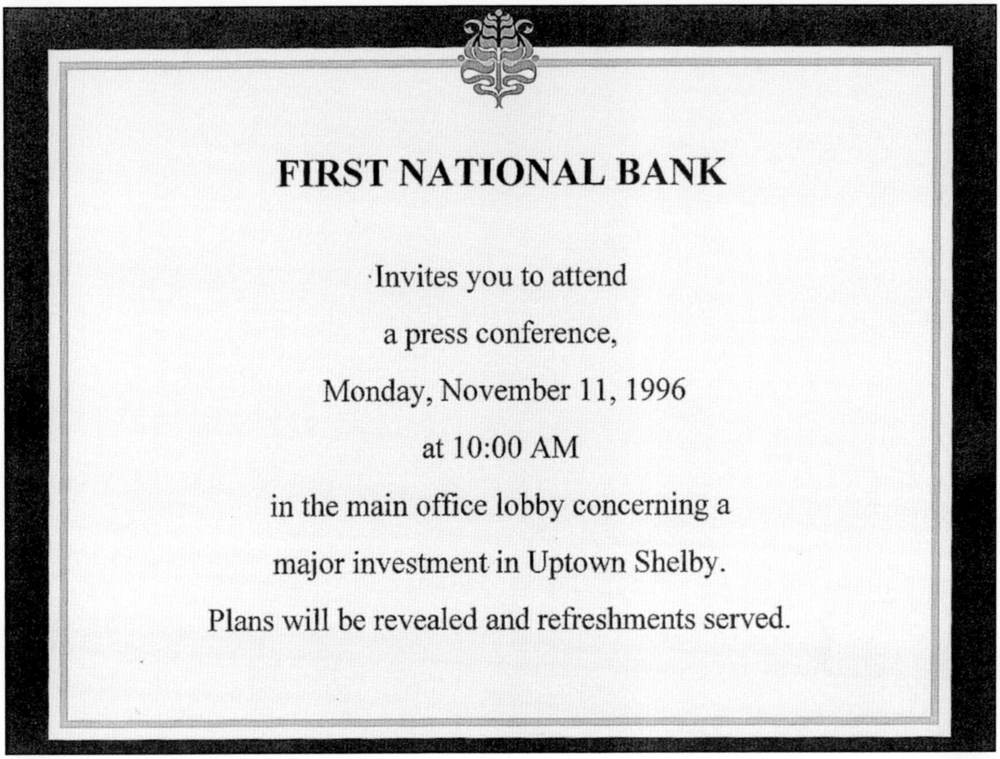

FIRST NATIONAL BANK

Invites you to attend

a press conference,

Monday, November 11, 1996

at 10:00 AM

in the main office lobby concerning a

major investment in Uptown Shelby.

Plans will be revealed and refreshments served.

In 1996, the bank was preparing for major physical changes. On November 11, 1996, First National unveiled its plans for the future.

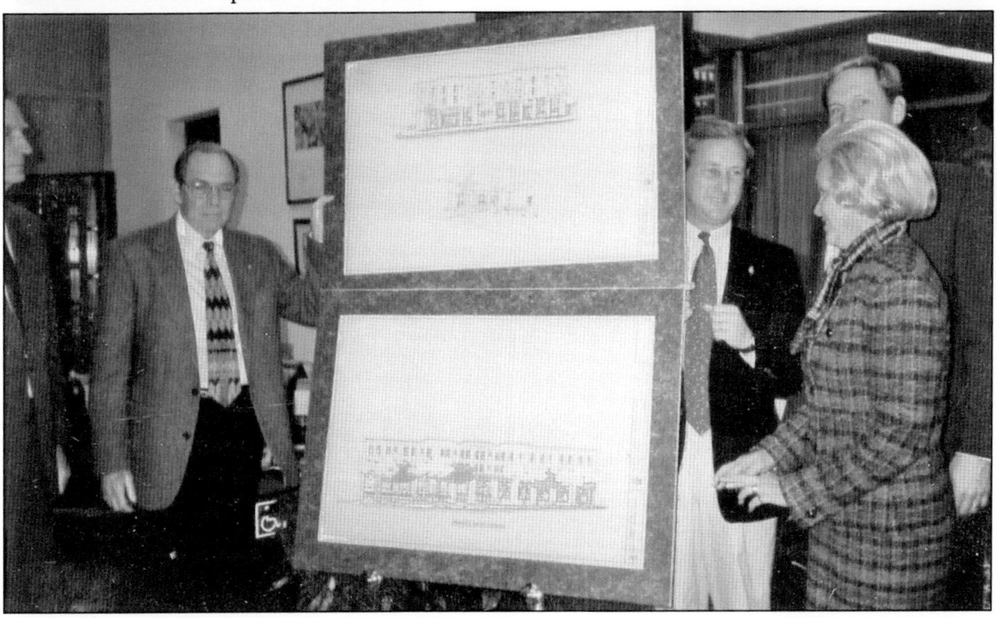

From left to right, contractor Carl Morrison, architects Roger Holland and Mark Patterson, and bank president Adelaide Craver present the architects' drawings for a major expansion of its uptown offices. The bank would expand its size as well as make major architectural changes in the Charles Building and the adjacent Blanton Building.

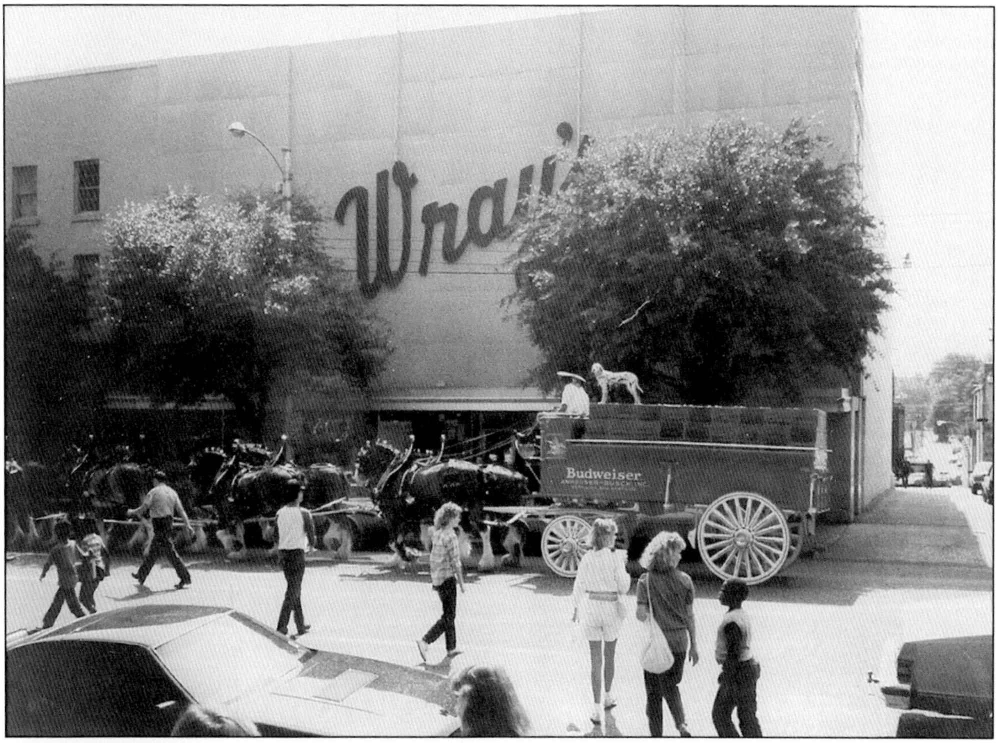

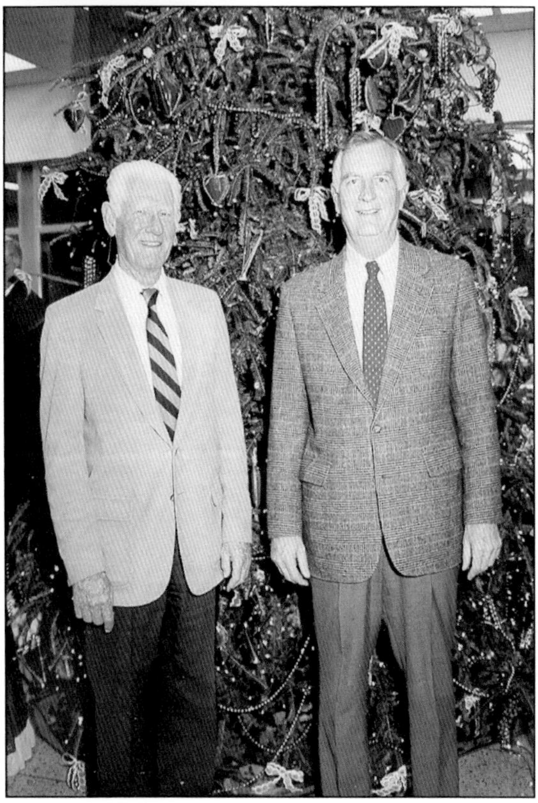

The Budweiser Clydesdales parade by the Blanton Building, which had housed A.V. Wray's for decades. When Wray's moved to another location, the building built by Burwell Blanton in 1884 would become a part of First National Bank. The plans called for redesigning both buildings to create a new First National Bank Center.

George Blanton Jr. (left) and Ed Hamilton stand together in this Christmas photo. Their 50 years of leadership at the head of the bank prepared it to expand to meet the needs of the 21st century.

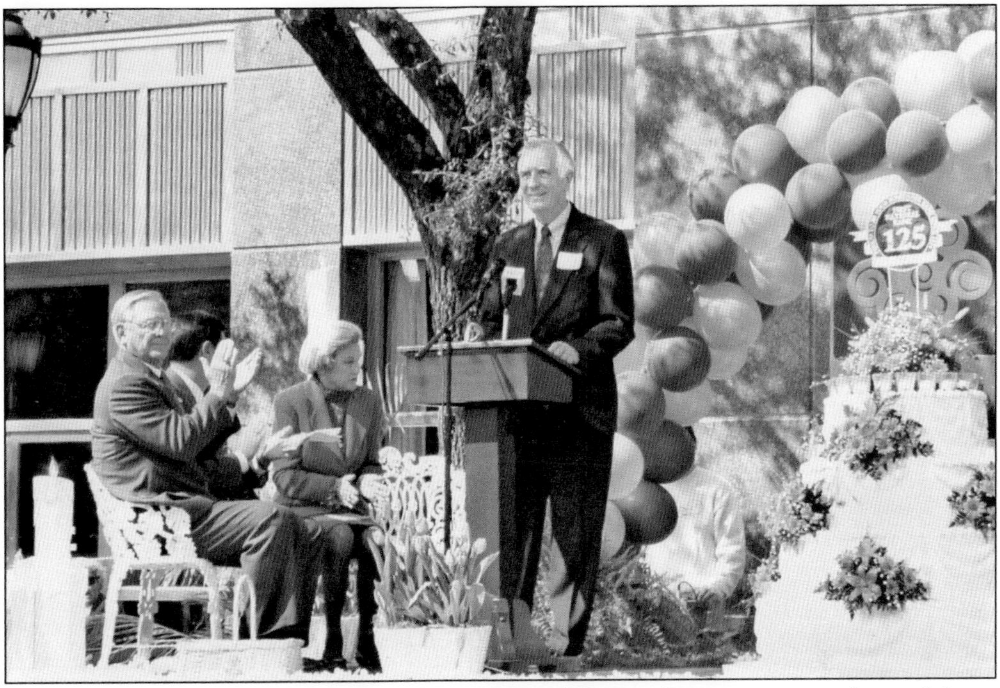

Just after the bank's expansion to Kings Mountain and Gaston County, it was ready to celebrate its 125th anniversary and display its expanded and remodeled quarters. Above, Chairman Ed Hamilton speaks as County Commissioner Jim Crawley and Pres. Adelaide Craver look on.

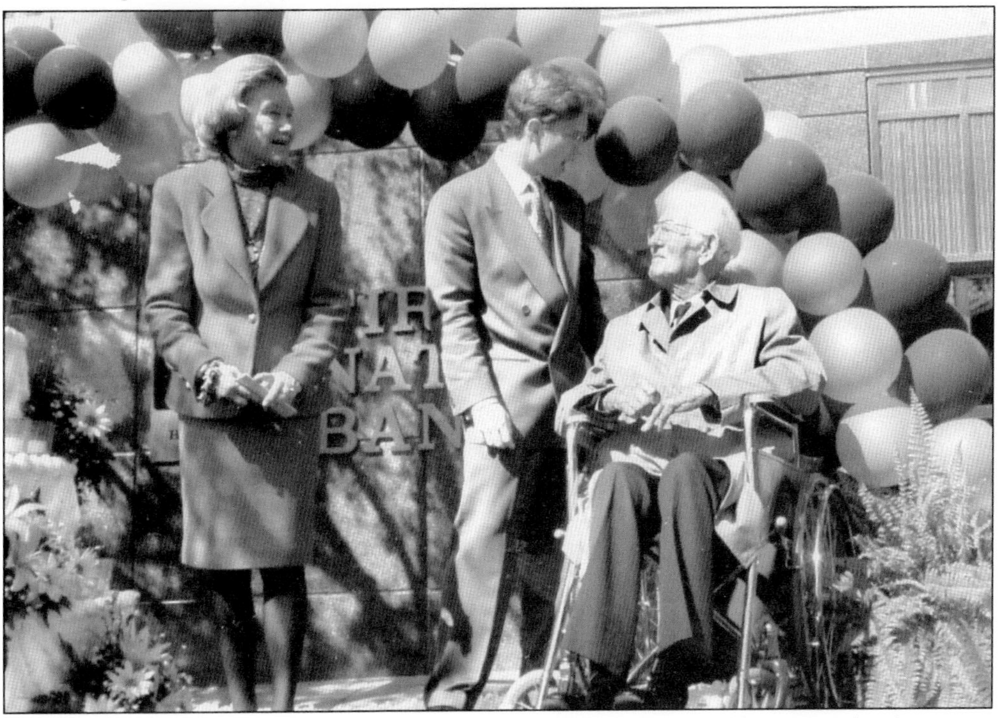

At the gala celebration in March of 1999, George Blanton Jr. was able to join the festivities. Mr. Blanton looks at his grandson, Sydney Freedberg Jr., and Adelaide Craver.

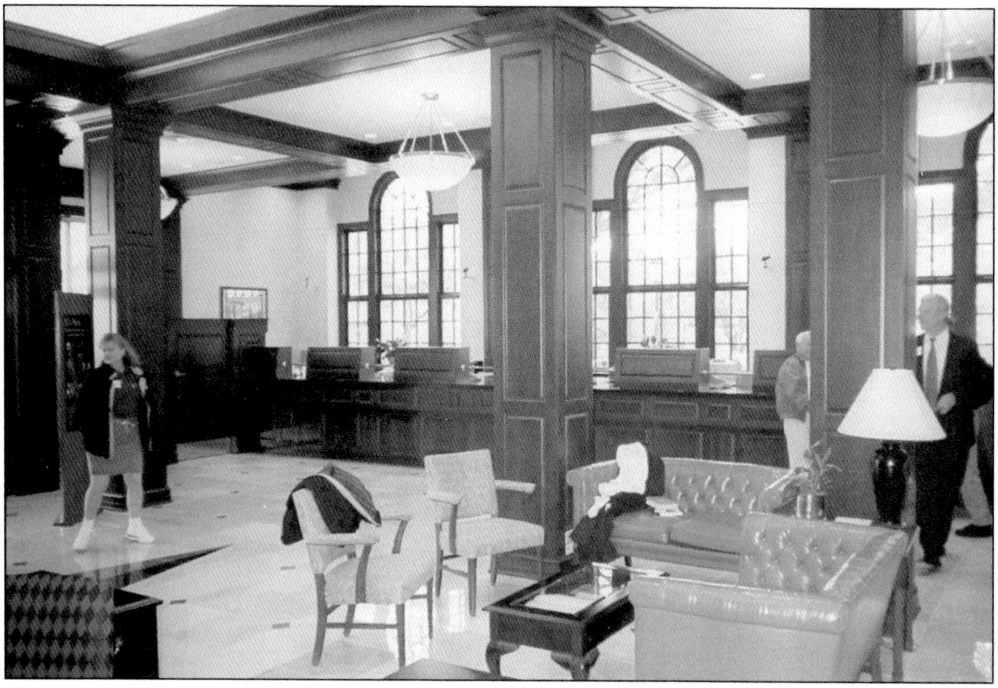

Customers were admitted to the newly renovated lobby. The windows that were covered in the 1960 remodeling reappeared with the same architectural style the earlier ones had had before they were covered.

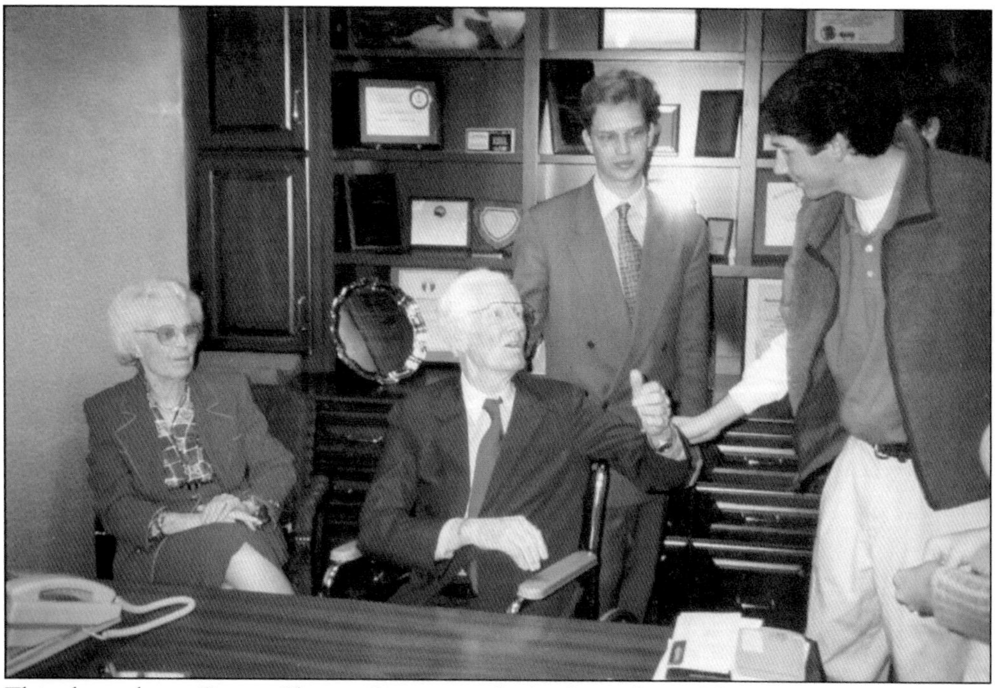

This photo shows George Blanton Jr. visiting the bank on the 125th anniversary celebration. With him are his wife, Nancy, and grandsons, Sydney Freedberg Jr. and Charles (Charley) Rush Hamrick IV (right).

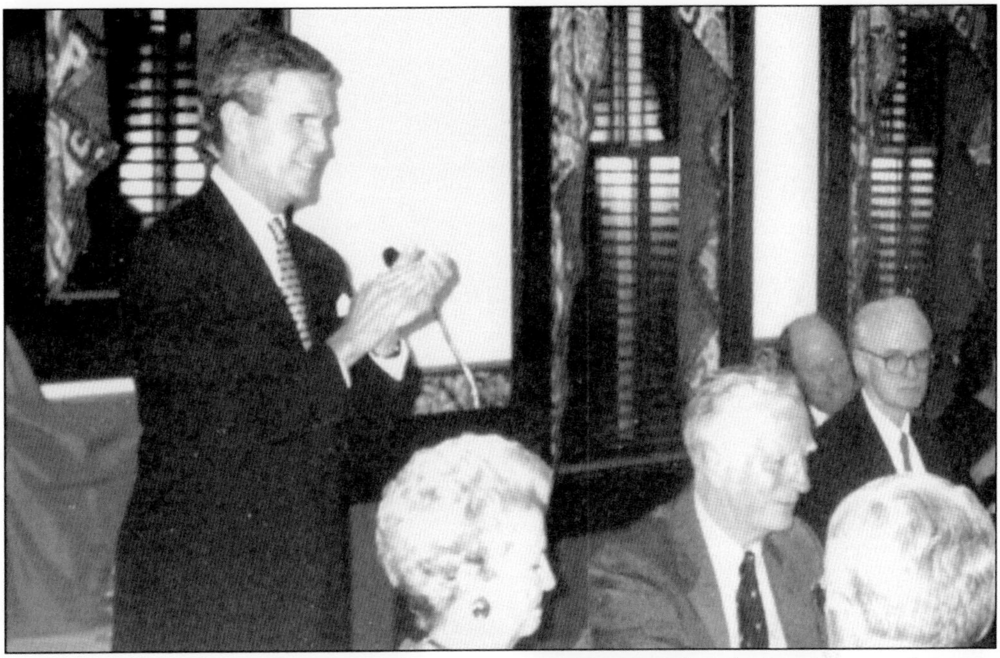

As a part of the 125th anniversary celebration, it was announced that the meeting room/banquet hall upstairs in the First National Bank Center would be named the Edgar Blanton Hamilton Hall in honor of Mr. Hamilton, current chairman of the board and former president and CEO of the bank. Shelby attorney Richard Craver speaks as Mr. Hamilton is honored.

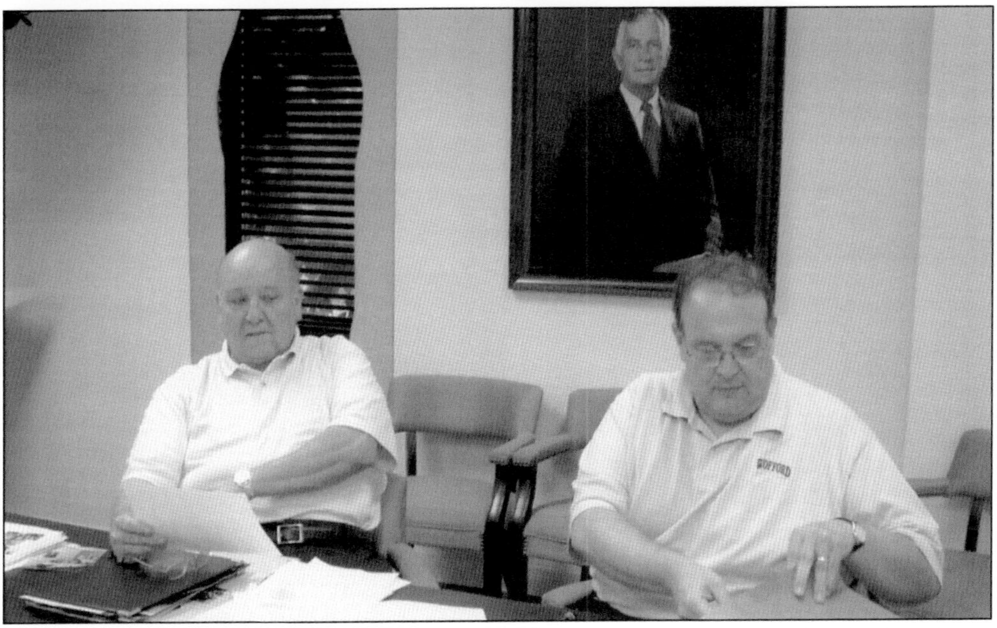

Mr. Hamilton has been recognized in many ways for his community activities. Authors Barry Hambright (left) and Rusty Patterson are seen here working in the Cleveland Community College conference room named in honor of Mr. Hamilton, whose portrait hangs on the wall in the photo. Ed Hamilton is an active supporter of the college and successfully chaired a bond referendum in support of the institution.

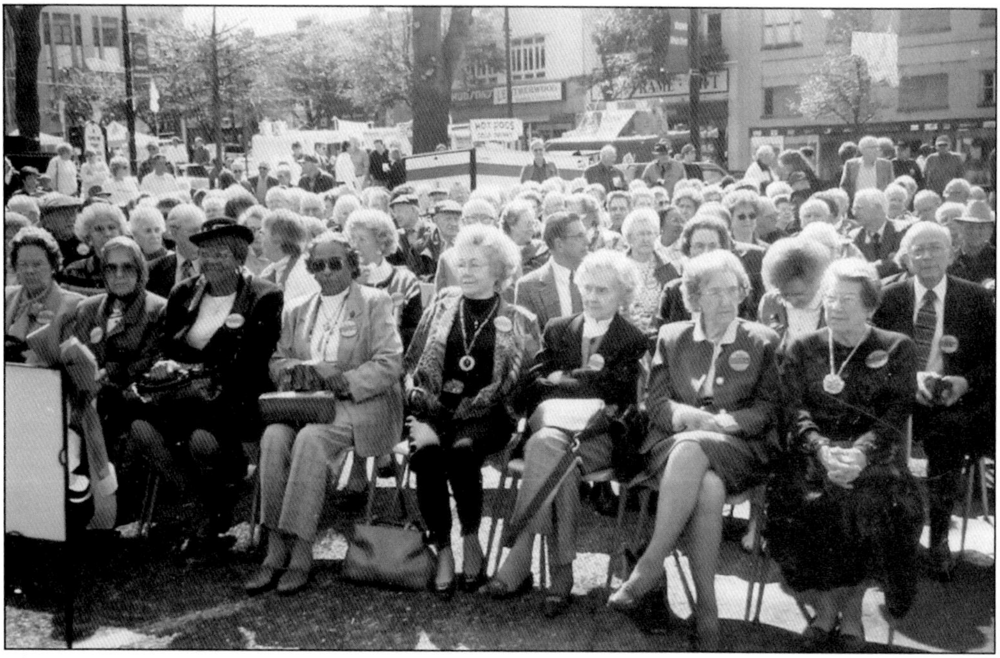

The anniversary day drew over 2,000 people to Uptown Shelby. First National emphasized its long-term service by creating a Heritage Club for customers who had banked with First National for over 50 years. A large group of these loyal customers were recognized at the event.

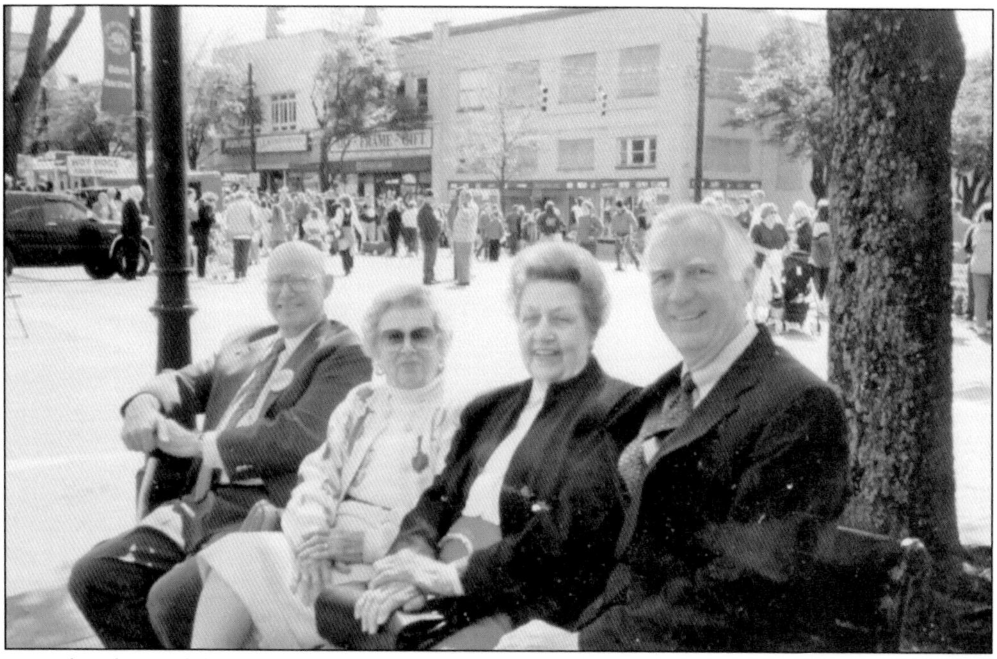

Seated in front of the bank with Board Chairman Ed Hamilton (right) are longtime customers (from left to right) William H. Withrow, Myrtle Rose, and Cornelia Barnett. Mr. Withrow is a retired naval commander and a retired Gardner-Webb University (GWU) political science professor. Although the Withrow family lives in Hollis in Rutherford County, they have banked at First National for five generations.

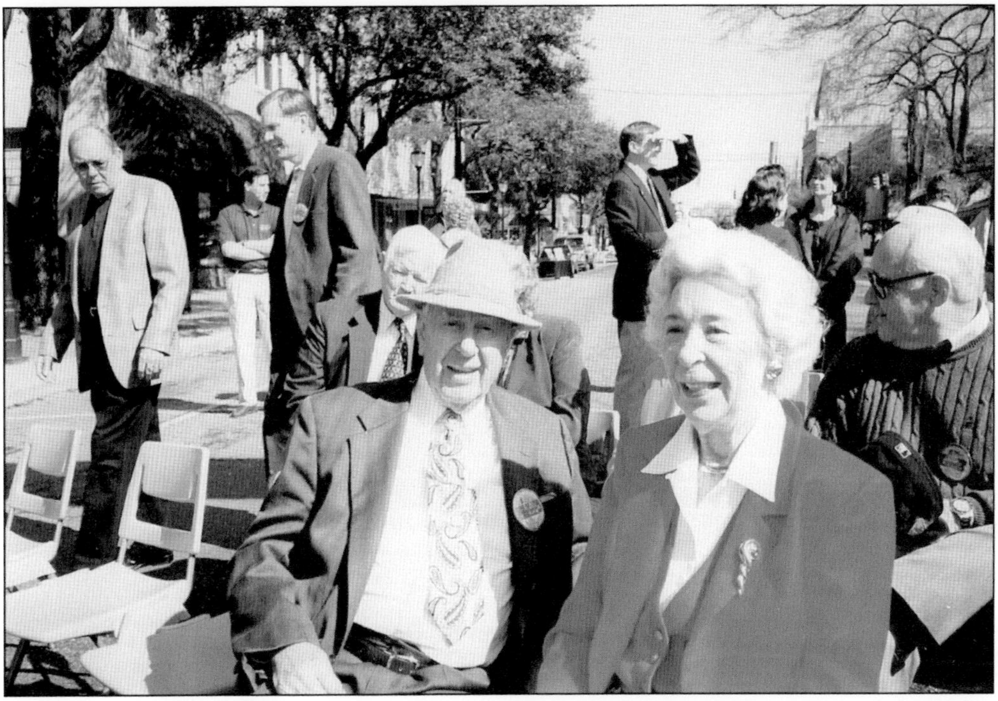

Among numerous leaders of the community in attendance were former editor of the *Shelby Daily Star* and bank director Henry Lee Weathers and his wife, Lillie.

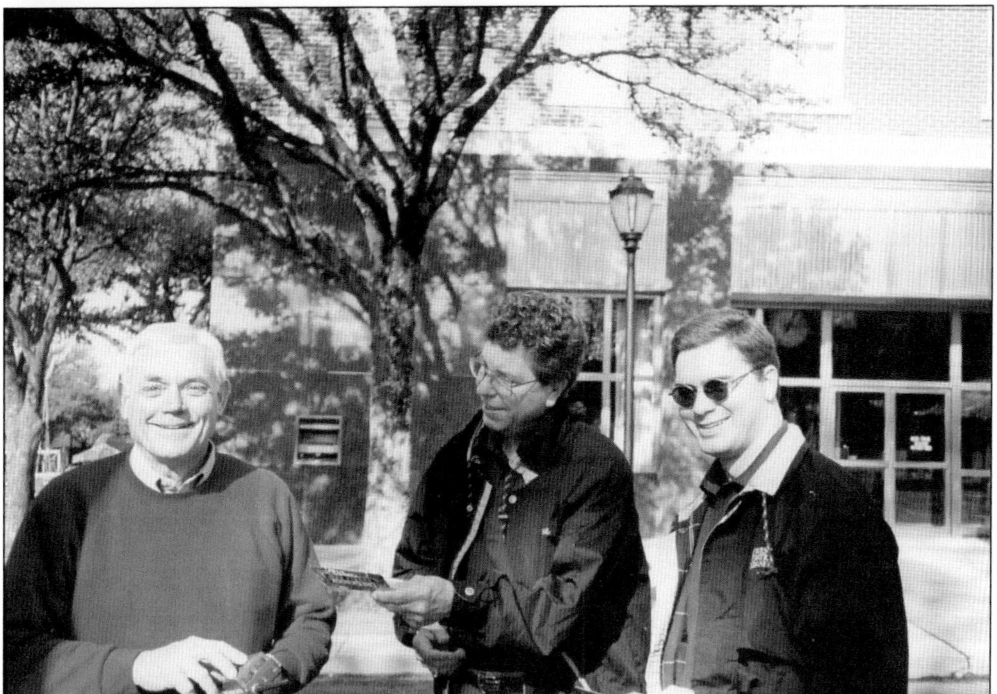

The front of the newly renovated bank is seen from across Lafayette Street. Enjoying the day, from left to right, are Morris Page, FNB Vice Pres. Hill Hudson III, and Steve Tharington.

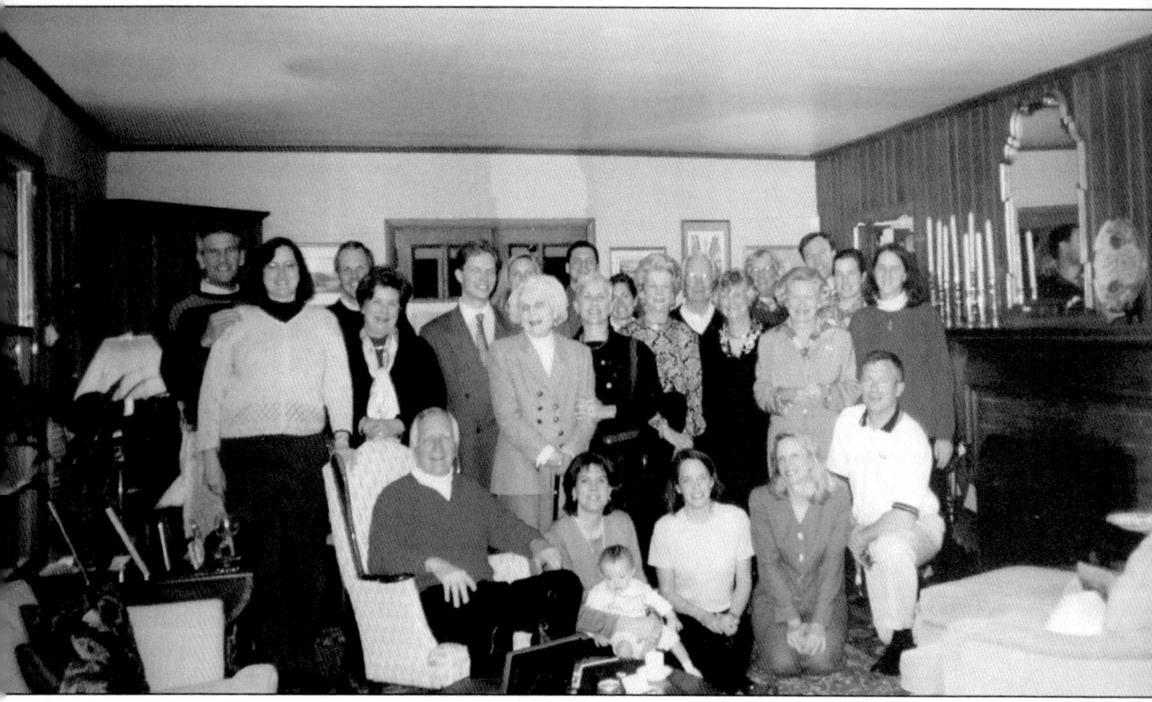

During the 125th anniversary celebration, the descendants of Burwell Blanton gathered for a photo. Pictured, from left to right, are the following: (front row seated) Ed Hamilton, Susan Hamilton (holding Parke Lovett), Betsy Hamilton, Catherine Blanton Freedberg, and Joe Hamilton III; (middle row) Caroline Chapell, Fran Moore, Sidney Freedberg, Nancy Blanton, Lydia Blanton, Margaret Hamilton, Edith Hamilton, Dede Hamilton, Adelaide Craver, Mildred Chapell, and Millie Thayer; (back row) Dick Craver, Dan Moore Jr., Adelaide Craver, Newton Craver, Joe Hamilton Jr., Helen Thayer Chapell, and Rick Lovett.

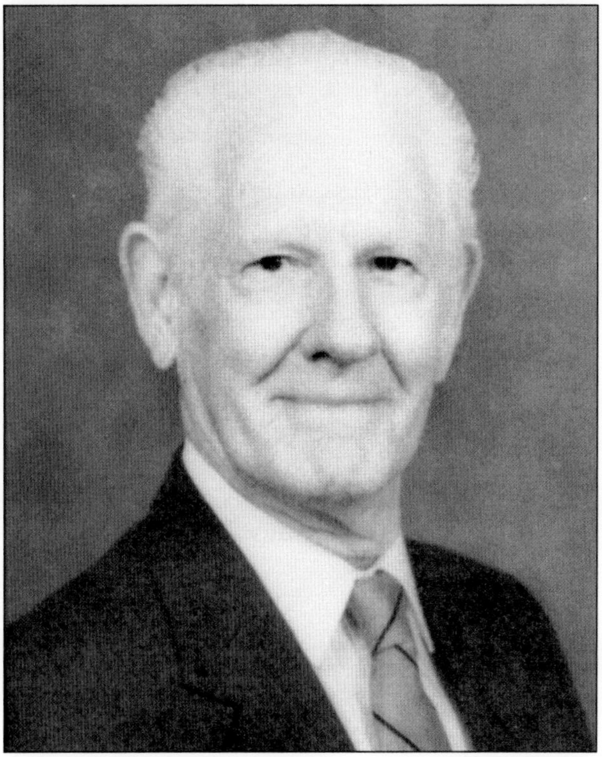

A sad note, as the bank completed 125 years of service, was that George Blanton Jr. became ill in 1999 and died in 2001. Mr. Blanton had been a part of the bank since 1936, and he had grown up with an uncle and a father who served as presidents of First National. For many who grew up in Shelby in the post–World War II era, George Blanton Jr. was First National Bank. Mr. Blanton was a man who truly loved people and sincerely tried to meet their needs. Those who knew him in other areas of his life saw a man who did not like dishonesty, loved his family, and served his community. His wife, Nancy, relates that he never brought the bank home; he had a life outside the bank's walls.

Mr. Blanton had a long and distinguished career. After graduating from the University of North Carolina, where he received a B.S. degree in business administration in 1935, and working for a year at American Trust Company in Charlotte, he returned to Shelby to work at First National in 1936. During World War II, he joined the United States Navy and served as ship service officer of the naval receiving station at Anacostia, D.C. He retired as lieutenant (jg) in 1946 and returned to the bank, where he became president in 1947 at the age of 32.

On a broader level, he became the first chairman of the North Carolina Young Bankers Association and served as a member of the board of directors of the Fifth Federal Reserve District and as a member of the Fifth Regional Advisory Committee of the OCC. In 1964, he was appointed to the board of the Federal Reserve Bank in Richmond, Virginia.

He was an advocate of the county's business and industrial life. He was instrumental in the development and organization of a number of businesses and industrial enterprises in the county. He was a strong community builder and displayed a keen interest in the people of Cleveland County. He was a charter member and officer in the Shelby Junior Chamber of Commerce as well as a director and vice president of the Shelby Chamber of Commerce. The press box at Shelby High School stadium is named in his honor.

He was actively involved in Gardner-Webb University, where he was twice elected chairman of the board of advisors. He was awarded a doctorate of humanities from GWU in 1997 and named trustee emeritus in 1999. In 2000, the Hamrick Hall auditorium was named in his honor.

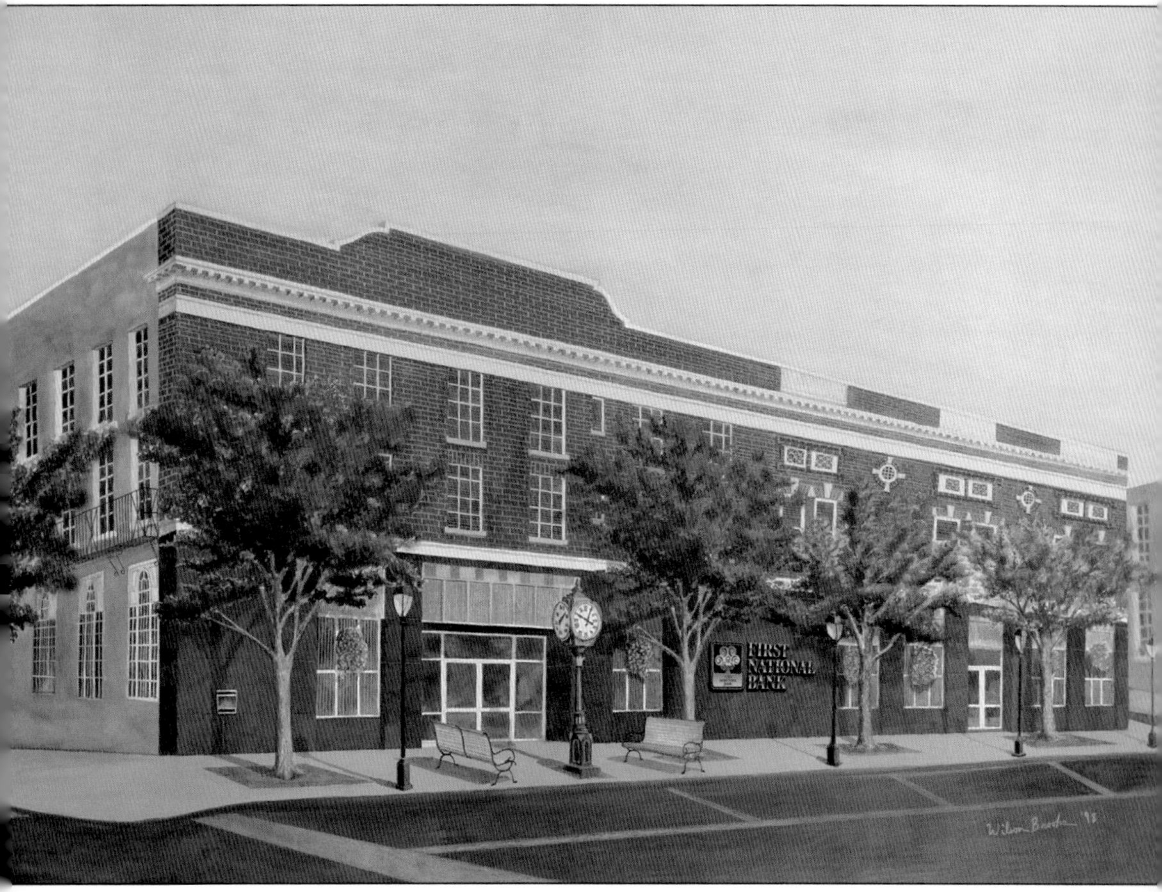

Shown above in an artist's rendering by Wilson Brooks commissioned for the bank's 125th anniversary celebration which captures the impressive new facade that characterized the solid institution George Blanton Jr. left to new generations. In 2000, the 1998 renovation received the L. Vincent Lowe Jr. Business Award presented by The Historic Preservation Foundation of North Carolina, Inc. for support and promotion of historic preservation.

Three

A Business Is Only as Good as Its People
The Bank's Extended Family

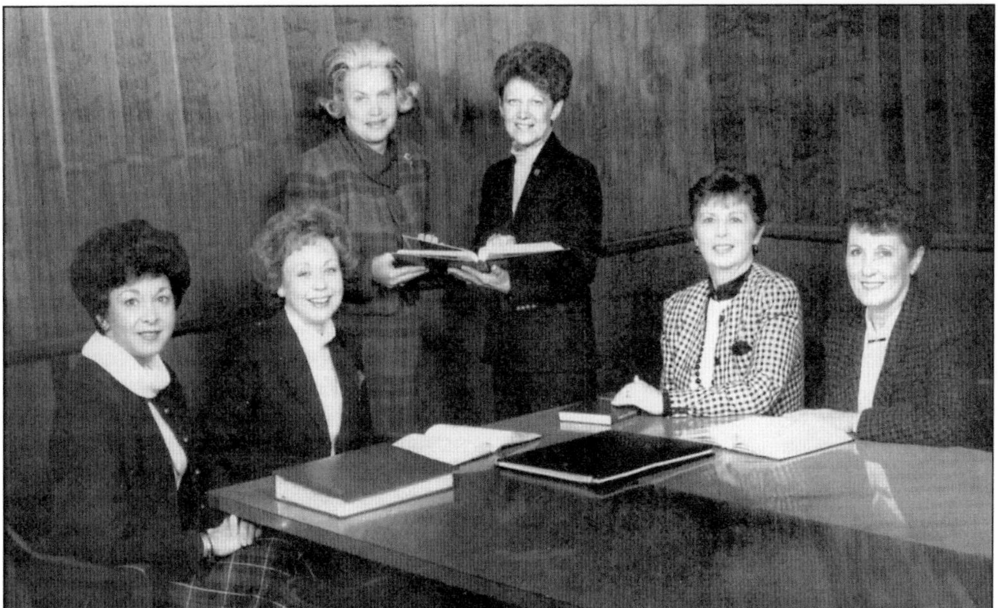

This photograph ran in an early 1990s promotional brochure that noted the management and staff are loaded with talented and capable women. Pictured from left to right are Helen Jeffords, Brenda Page, Adelaide Craver, Carol Treharne (Wood), Barbara Allen, and Dorothy Pearson.

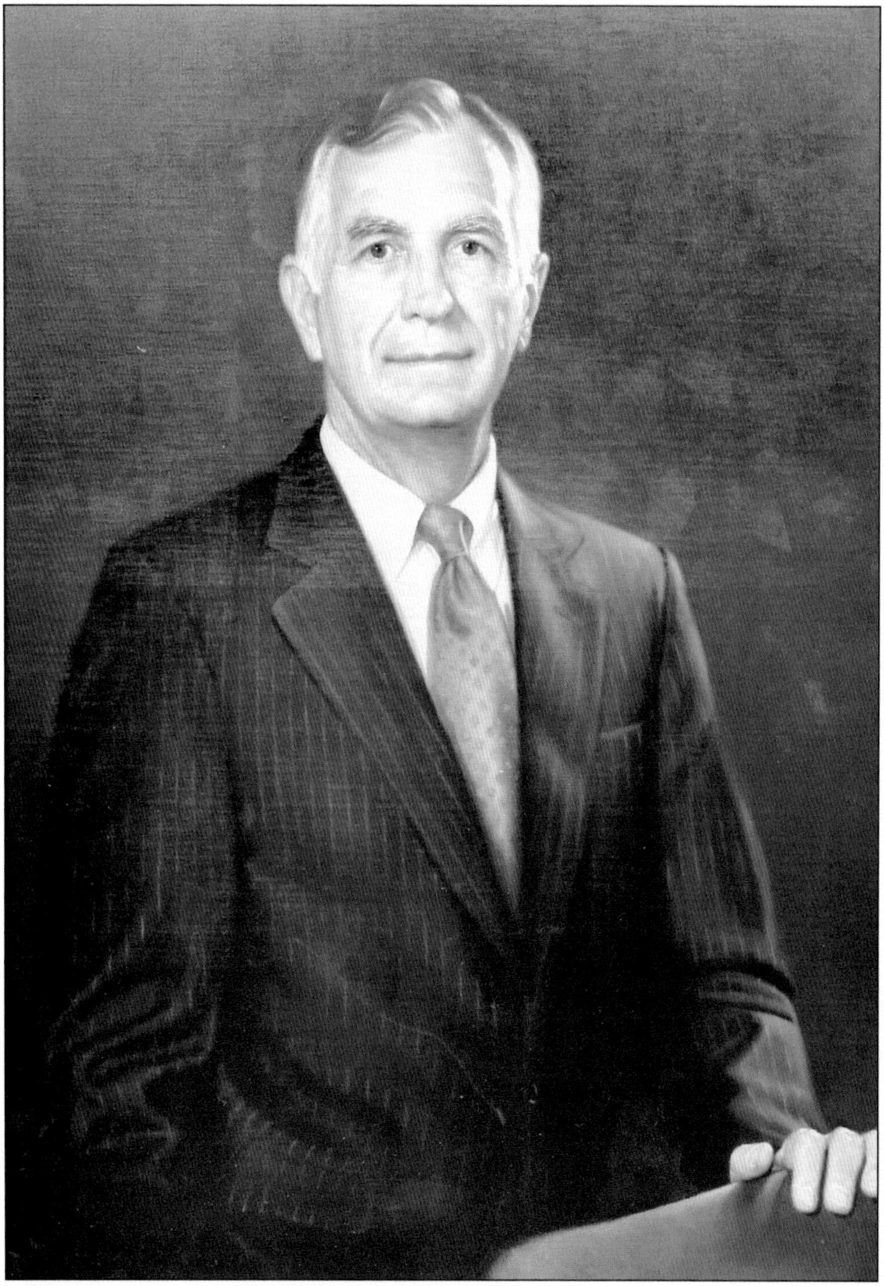

Edgar Blanton Hamilton joined First National in 1961 at the invitation of his cousin, George Blanton Jr. The son of Joseph and Betty Blanton Hamilton, Ed spent his early childhood in Charlotte and grew up in Atlanta. He graduated from the Georgia Institute of Technology before serving in Germany as a second lieutenant in the army. Hamilton worked in sales with Westinghouse Electric Corporation before joining the bank. Ed is a graduate of the Carolinas Banking School, the Stonier Graduate School of Banking, Rutgers University, and the Kenan-Flagler Executive Management Program at the University of North Carolina in Chapel Hill. Ed succeeded George Blanton Jr. as president of First National Bank in 1979, CEO in 1985, and chairman of the board in 1996.

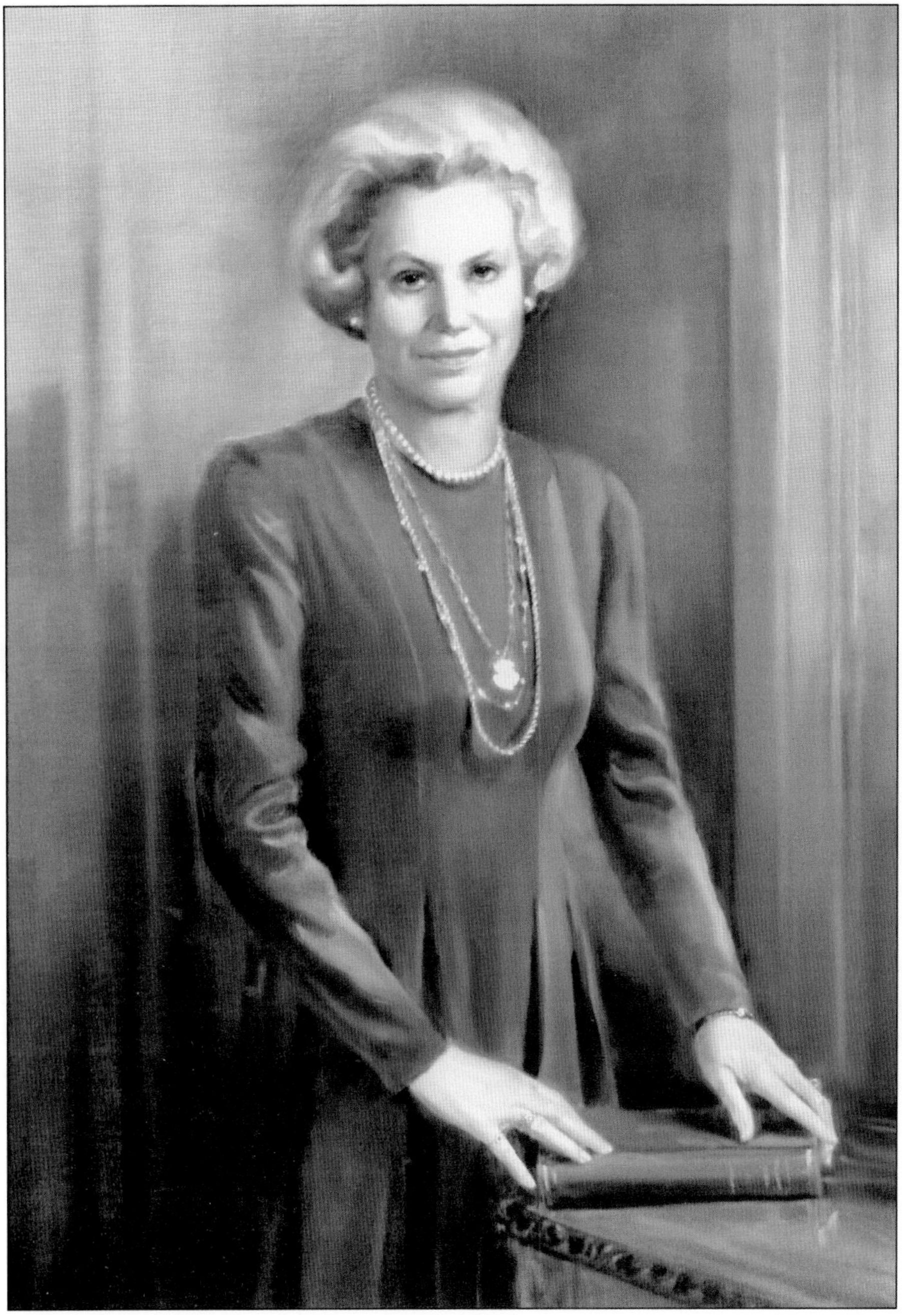

Adelaide Austell Craver joined First National Bank in 1981 as vice president and cashier after 14 years of banking experience in the trust department of First Union National Bank in Charlotte. The daughter of Charles and Mary Adelaide Austell, she grew up in Shelby. Adelaide is a graduate of Duke University, with a B.A. degree in economics, and the University of North Carolina in Chapel Hill Law School, with a J.D. degree. After joining First National, she graduated from the Kenan-Flagler Executive Management Program at the University of North Carolina in Chapel Hill. Adelaide became the bank's eighth president in 1996. She added CEO to her duties in 1998.

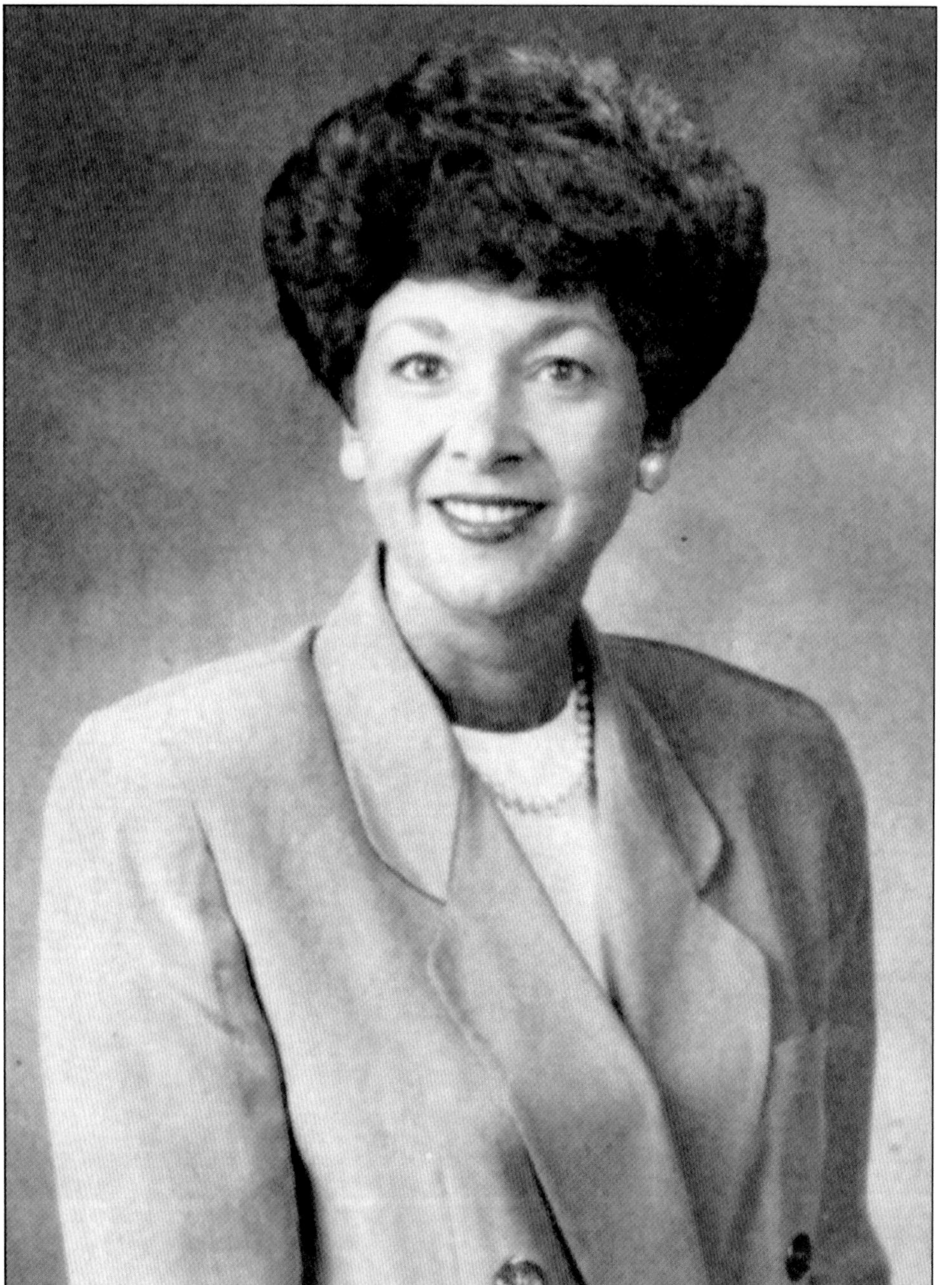

Helen A. Jeffords grew up in Pensacola, Florida, and is a graduate of the University of Georgia with a B.A. degree in accounting. Helen, a certified public accountant in Pennsylvania and North Carolina, had 15 years experience in public accounting and health services before joining First National in 1983. Seeing the need for a highly trained financial officer, Ed Hamilton hired Helen in 1983 as vice president and comptroller. Today, she serves as executive vice president and chief financial officer for the bank and is on the board of directors. Her duties include managing financial services and the bank's investment portfolio, and she is instrumental in the bank's general operation.

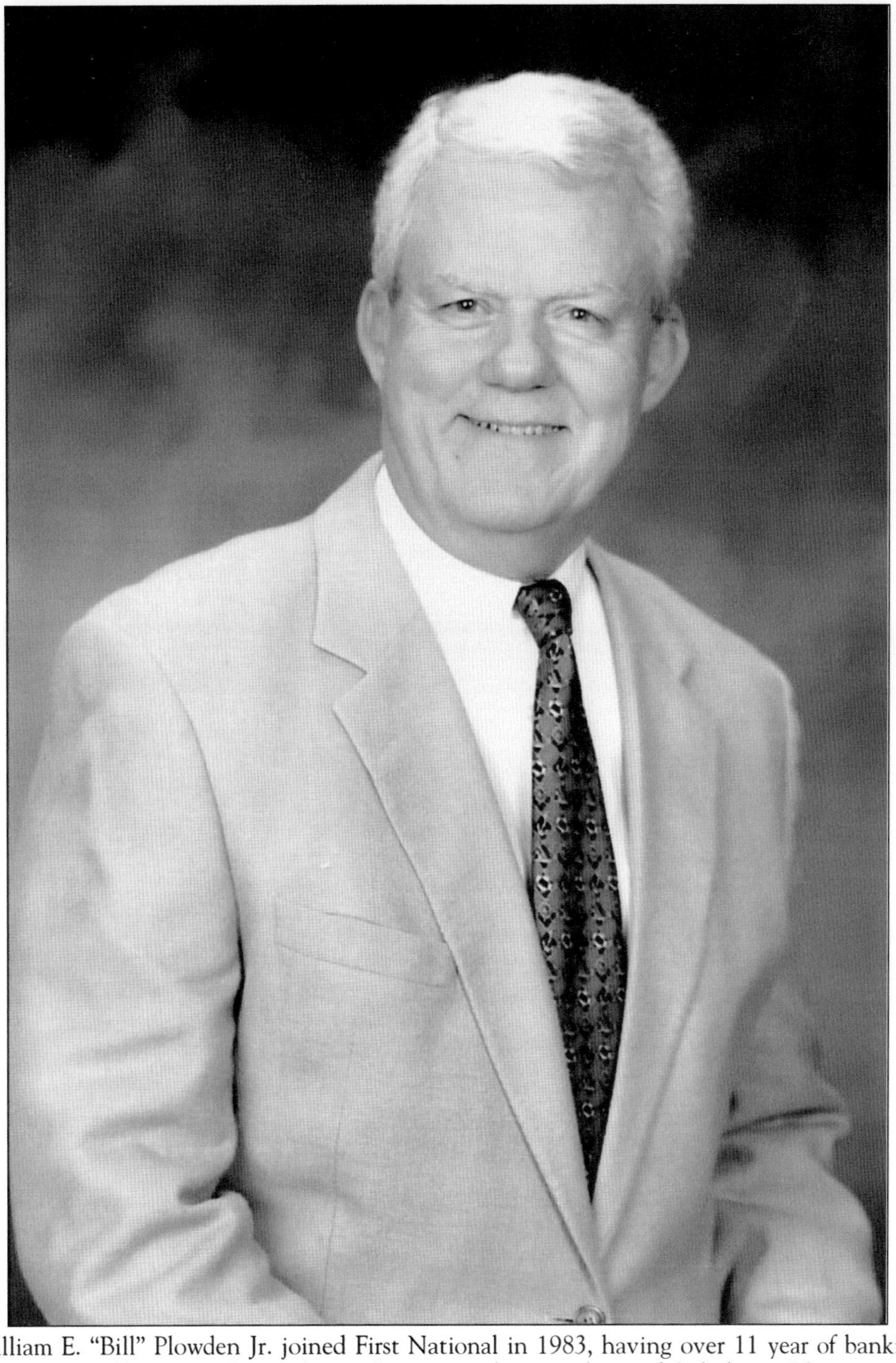

William E. "Bill" Plowden Jr. joined First National in 1983, having over 11 year of banking experience. Bill was raised in Atlanta, Georgia, and is a graduate of Oglethorpe University in Atlanta, with a dual major in business and economics; Woodrow Wilson College, with a J.D. degree; and the National Trust School at Northwestern University. Today, Bill serves as vice chairman of the board and senior trust officer for the bank. In addition to his duties as the head of the trust department, he oversees the brokerage and financial planning.

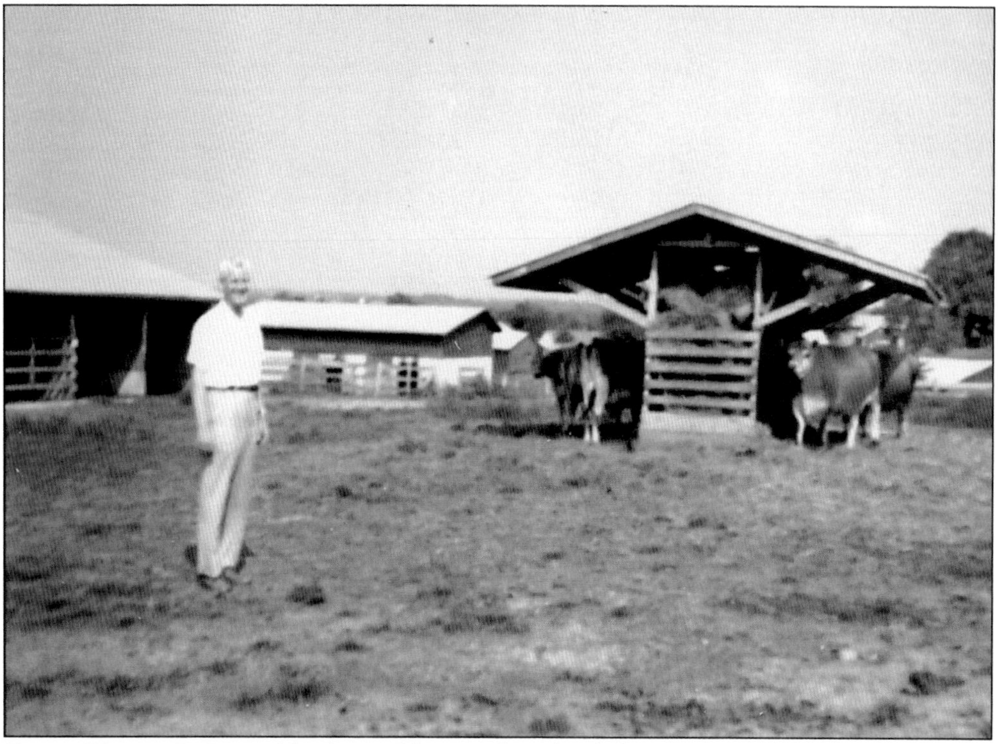

George Blanton Jr. learned his love of farming from his father. It is said that some of George's happiest moments were spent on the farm.

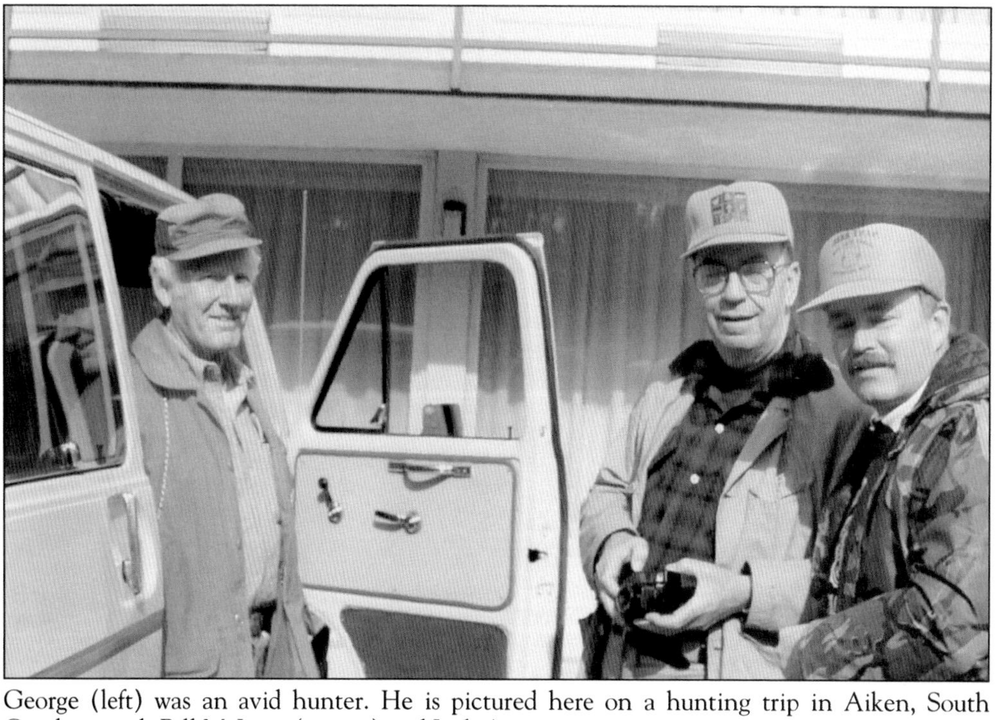

George (left) was an avid hunter. He is pictured here on a hunting trip in Aiken, South Carolina, with Bill McLean (center) and Jack Arey.

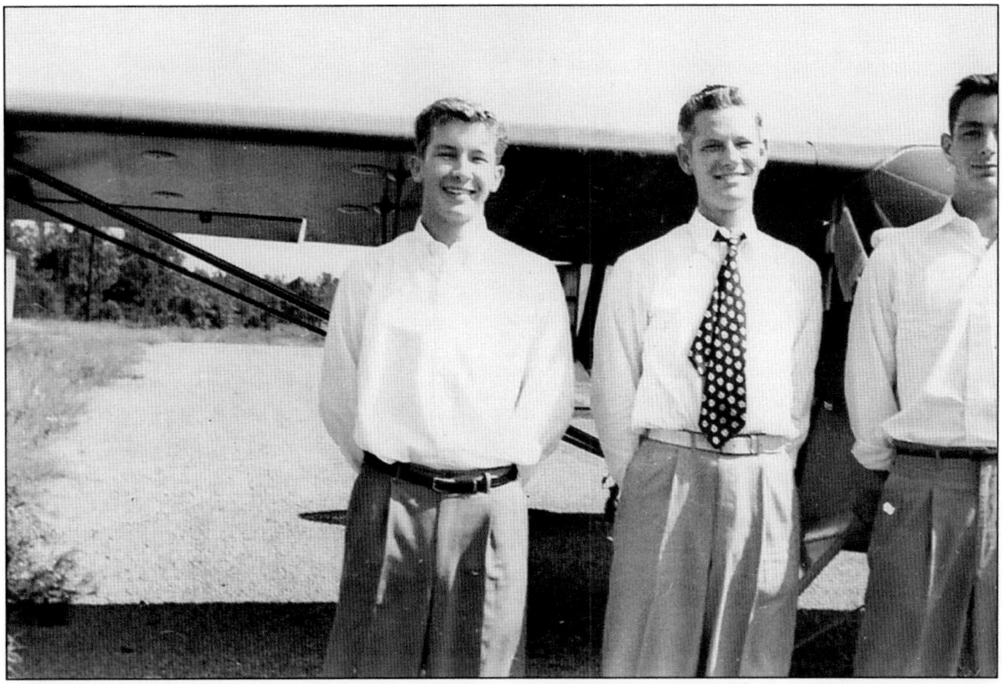

In August of 1949, George Blanton Jr. (center) flew to Atlanta to visit Joe Hamilton Jr. (left) and Joe's brother Ed Hamilton.

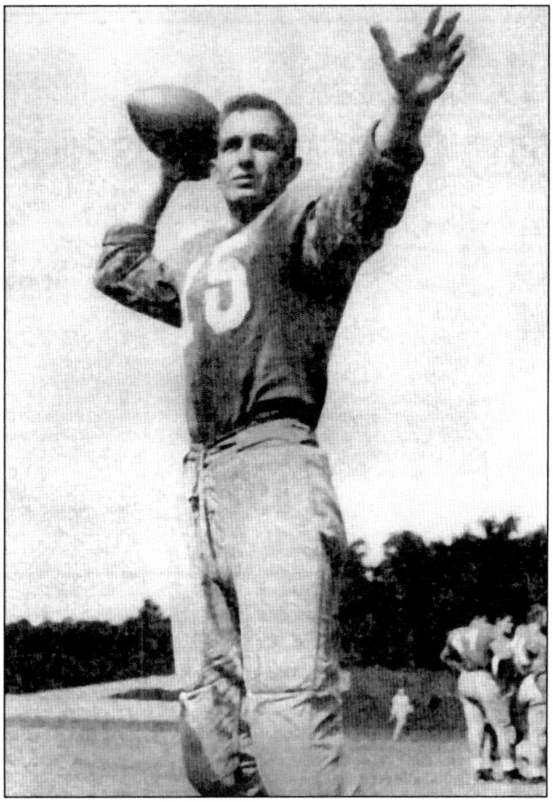

Ed Hamilton played football at Georgia Tech. "Irish Eddie" once threw four touchdowns before nearly 40,000 fans at Grant Field in Atlanta. Fortunately for the citizens of Cleveland County, Ed gave up his football career and concentrated on academics.

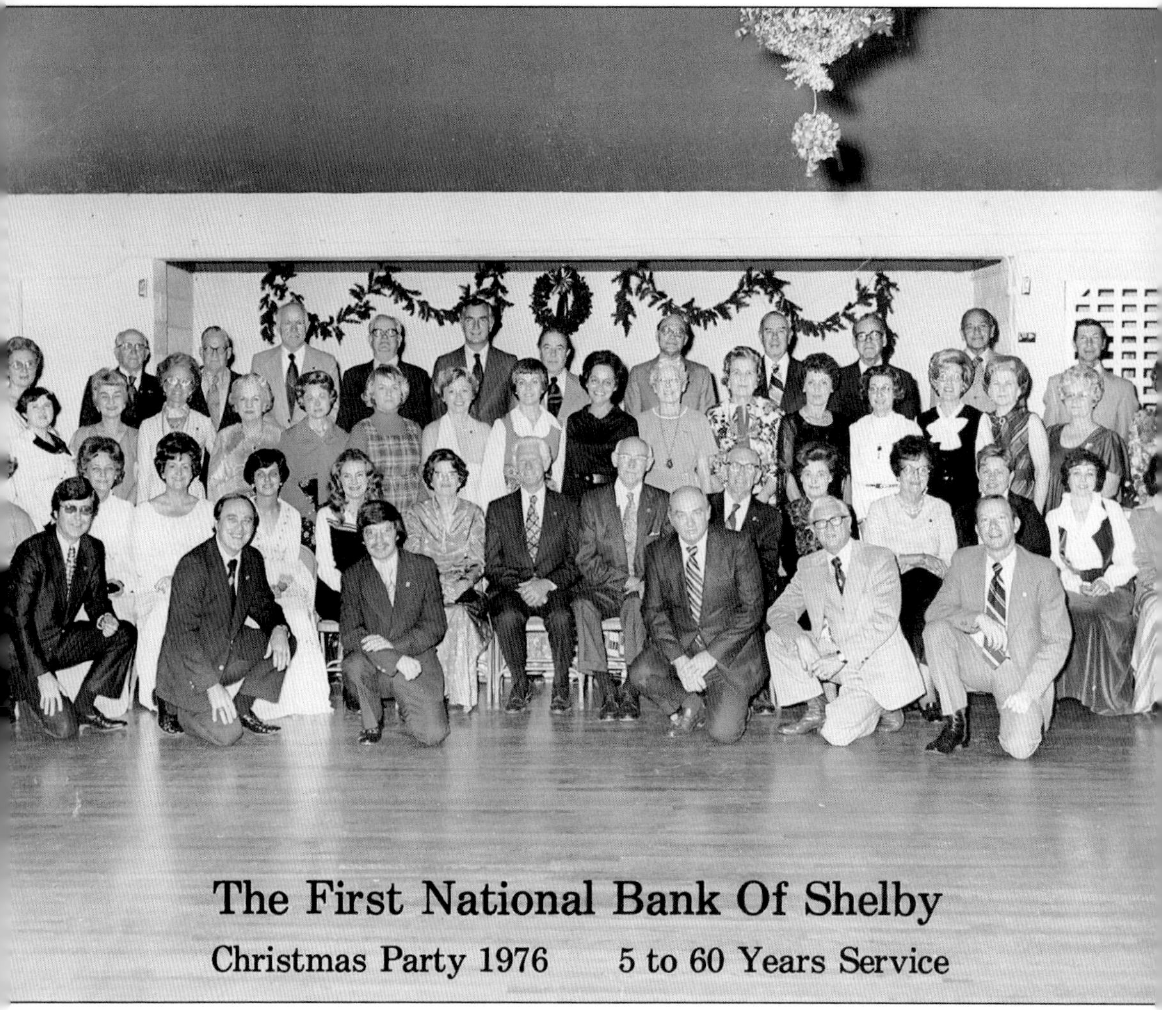

This group photograph was taken at the former Elks Club during the bank's 1976 annual Christmas party. The group represented 5 to 60 years of service with the bank. Pictured, from left to right, are the following: (first row) Bobby Smith, Jack Creech, Tommy Dorsey, David Putnam, Max Wallace, and Bobby Guffey; (second row) Nina Price, Estelle Ledford, Ruth Champion, Debbie Greene-Horn, Mary Ivester, Mabel Elliott, George Blanton Jr., Paxton Elliott, C.S. Mull, Dorothy Shytle, Louise McBrayer, Mary Rudisill, Brenda Page, and Rita Lowe; (third row) Diane Hines, Libby Watson, Katherine Dayberry, Juanita Webb, Eloise Wright, Edrie Ramsey, Brenda Roberts, Betty Ledbetter, Jean Greene, Clara Greene, Mary Harrill, Dot Pearson, Edna Wright, Betty Walker, Ruth Wilkie, Lib McSwain, and Hanson Lineberger; (fourth row) Mozelle Ingle, Joe Whisnant, Fred Morehead, Dan Jones, Flay Gardner, Ed Hamilton, Bill Pearce, Rush Hamrick Jr., Henry Weathers, Horace Carter, R.T. LeGrand Jr., and Vaughn Whitaker.

George Blanton Jr. (seated), Mabel Elliott, and Bobby Smith pose for this photograph in Mr. Blanton's office. The image represents over 150 years experience in banking at First National.

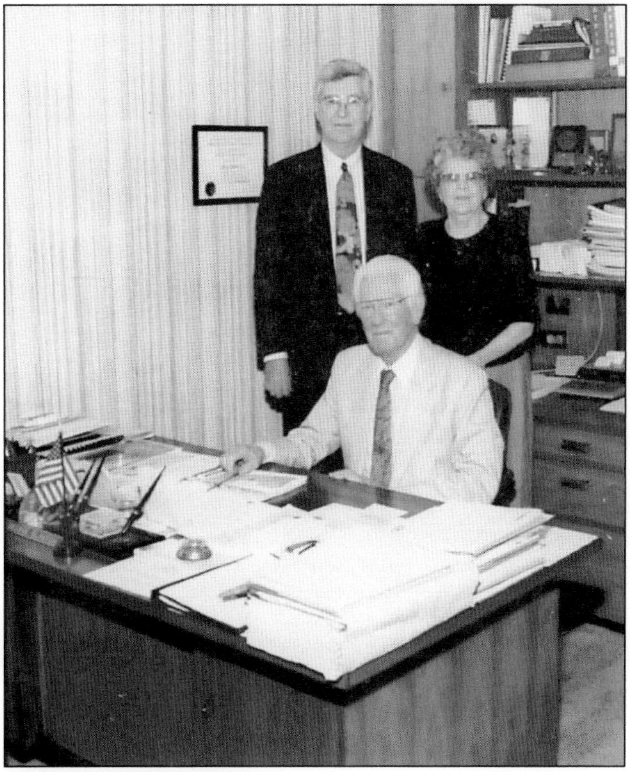

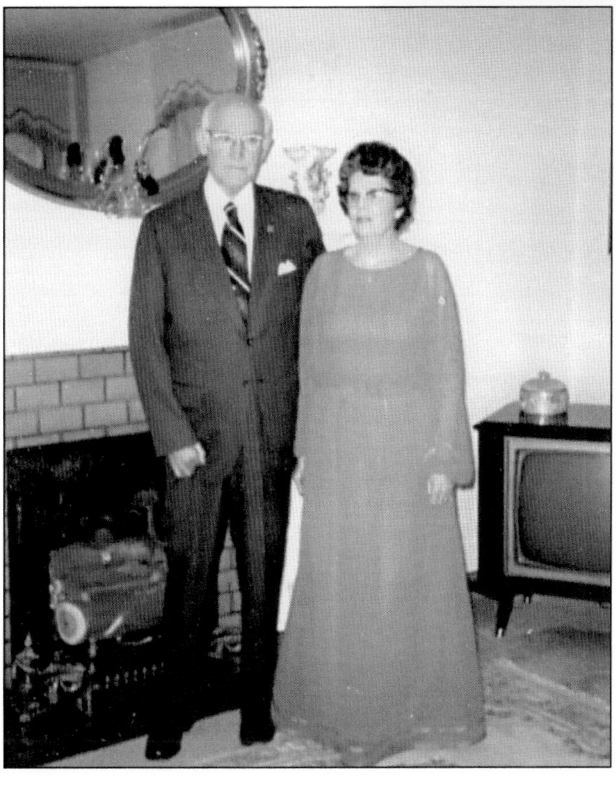

Paxton and Mabel Elliott are pictured at their retirement party on February 19, 1979. Paxton worked at First National for 60 years, having started in 1919. Mabel started with the bank in 1942. She returned to the bank after a short retirement and, after 62 years, still holds a position in customer relations today.

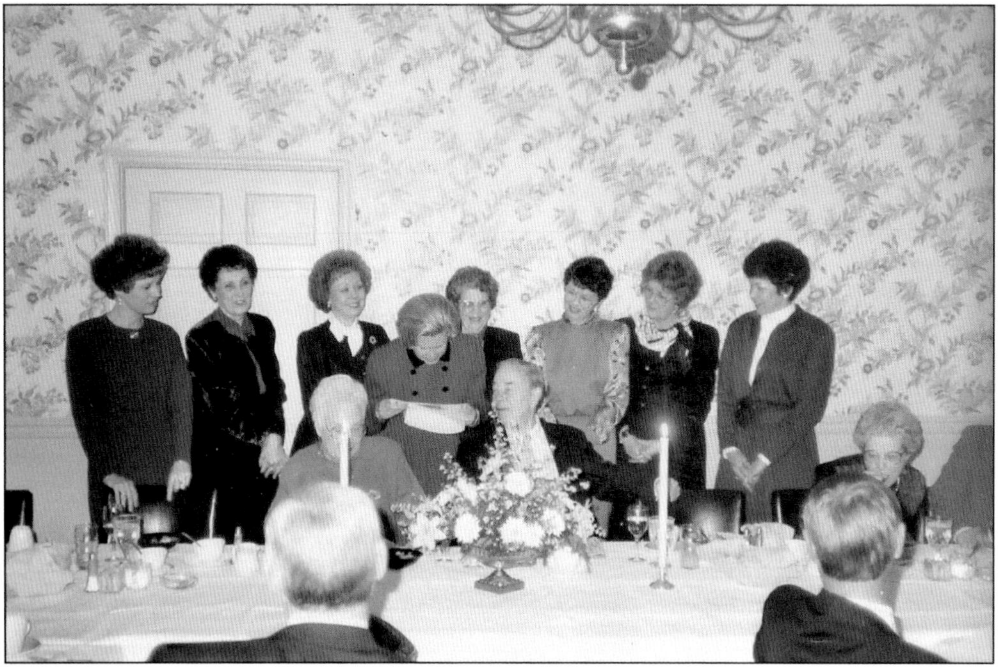

The bank celebrated Bill Pearce's retirement with a party on January 31, 1991. Pictured, from left to right, are the following: (seated) Sue and Bill Pearce; (standing) Sharon Owens, Dorothy Pearson, Brenda Page, Adelaide Craver, Mabel Elliott, Barbara Allen, Ruth Champion, and Helen Jeffords.

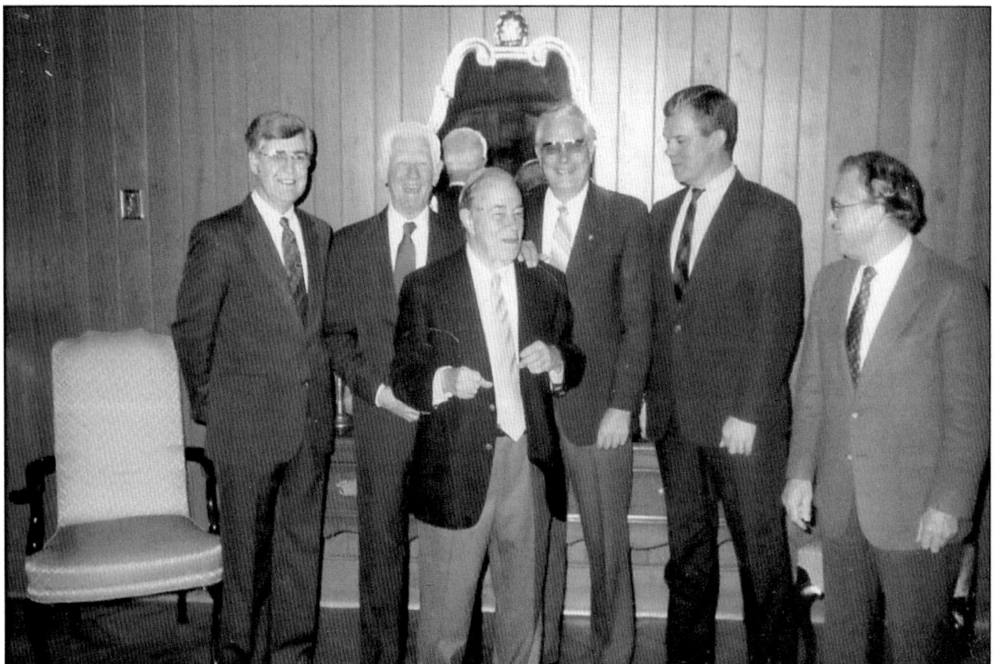

Pictured with Bill at his retirement party are, from left to right, Bobby Smith, George Blanton Jr., Bill, Ken Gibson, Bill Plowden, and Calvin Blalock.

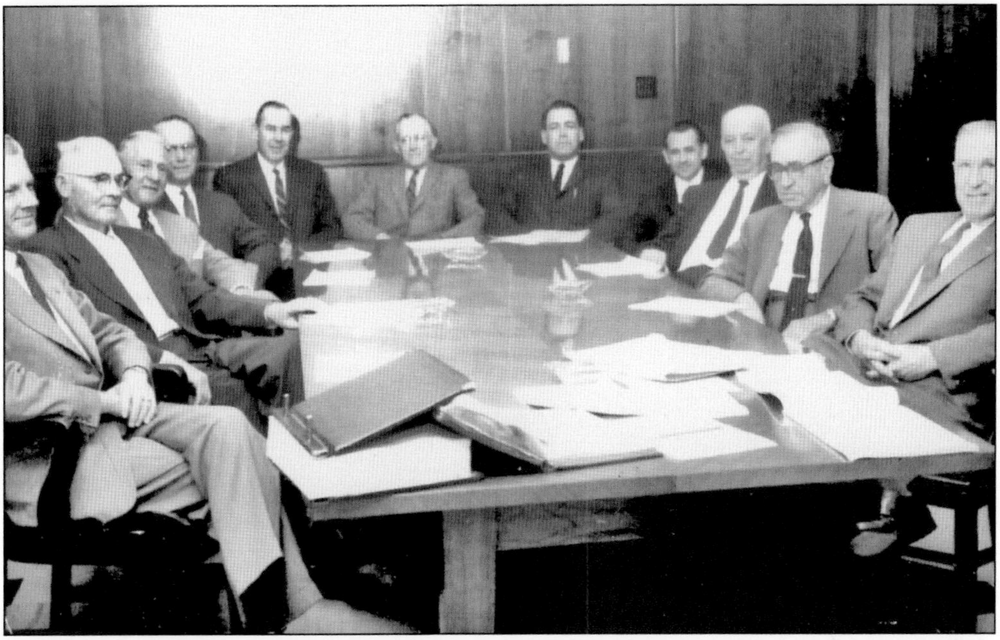

The board of directors of First National took a moment from a 1958 meeting for this photo opportunity. Pictured, from left to right, are George Blanton Jr., Tom M. Cornwell, Jean Schenck, J.R. Dover Jr., Henry L. Weathers Sr., Joseph C. Whisnant, Horace H. Carter, Fred W. Alexander, D.W. Royster Sr., R.T. LeGrand Sr., and Clarence S. Mull. Absent from the meeting were George Blanton Sr., Otis Mull, and Don Carpenter.

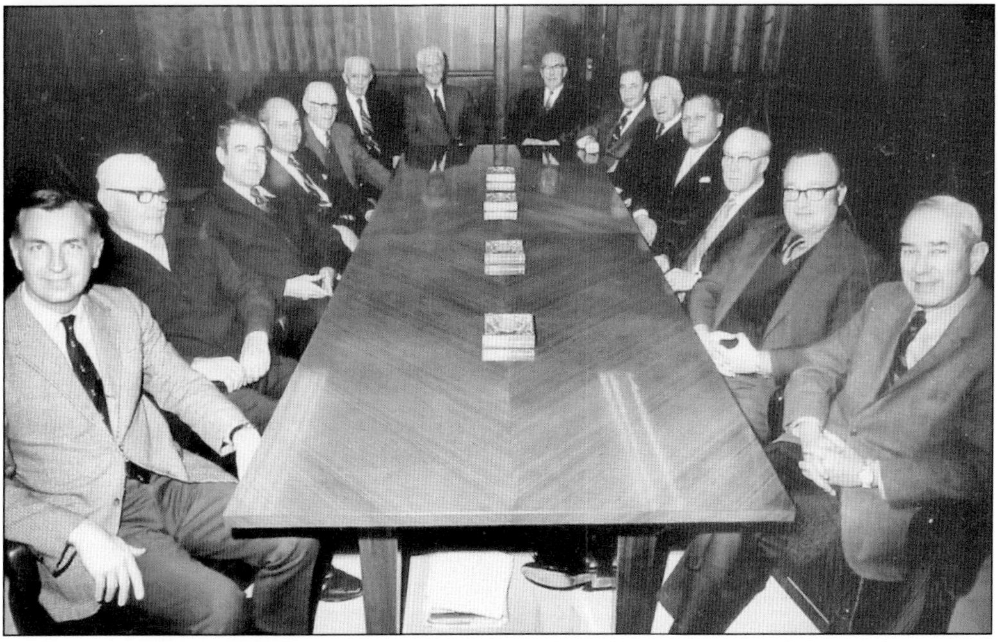

In 1971, the board of directors was comprised of the following, pictured from left to right: Edgar Blanton Hamilton, Tom M. Cornwell, Horace H. Carter, R.T. LeGrand Jr., Joseph C. Whisnant, D.W. Royster Sr., George Blanton Jr., C.S. Mull, William Pearce, Jean Schenck, R. Patrick Spangler, Charles I. Dover, J.R. Dover III, and Henry Lee Weathers Sr.

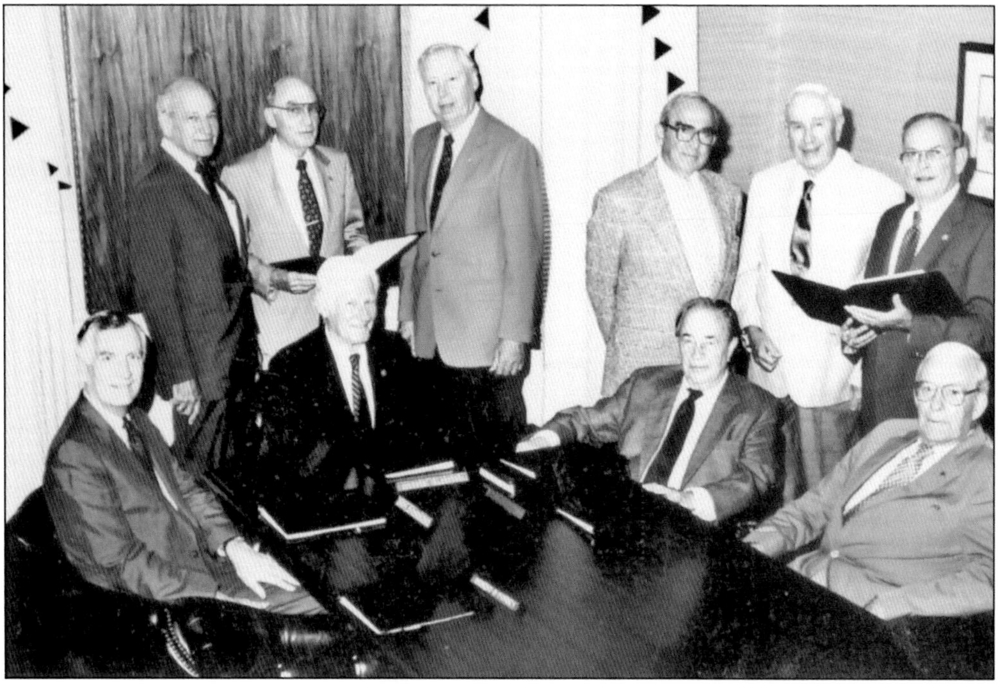

The board of directors, pictured in this 1989 photograph, are as follows, from left to right: (seated) Edgar B. Hamilton, president and CEO; George Blanton, Jr., chairman of the board; William E. Pearce, senior vice president; and Robert R. Forney; (standing) R.T. LeGrand Jr.; C. Rush Hamrick Jr.; Lloyd C. Bost; G.J. Vincent; Henry Lee Weathers Sr.; and Newlin Schenck.

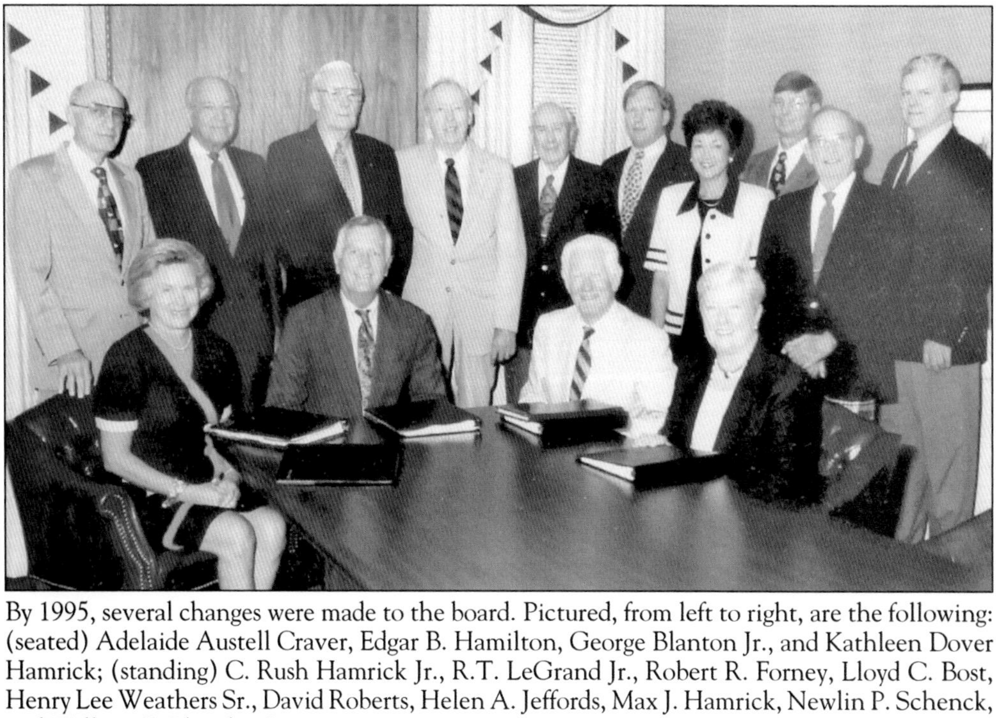

By 1995, several changes were made to the board. Pictured, from left to right, are the following: (seated) Adelaide Austell Craver, Edgar B. Hamilton, George Blanton Jr., and Kathleen Dover Hamrick; (standing) C. Rush Hamrick Jr., R.T. LeGrand Jr., Robert R. Forney, Lloyd C. Bost, Henry Lee Weathers Sr., David Roberts, Helen A. Jeffords, Max J. Hamrick, Newlin P. Schenck, and William E. Plowden Jr.

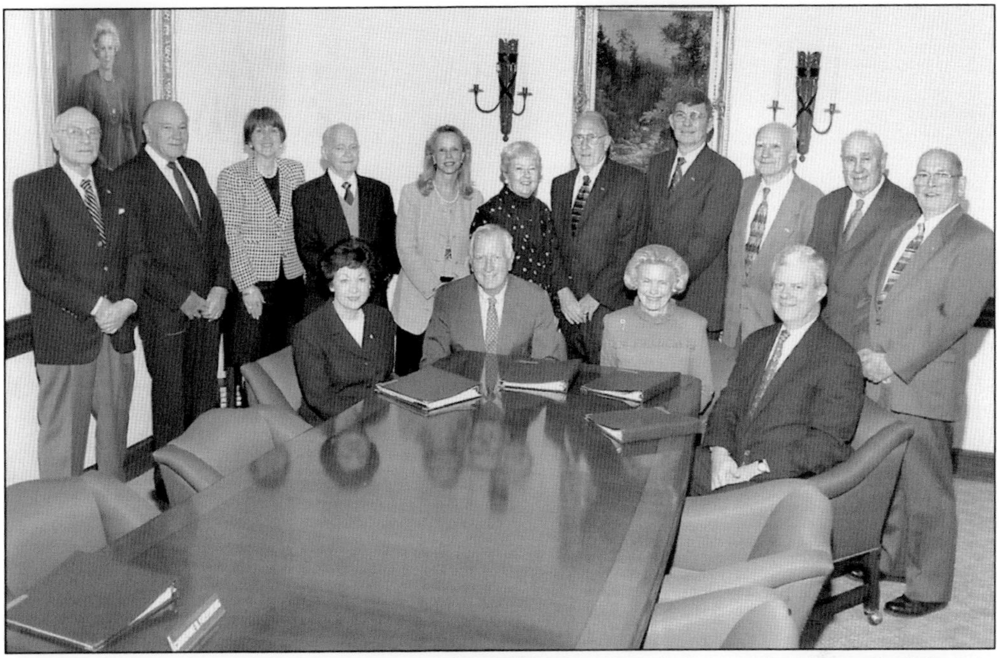

Pictured in this 2001 board meeting are the following, from left to right: (seated) Helen A. Jeffords; Edgar B. Hamilton; Adelaide Austell Craver; and William E. Plowden Jr.; (standing) C. Rush Hamrick Jr.; R.T. LeGrand Jr.; Martha R. Plaster; Henry P. Neisler; Catherine Blanton Freedberg, Ph.D.; Kathleen Dover Hamrick; Glee E. Bridges; Max J. Hamrick; Dr. John C. McGill; Henry Lee Weathers Sr.; and Newlin P. Schenck.

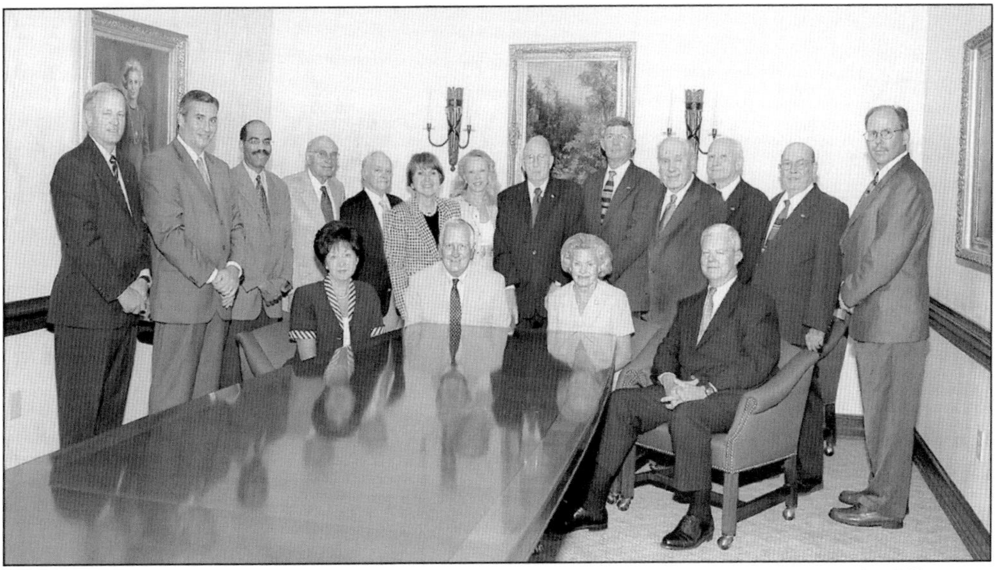

The 2004 board of directors of First National is pictured here. From left to right are the following: (seated) Helen Jeffords; Edgar B. Hamilton; Adelaide Austell Craver; and William E. Plowden Jr.; (standing) David W. Royster III; John O. Harris III; Dr. Kevin T. James; C. Rush Hamrick Jr.; Henry P. Neisler; Martha R. Plaster; Catherine Blanton Freedberg, Ph.D.; Glee E. Bridges; Max J. Hamrick; Henry Lee Weathers Sr.; Dr. John C. McGill; Newlin P. Schenck; and John E. Young.

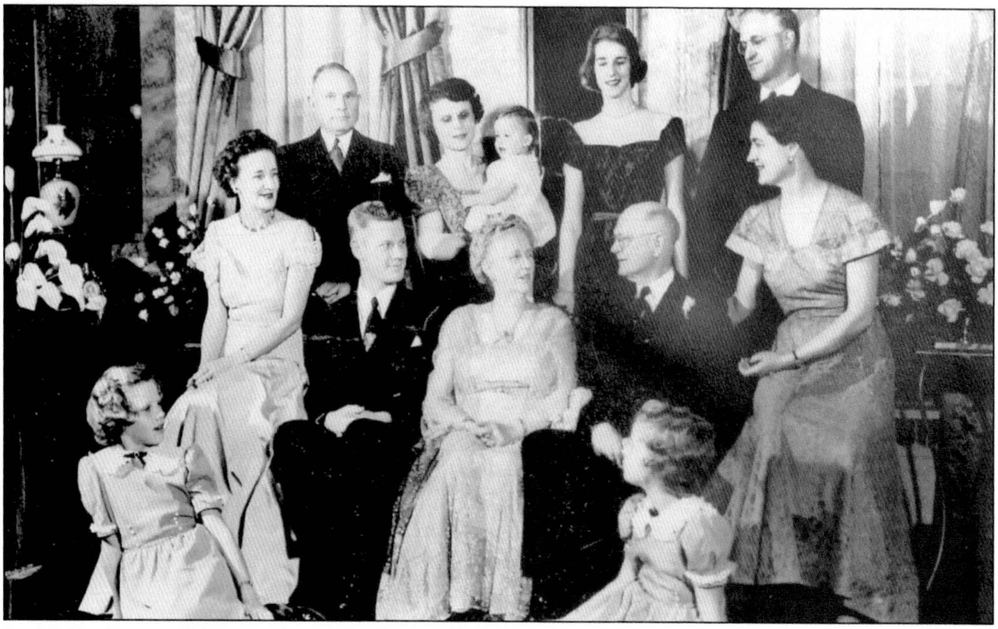

In 1950, George Blanton Sr. and Ida Estelle Wood Blanton celebrated their golden wedding anniversary. Gathered for the family photograph were the following, pictured from left to right: (seated on floor) Nancy D. Blanton and Catherine W. Blanton; (seated on the sofa) Millicent Blanton Thompson, George Blanton Jr., Mrs. George Blanton Sr., George Blanton Sr., and Caroline Blanton Thayer; (standing) Reggie Thompson, Nancy Blanton (holding Lydia Blanton), Helen Thayer Chapell, and Sherman Thayer.

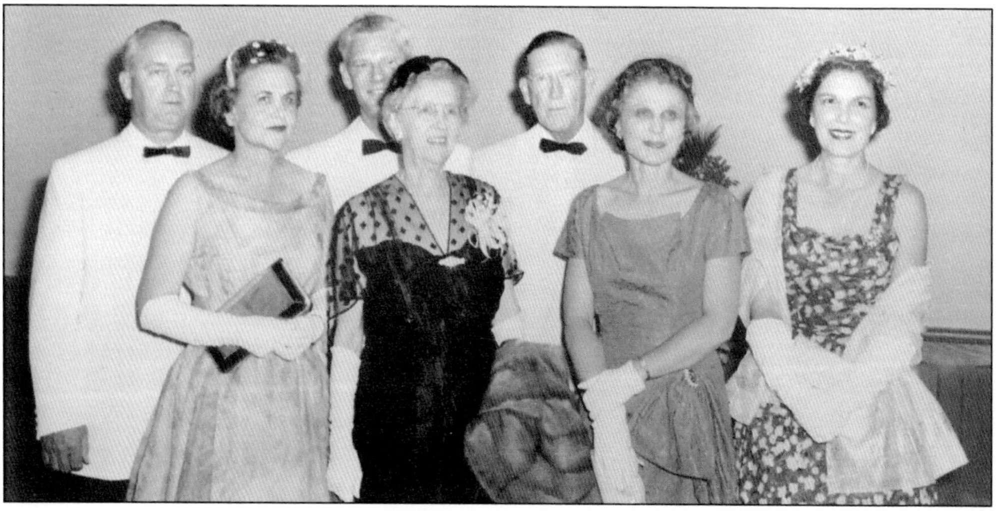

Descendants of Burwell Blanton gathered at the wedding of Joe and Dede Hamilton Jr. in Atlanta, Georgia, in 1957. They are, from left to right, as follows: (front row) Mary Adelaide Roberts Austell (granddaughter of Burwell Blanton's daughter Mary Judith and Richard Eskridge and the daughter of Frances Eskridge and W.J. Roberts Jr.), Ida Wood Blanton (Mrs. George Blanton Sr.), Nancy Dicks Blanton (Mrs. George Blanton Jr.), and Julia May (Mrs. Charles Webb); (back row) Charles B. Austell (husband of Mary Adelaide Austell), George Blanton Jr. (grandson of Burwell Blanton and son of George Blanton Sr. and Ida Wood Blanton), and Charles Webb (son of Burwell's daughter Margaret and George Webb Jr.)

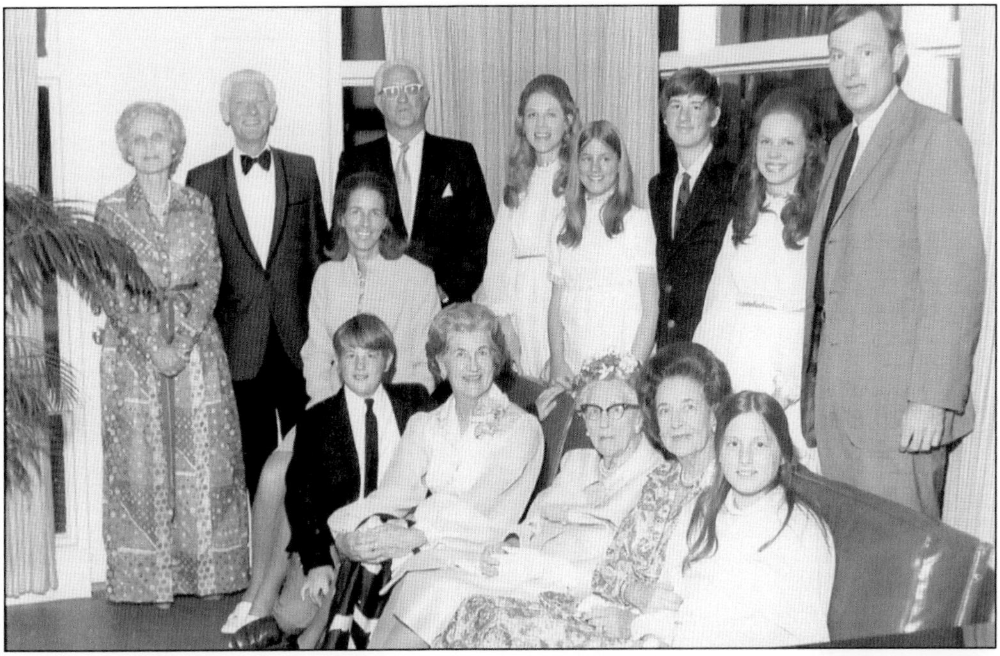

North Lake Country Club was the setting for this April 29, 1972 wedding reception honoring Adelaide Austell and Richard Craver. From left to right are the following: (seated) Helen Thayer Chapell, Richard Chapell, Caroline Blanton Thayer, Ida Blanton, Millicent Blanton Thompson, and Caroline Blanton Chapell; (standing) Nancy and George Blanton Jr., Sherman Thayer, Nancy Dicks Blanton, Mildred Chapell, George Chapell, Catherine Blanton Freedberg, and Dick Chapell.

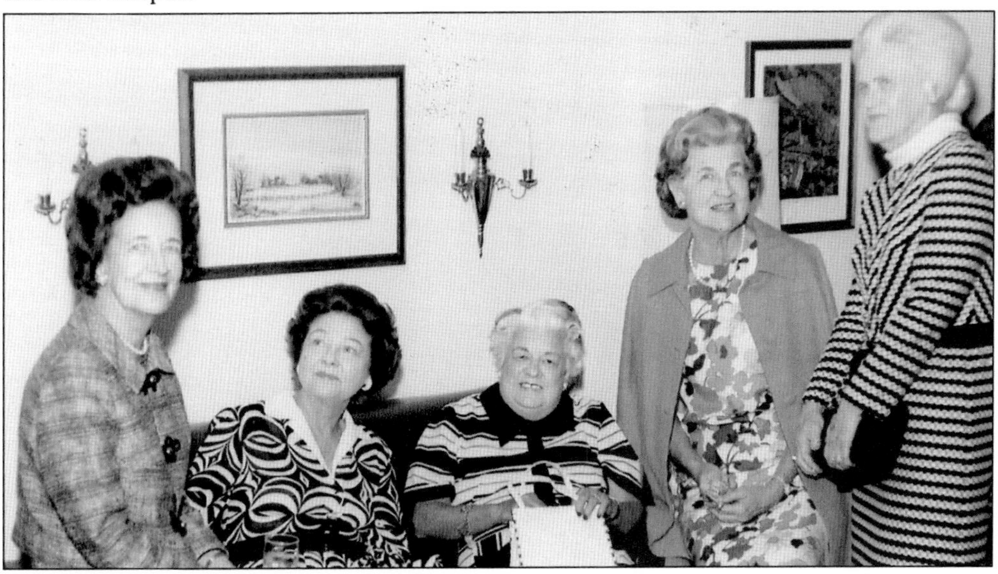

Descendants of Burwell Blanton pose for this photograph at the wedding breakfast held for Adelaide and Dick Craver. They are, from left to right, Millicent Thompson, sister of George Blanton Jr.; Jean Dewey (Faison), cousin of Ed Hamilton; Betty Blanton Hamilton, mother of Ed Hamilton; Caroline Thayer, sister of George Blanton Jr.; and Minnie Eddins Carpenter, aunt of Adelaide Austell Craver.

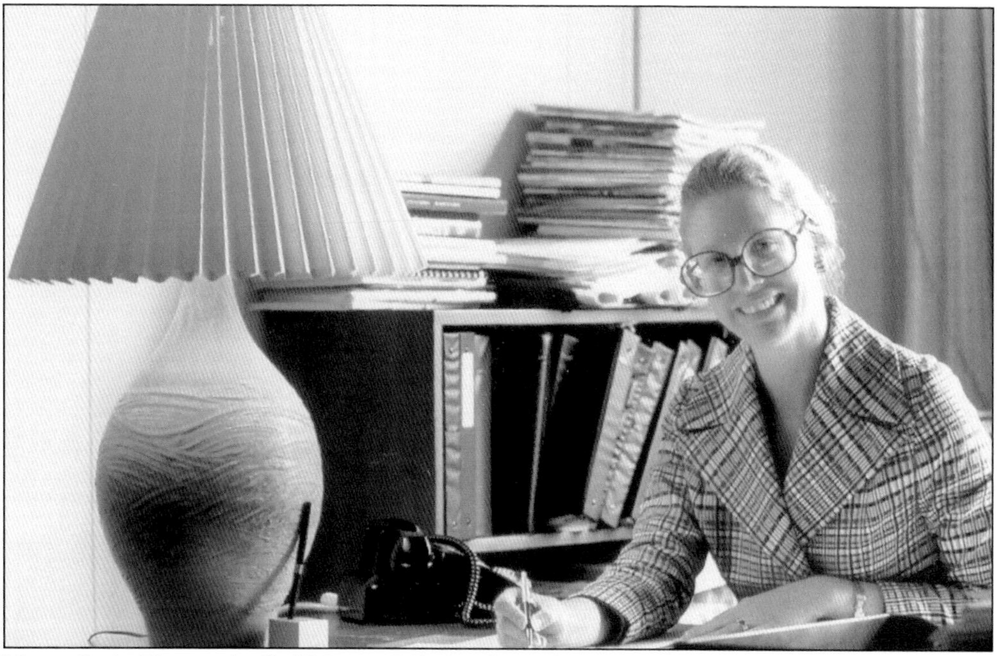

Nancy Dicks Blanton (called "Nancy D"), daughter of George and Nancy Blanton Jr., is pictured here in her office at Citibank, where she was a vice president in New York City in 1976. She was married to Pendleton Siegel and was tragically killed in a train crash on July 13, 1976, on her way from New York City to their home in Connecticut. She had worked for First National for two years in the 1960s before going to the University of Virginia for her MBA.

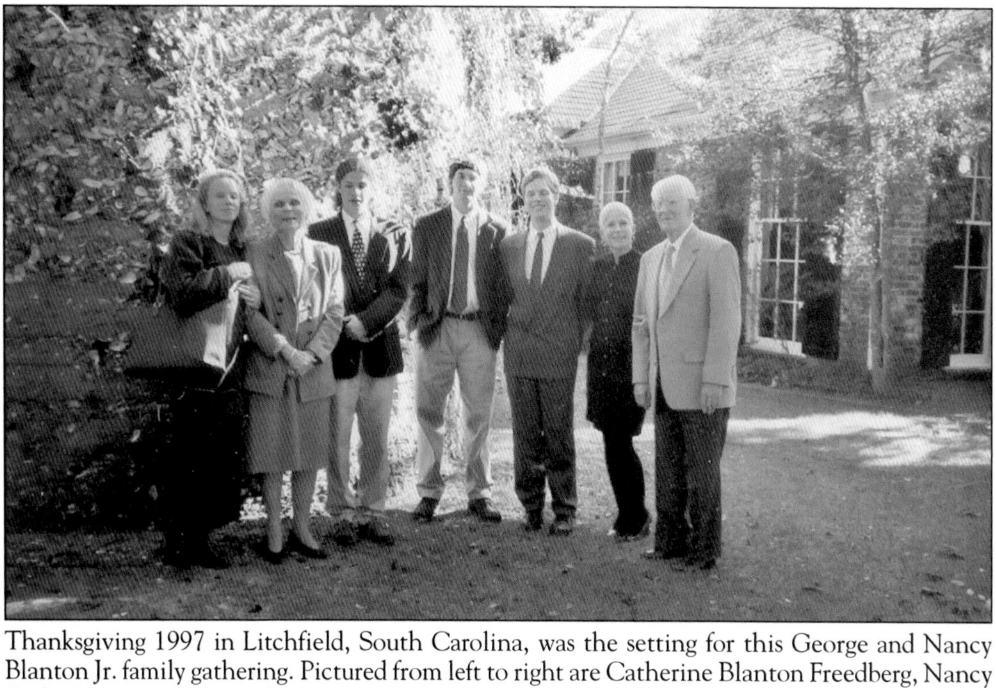

Thanksgiving 1997 in Litchfield, South Carolina, was the setting for this George and Nancy Blanton Jr. family gathering. Pictured from left to right are Catherine Blanton Freedberg, Nancy Dicks Blanton, George Blanton Hamrick ("Blanton"), Charles Rush Hamrick IV ("Charley"), Sydney Joseph Freedberg Jr., Lydia L. Blanton, and George Blanton Jr.

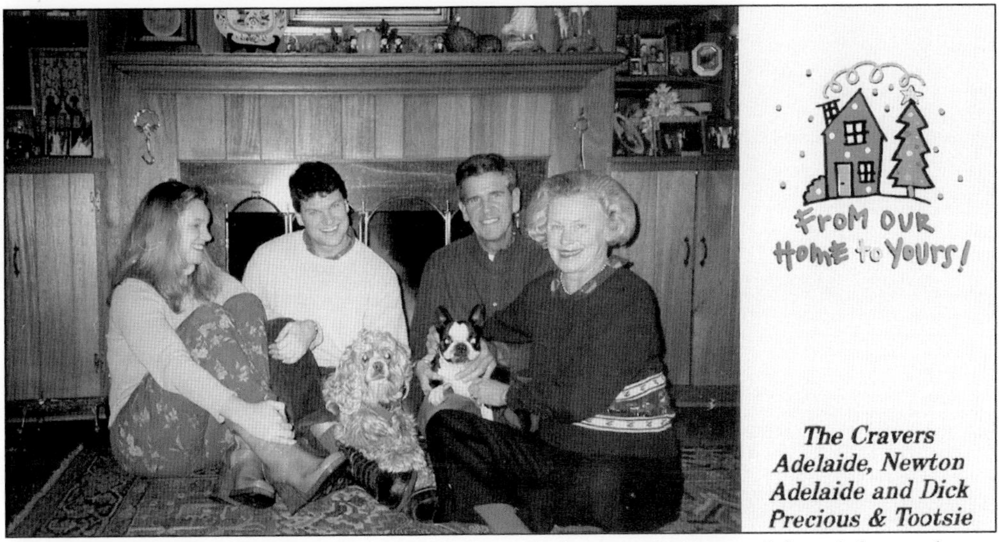

The Craver family is captured in a Christmas card photograph. Pictured from left to right are daughter Adelaide, son Newton, Adelaide, and Richard (Dick) Craver, along with family pets Precious and Tootsie.

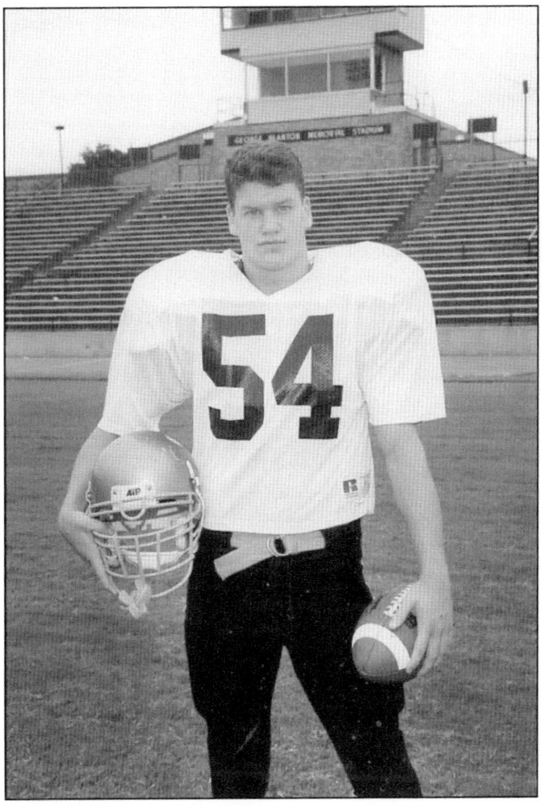

Newton Craver poses for his senior high school football photo in George Blanton Memorial Stadium. Newton is a sixth-generation member of the Blanton family to work at First National. He joined the bank in 2003 after receiving his MBA from Wake Forest University.

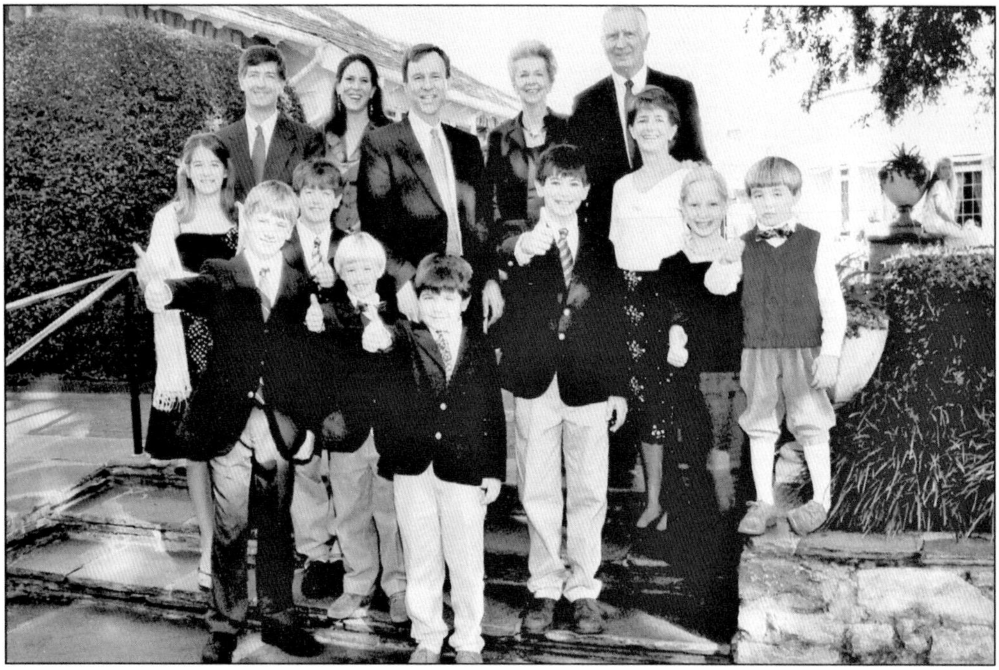

The family of Ed and Edith Hamilton gathered for this photo at a recent wedding. Their grandchildren, pictured from left to right, are Eloise Hamilton, Jared Lovett, Wake Hamilton, Hayden Lovett, Blanton Hamilton III, Moore Hamilton, Hamilton Lovett, and Parke Lovett. The adults, from left to right, are Blanton Hamilton Jr., Susan Hamilton, Rick Lovett, Edith Hamilton, Ed Hamilton, and Jeanelle Lovett.

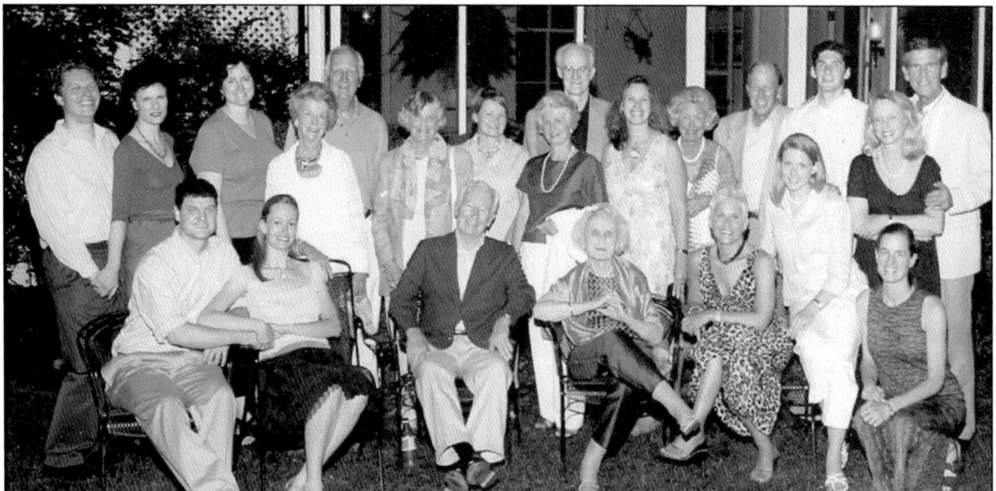

The Blanton family gathered at Mrs. Blanton's home in June of 2003 for a party honoring Newton Craver and Kendalyn Lutz. Pictured from left to right are the following: (front row) Newton Craver, Kendalyn Lutz, Joe Hamilton, Nancy Blanton, Lydia Blanton, Christine Hamrick, and Mildred Chapell; (back row) Sydney Freedberg, Martha Freedberg, Caroline Chapell, Edith Hamilton, Ed Hamilton, Dede Hamilton, Emmy Holt, Robin Cochran, Bill Holt, Adelaide Craver, Adelaide Craver, Jim Cochran, Charley Hamrick, Catherine Blanton Freedberg, and Dick Craver.

Four

A Community-Oriented Bank

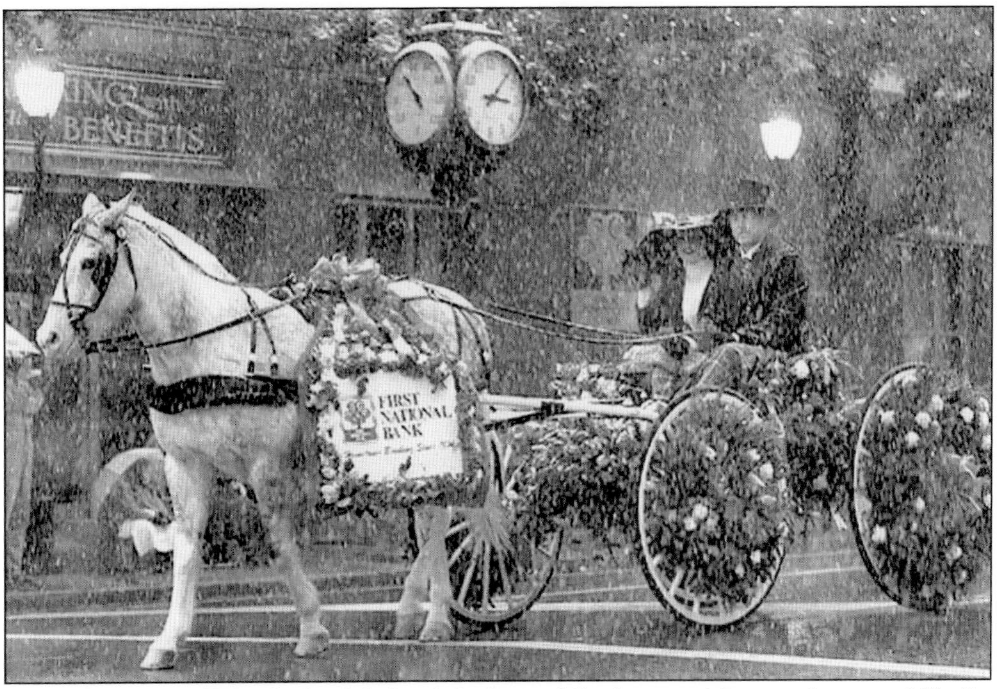

This snowy scene shows the bank behind the beautifully decorated float in the annual Shelby Christmas parade. Riding are bank team members Holly Denton (Wall) and her father, Danny Denton.

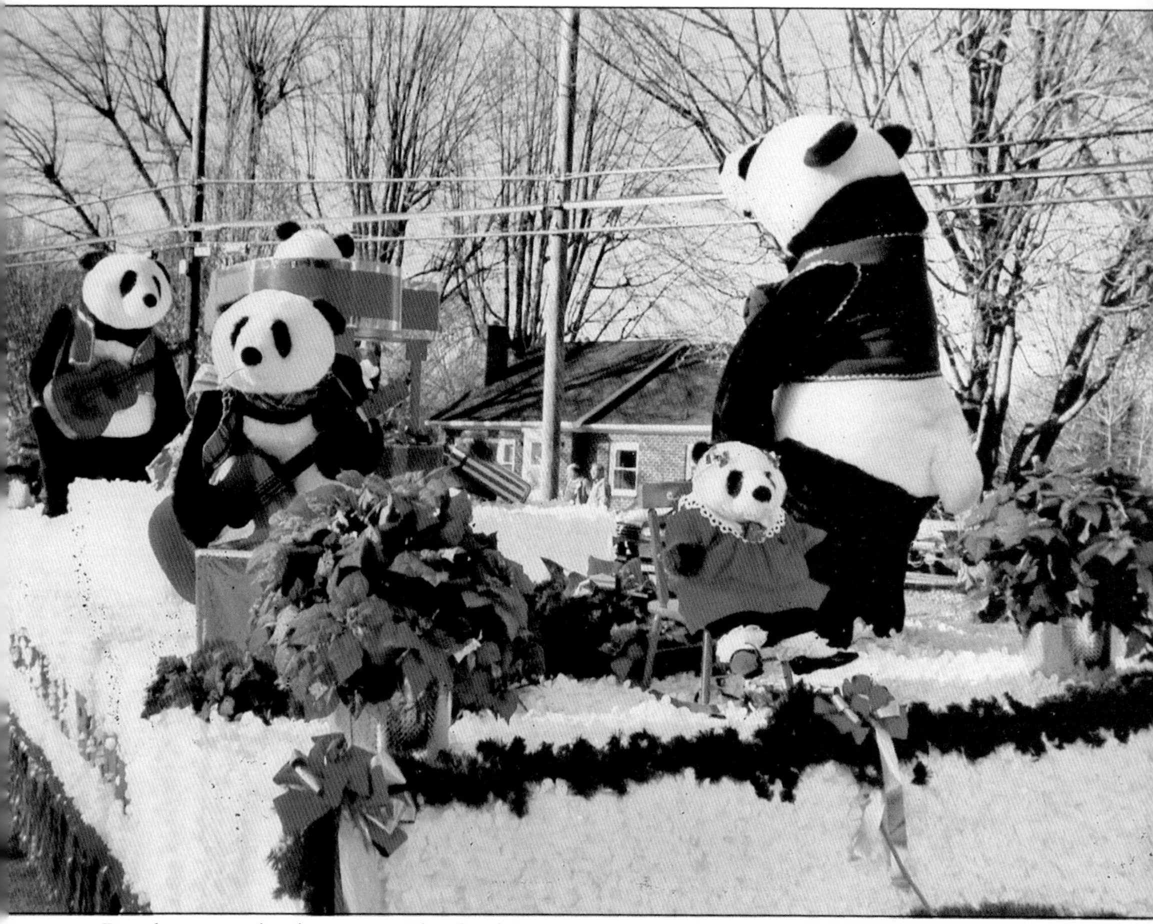

People expect banks to provide checking accounts, savings accounts, credit cards, and loan programs. After all, banks are to make money by offering a product or whole series of products to customers. Banks obviously must treat their customers fairly or they will cease to survive as businesses. We have shown that First National Bank does these things in a successful way. However, "Your Hometown Bank" has been and needs to be involved in the community it serves. This means bank team members as well as the bank itself need to reach out and serve.

Small-town Christmas parades are still important to thousands of youngsters (and oldsters). First National has developed a tradition of producing outstanding floats for the enjoyment of all. This cost brings in no direct revenue, but it adds to the beauty of Christmas each year. This is the 1995 float.

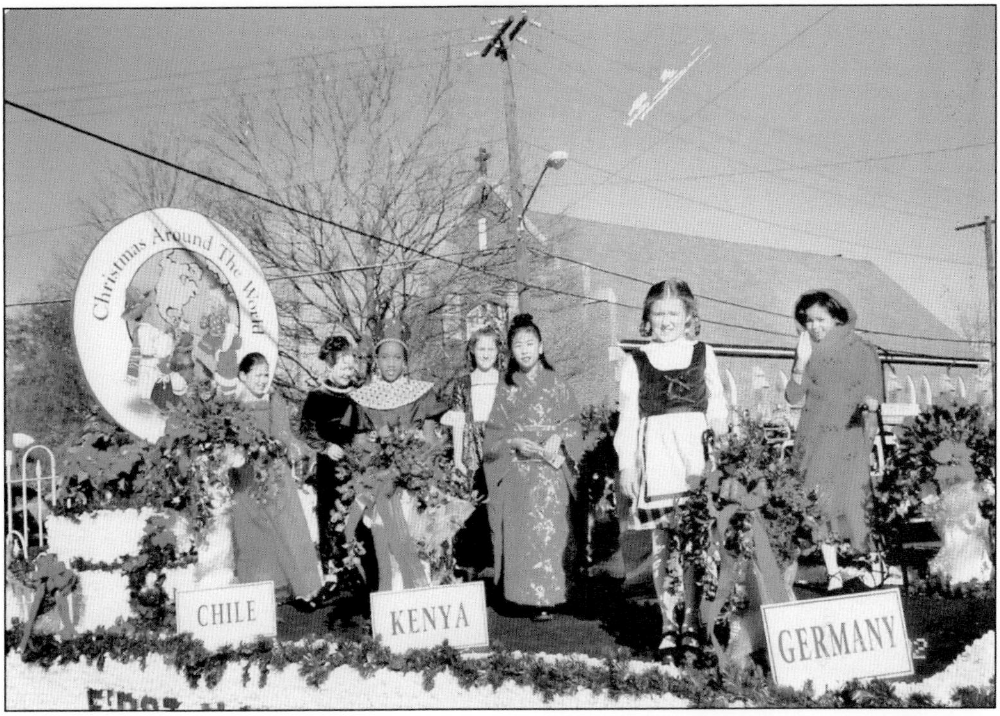

This float moves past the Lutheran church on its journey down Lafayette Street to the center of Uptown Shelby. Children are dressed in costumes of various countries in keeping with the theme "Christmas Around the World."

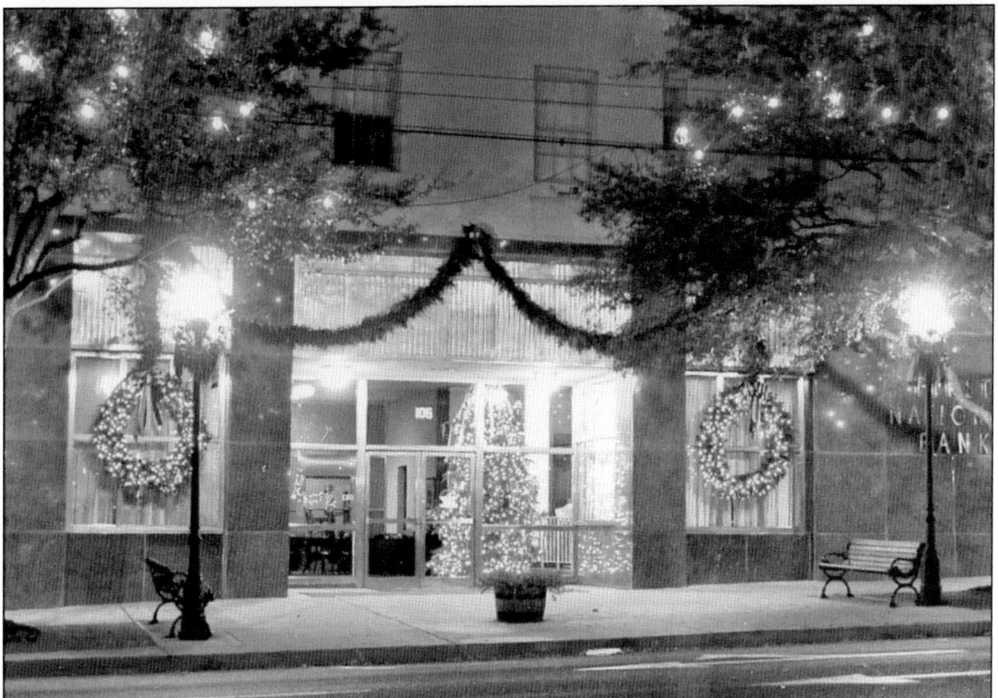
First National presents a beautiful picture with its lights at Christmas.

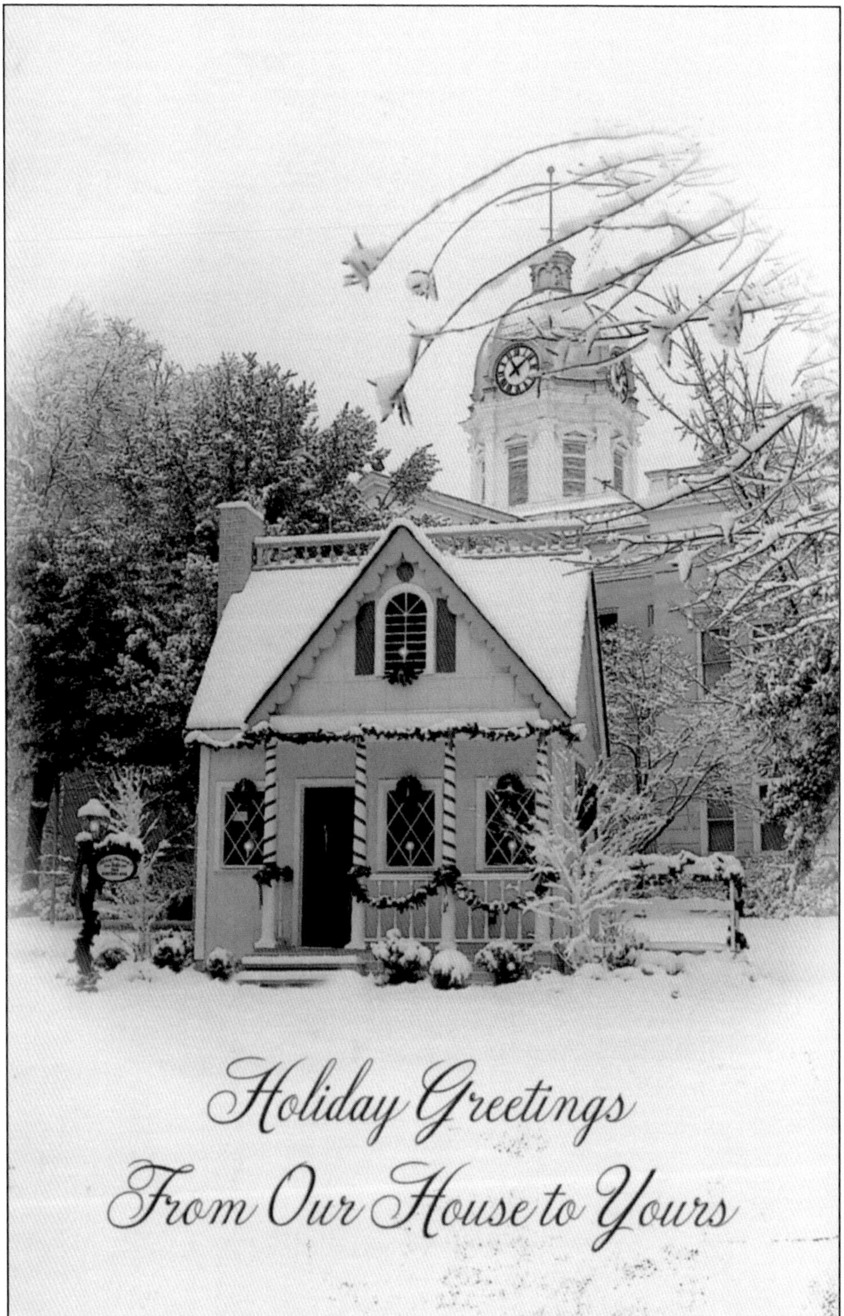

Each Christmas, First National Bank's Santa's House appears on the old court square (now the Cleveland County Historical Museum) lawn. This photo graced the front of the bank's 2002 Christmas card to its customers. The house is set up in November, and children visit it during the holidays. Senior Vice Pres. Brenda Page claims that she lost several nights' sleep when she realized how much over budget the house was going to be. She finally went to Pres. Ed Hamilton apologizing and hoping to avoid being fired. She is still with the bank, and the house has become an annual part of Christmas in Shelby.

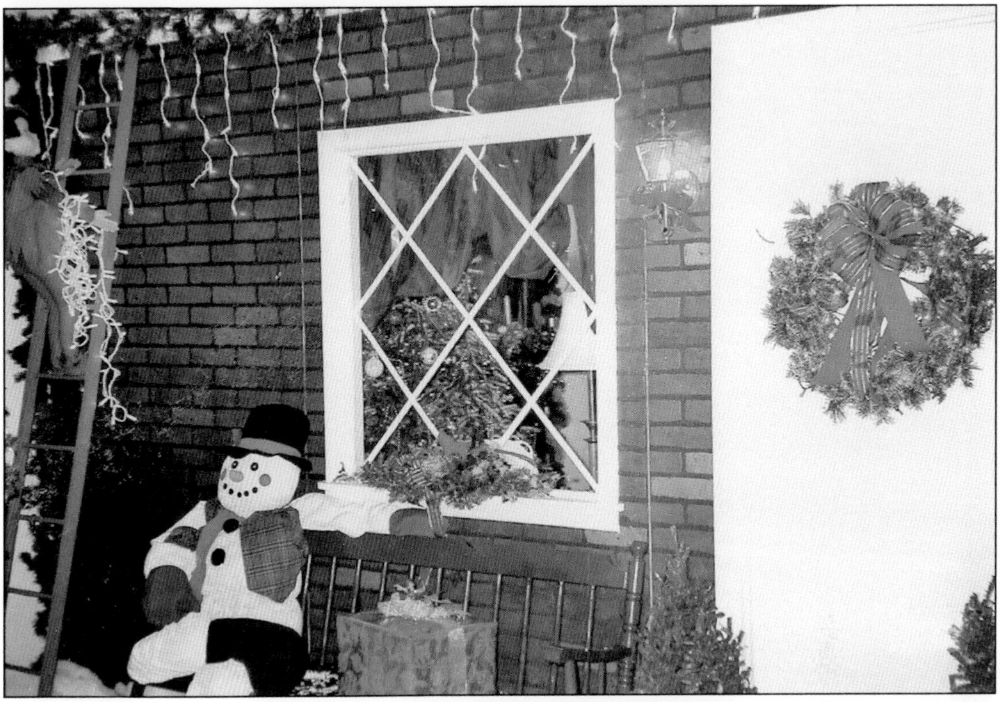

Each Christmas, First National opens a toy land at some vacant location in Uptown Shelby. Children are invited to enjoy the wonders of Christmas each year.

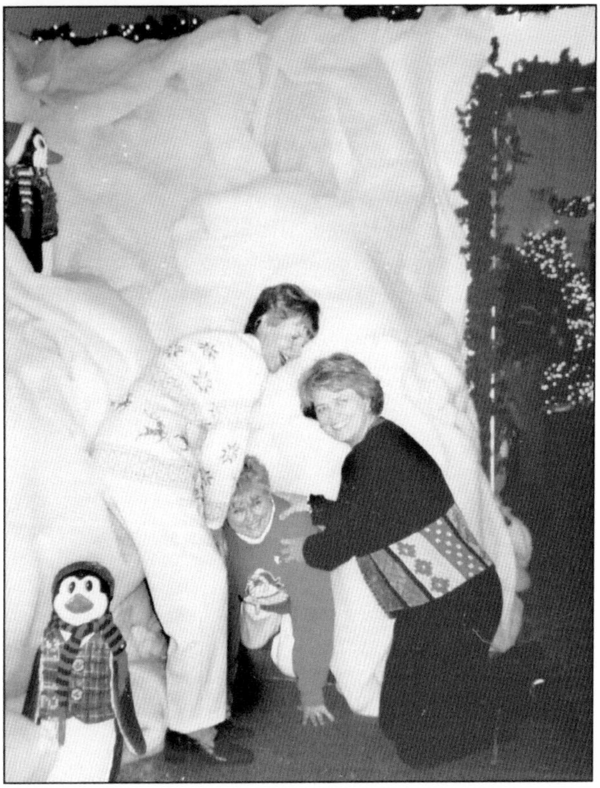

Employees Nina Price (left), Diane Hines (center), and Rita Lowe enjoy getting the house ready for the children. These First National team members have each served the bank for over 30 years.

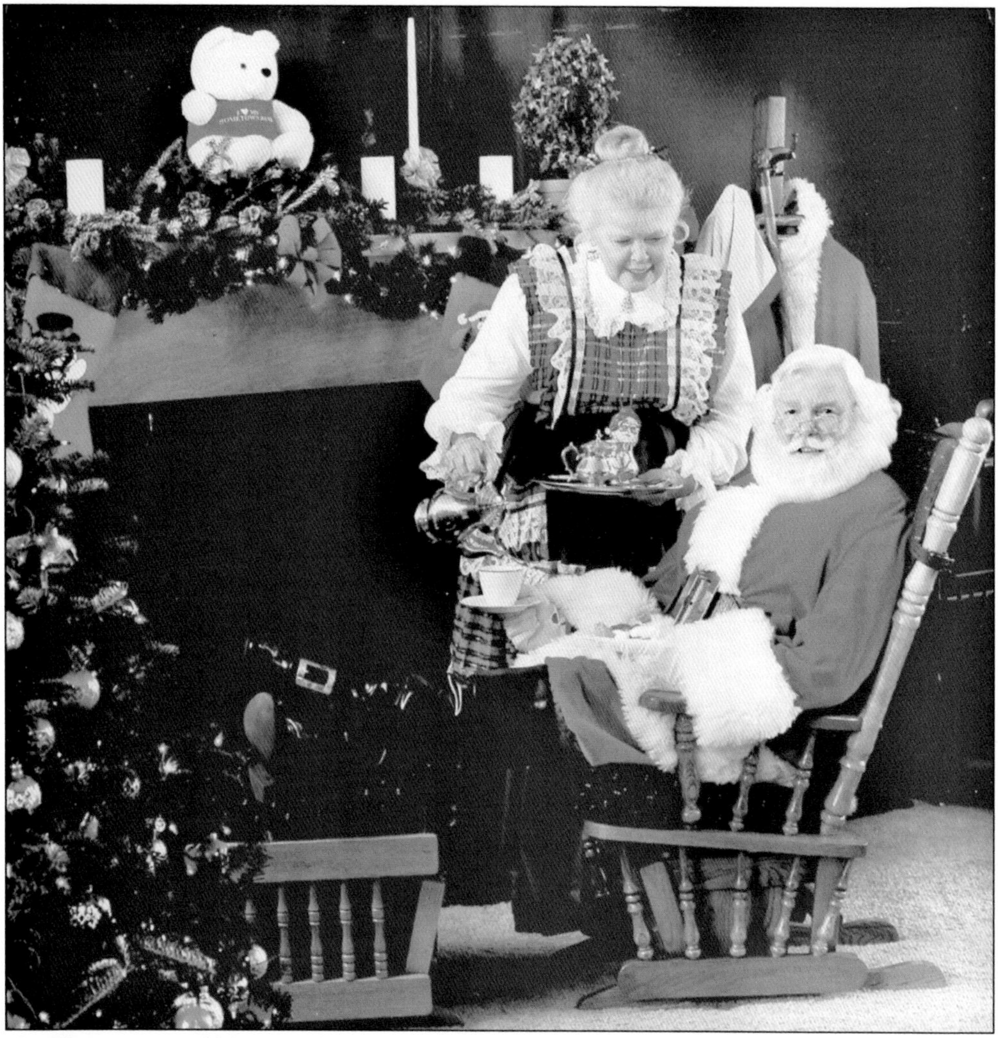

No Christmas would be complete without Santa. First National provides the real thing. Here Mrs. Claus serves hot tea to Santa as he relaxes from the hard work at the North Pole.

A program that has become common in both Cleveland and Gaston Counties at Christmas is known by the title "Angel Tree." The names of children whose families have little prospect of a happy Christmas are put on Christmas trees so that some "angel" will have an opportunity to make a difference and provide a happy Christmas. Churches and businesses often promote the program. First National employee Holly Wall stands with a set of presents for some fortunate child at Christmas in 2002.

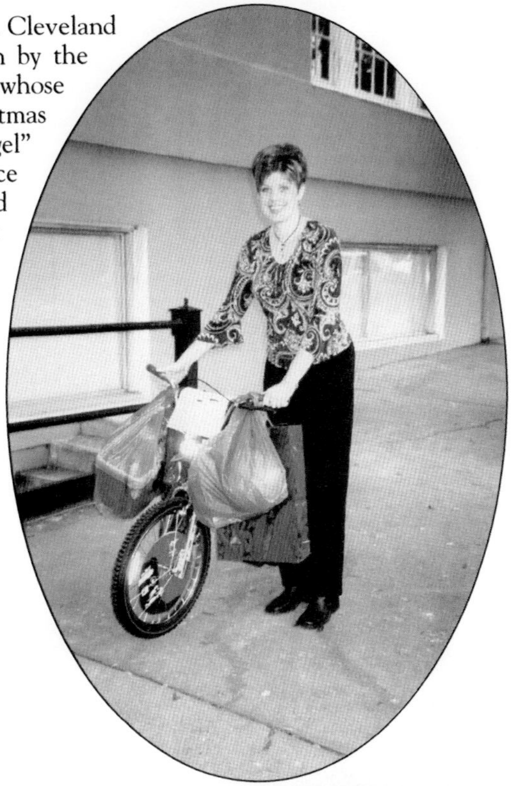

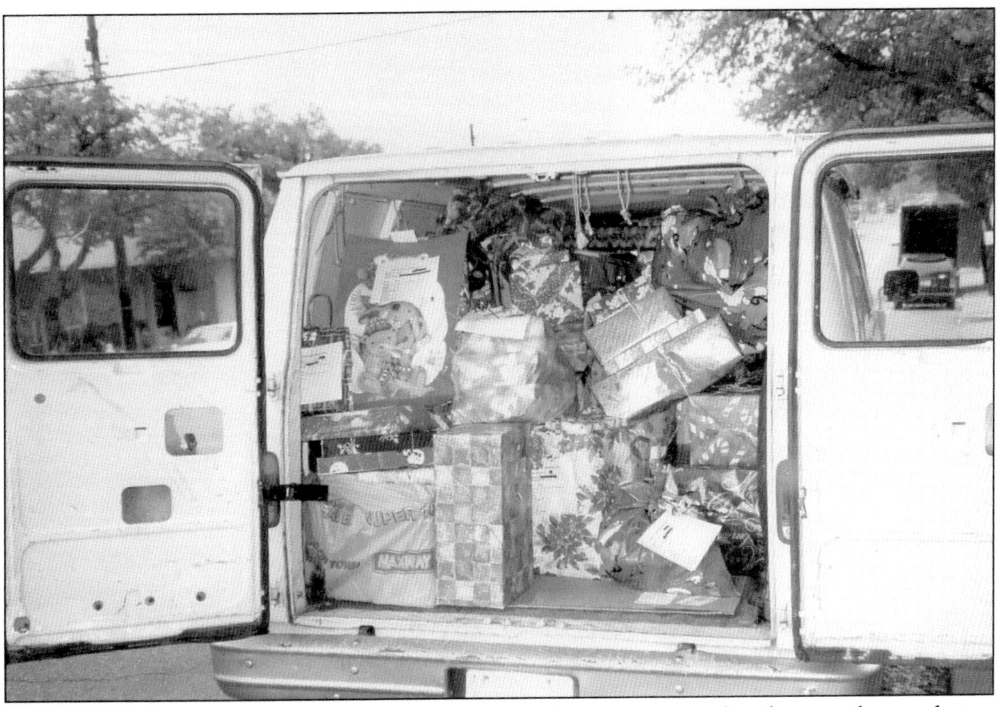

This loaded van shows some of the effort put forth by First National and its employees during Christmas in 2002.

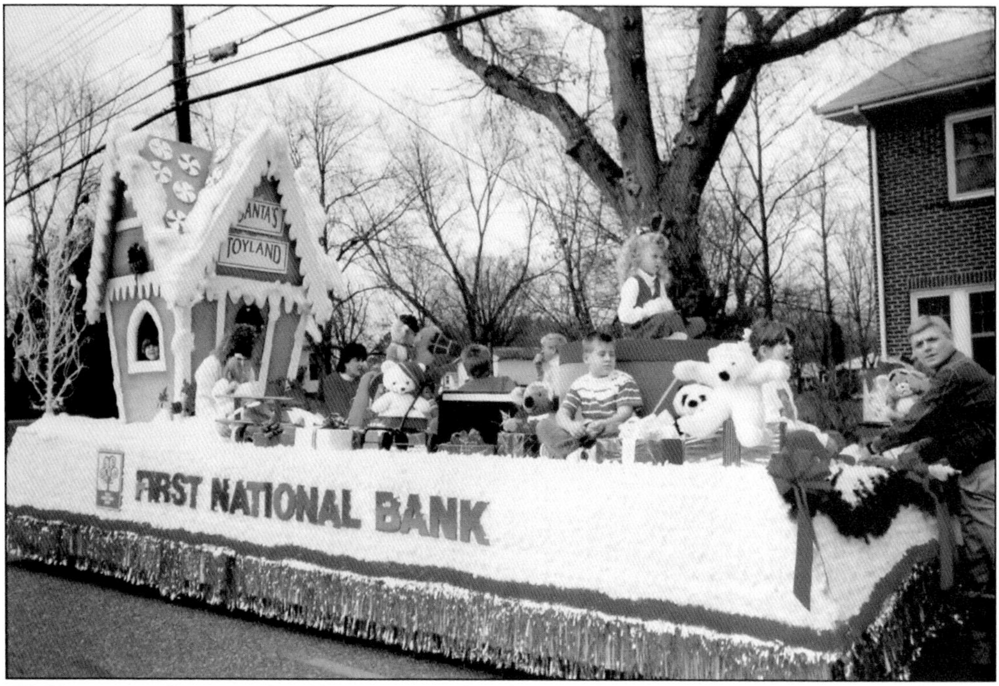

Children enjoy being in the Christmas parade. These children enjoy Santa's Toyland under the watchful eye of Morris Page (an honorary bank employee), who is the husband of Brenda Page.

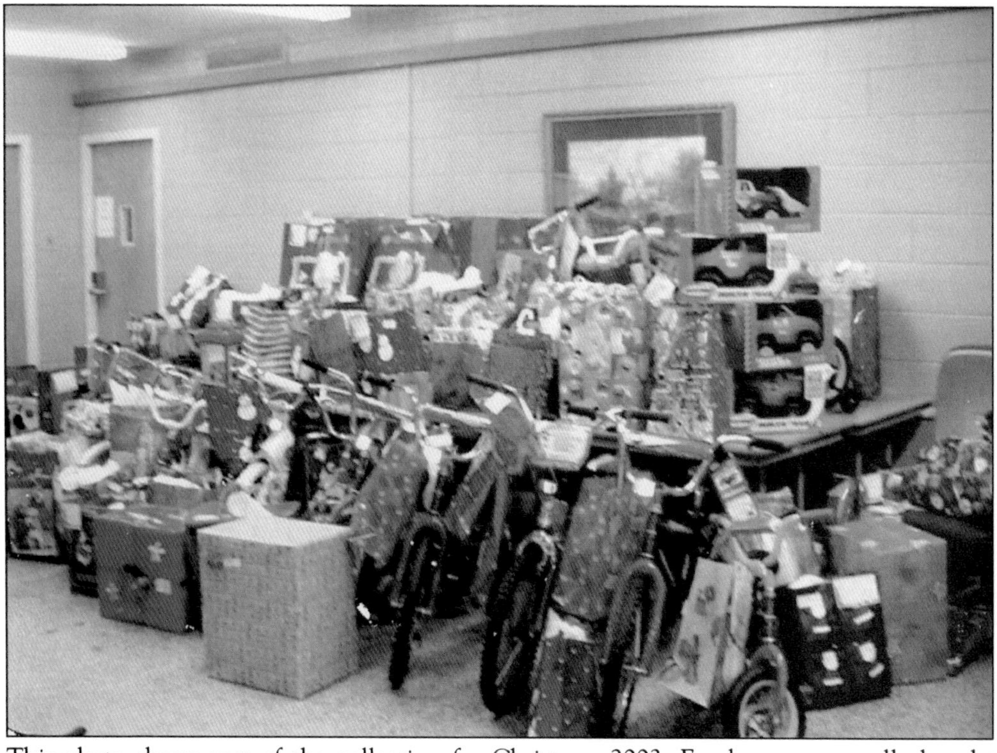

This photo shows part of the collection for Christmas 2003. Employees personally bought presents, as did the bank. Approximately 168 children benefited from the bank's 2003 effort.

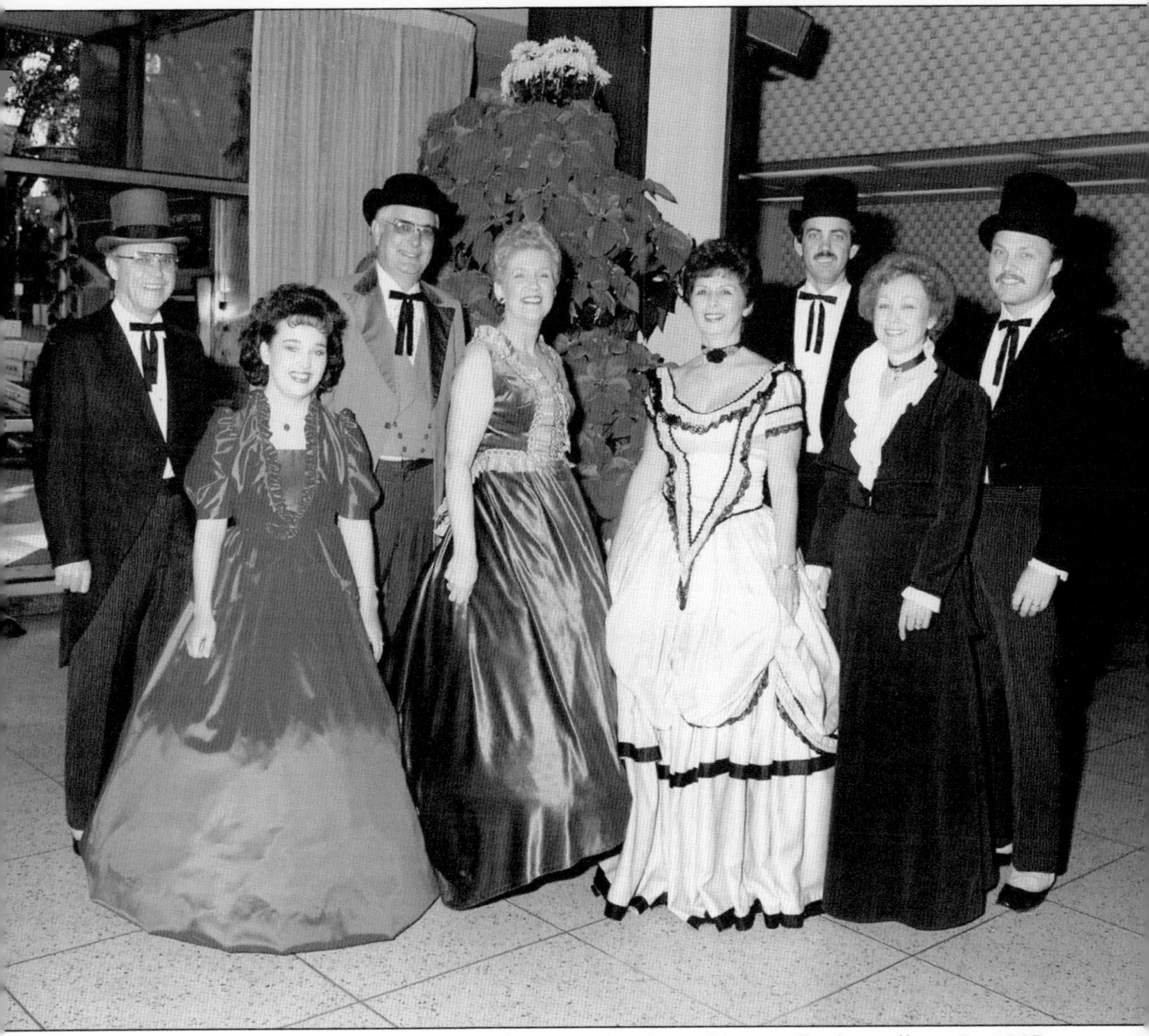

First National has an open house each Christmas for the public at all of its offices. In 1987, employees dressed in old-fashioned clothes. Pictured with the red poinsettia tree, from left to right, are Calvin Blalock, Donna Sisk, Ken Gibson, Betty Walker, Barbara Allen, Danny Denton, Brenda Page, and Cecil Clark. Bank team ladies in the 1980s and the 1990s dressed dolls for Christmas gifts for needy children.

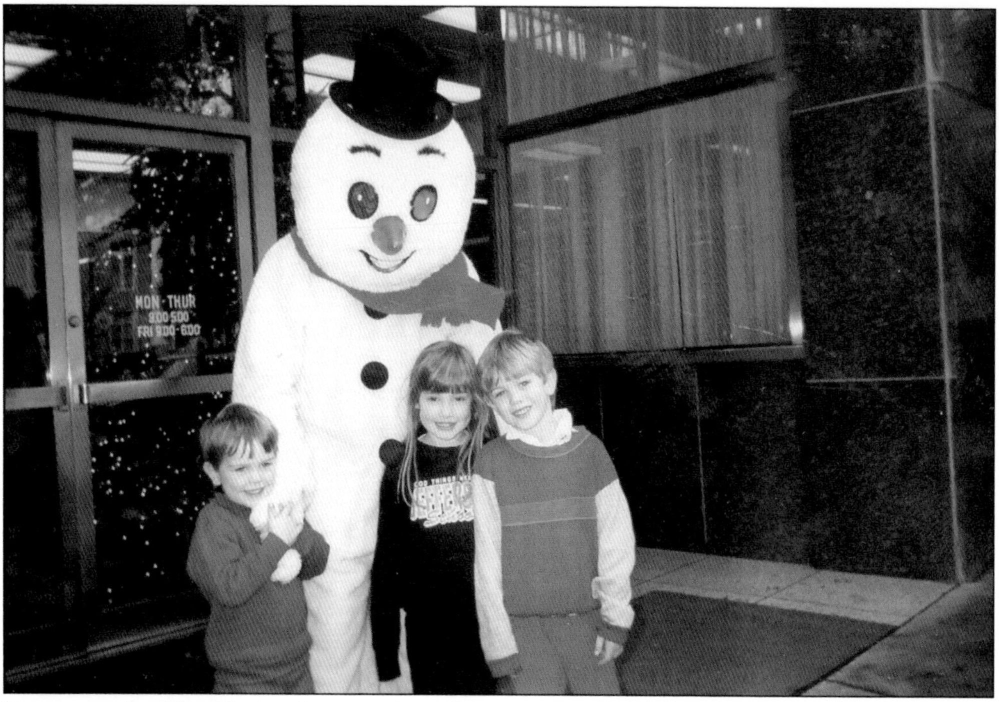

Frosty, another First National personality who appears each Christmas, poses with John Jackson Royster, Natalie Anthony, and David W. Royster IV.

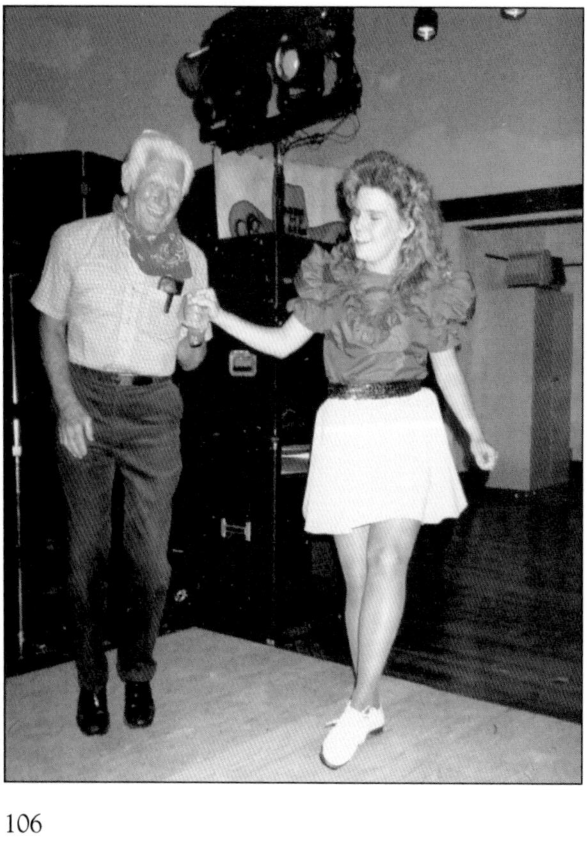

George Blanton Jr. shows another side as he dances with a professional clogger at a bank event.

Governor James G. Martin
cordially invites you to a reception
at two o'clock
followed by
the 1991 Governor's Volunteer Awards Ceremony
from three until four o'clock
Friday, the sixth of September
at the Great Smokies Hilton
Asheville, North Carolina

Christmas activities are fun and provide help for many children at Christmas; however, First National is involved with the community year-round. In 1991, the bank was recognized by Gov. Jim Martin for its service to the community. This is only one of many awards that the bank has received. Many organizations recognize the time and money that First National contributes to the community. CEO Adelaide Craver emphasizes that First National regularly supports charities and special projects in the community. She adds that Brenda Page has been invaluable in involving the bank in the needs of the community and in sponsoring community events. Brenda is joined by a staff that includes Phyllis Monteith, Roger Humphries, Holly Wall, and Jack Horner.

HOMETOWN PEOPLE

HELPING OTHERS

ne thing we've learned in over 125 years of service is that loyalty to our community is to the benefit of all.

East Kings Mountain Elementary, rated as one of North arolina's top primary schools, had a strong need for adult lunteers. In 2000 - 2001, sixteen First National Bank nployees decided to adopt the school, volunteering as tutors, aching assistants, and lunch buddies.

As a result, First National also volunteered its people and sources to start a computer training program for academically fted students at East. Nine students completed the course and ceived framed Certificates of Completion along with their mputer workbooks.

At First National Bank, we are proud of the giving spirit of our nployees. Serving the community is something they do well. ur Caring Volunteers Program was awarded the Governor's ward in 1997, and The Giving Heart Award in 2001 for community volvement. We believe that making an investment in tomorrow takes ore than money … it takes people helping other people.

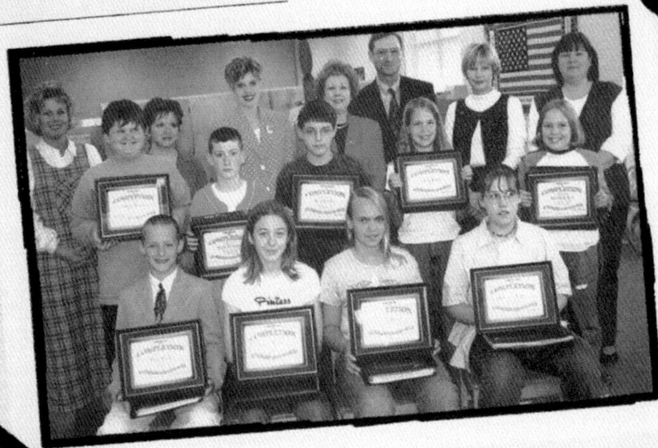

"At every step the child should be allowed t meet the real experiences of life"

— Ellen Key

FIRST NATIONAL BANK

YOUR HOMETOWN BANK

Hometown Banking Since 1874

Bank employees devote personal time to helping in schools around the county. During the 2000–2001 school year, 16 First National employees served as tutors, teaching assistants, and lunch buddies at East Kings Mountain Elementary School. The photo shows the students who completed a computer course led by First National employees.

April 18, 2002

Dear Ms. Adelaide Craver,

We appreciate all the support you provided for Math Day. We know you may have had to take time off your busy schedule and we thank you. We had a wonderful time competing and enjoying the refreshments. The Math Day competition would not have been possible without you. Thank you!

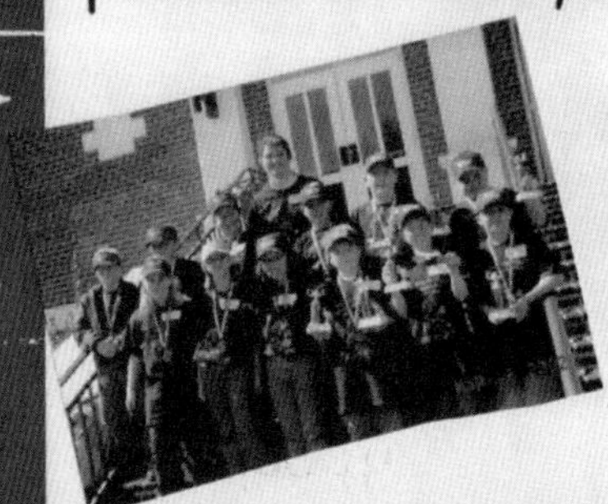

Sincerely,
Boiling Springs
Elementary
Math Team

This letter was received by First National CEO Adelaide Craver from the students at Boiling Springs Elementary School. The bank supported the Math Day competition for students.

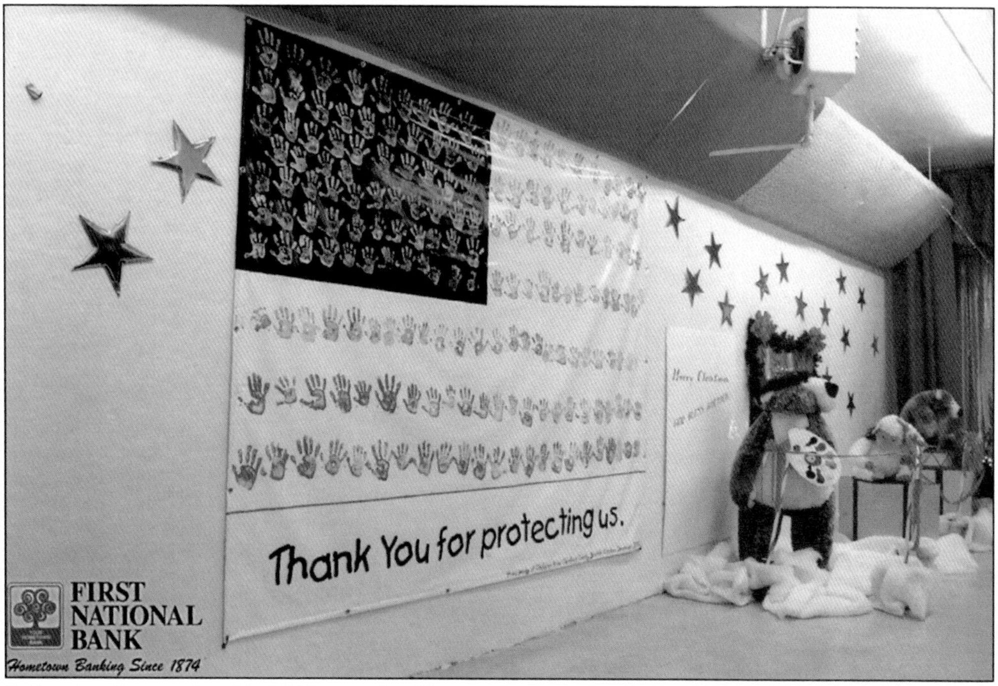

Following September 11, 2001, people all over the nation expressed support in many ways. First National Bank, under the leadership of Brenda Page, helped local children make a flag with the children's handprints representing stars and stripes.

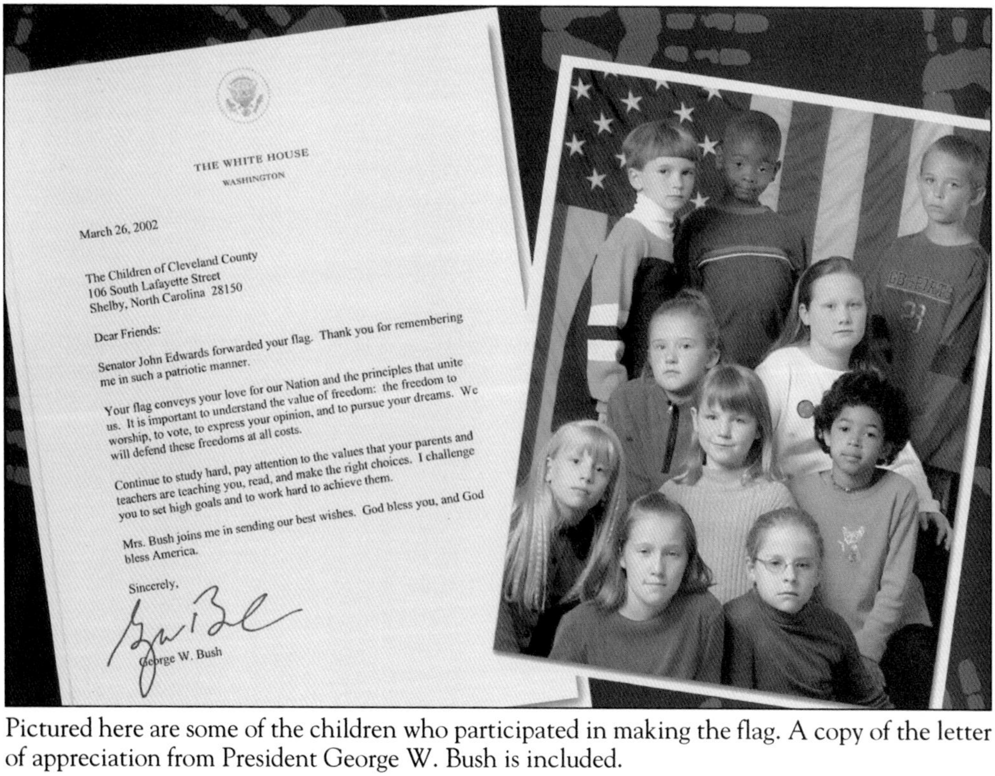

THE WHITE HOUSE
WASHINGTON

March 26, 2002

The Children of Cleveland County
106 South Lafayette Street
Shelby, North Carolina 28150

Dear Friends:

Senator John Edwards forwarded your flag. Thank you for remembering me in such a patriotic manner.

Your flag conveys your love for our Nation and the principles that unite us. It is important to understand the value of freedom: the freedom to worship, to vote, to express your opinion, and to pursue your dreams. We will defend these freedoms at all costs.

Continue to study hard, pay attention to the values that your parents and teachers are teaching you, read, and make the right choices. I challenge you to set high goals and to work hard to achieve them.

Mrs. Bush joins me in sending our best wishes. God bless you, and God bless America.

Sincerely,

George W. Bush

Pictured here are some of the children who participated in making the flag. A copy of the letter of appreciation from President George W. Bush is included.

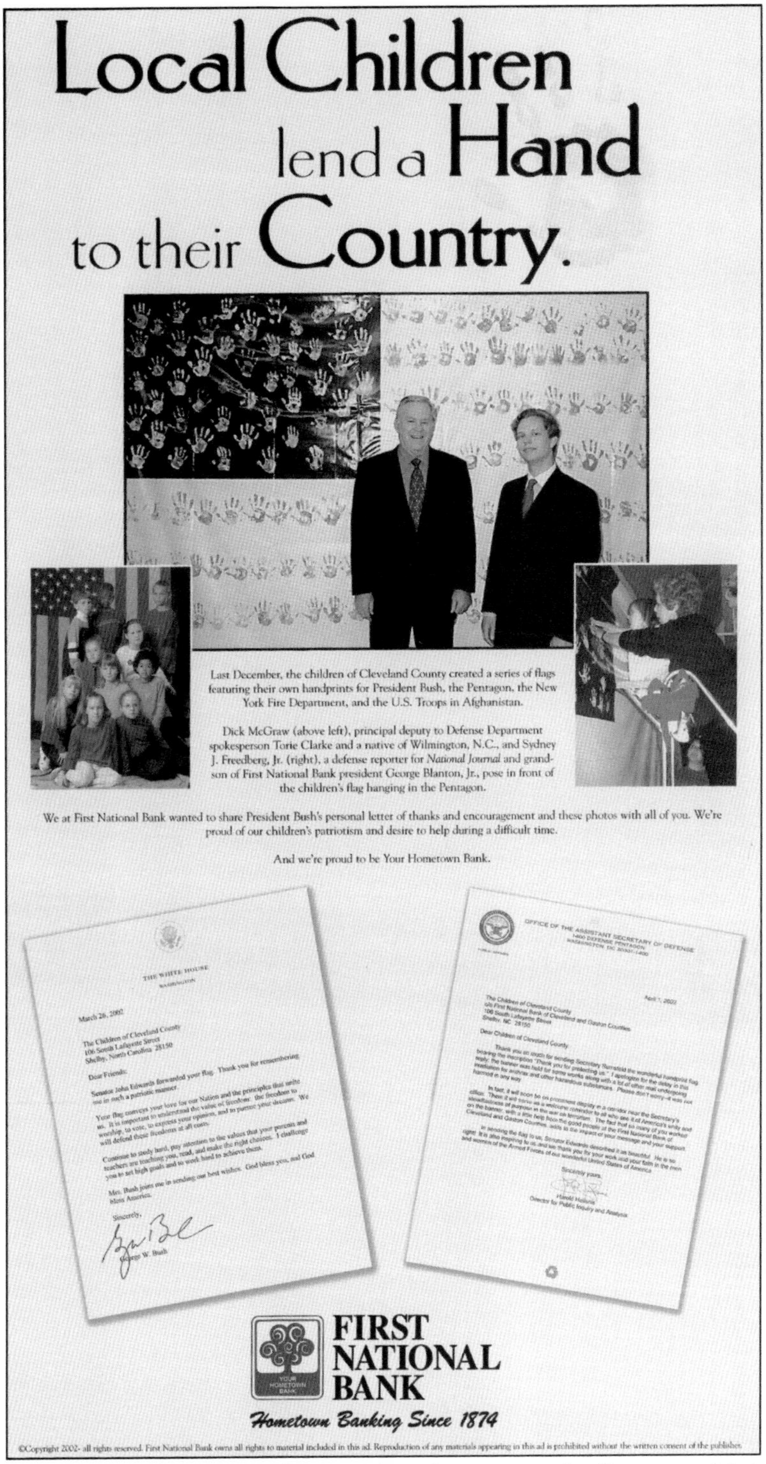

The flag was sent to Washington and is seen here hanging in the Pentagon. *National Journal* defense reporter Sydney J. Freedberg Jr., who is a grandson of George Blanton Jr. and a son of Bank Director Catherine Blanton Freedberg, is pictured with Pentagon official Dick McGraw.

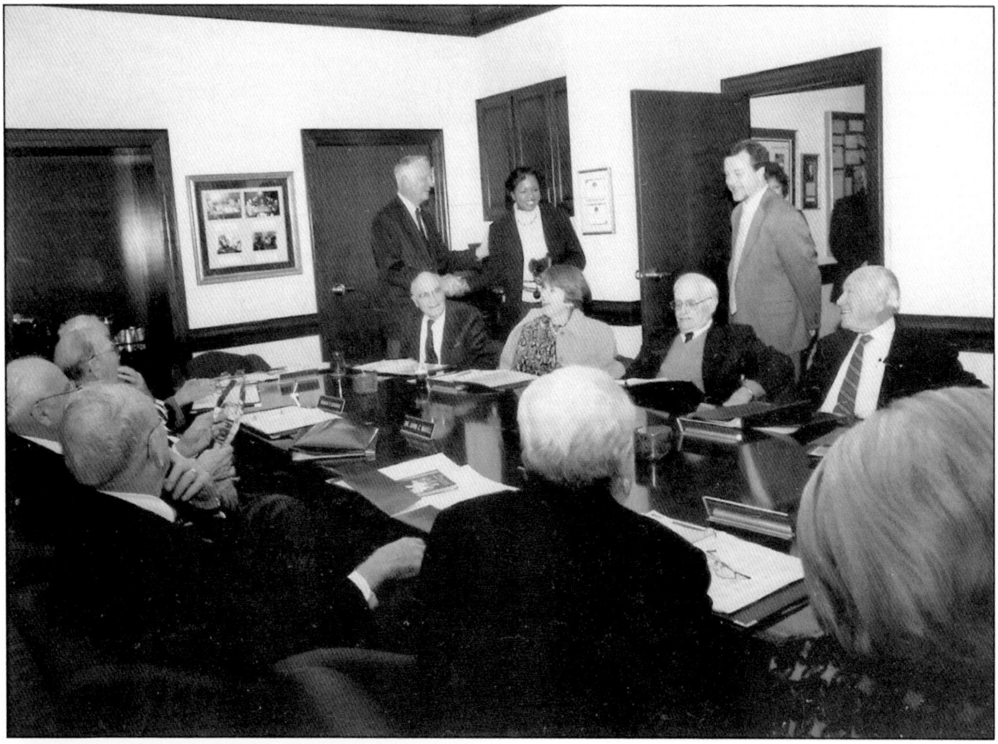

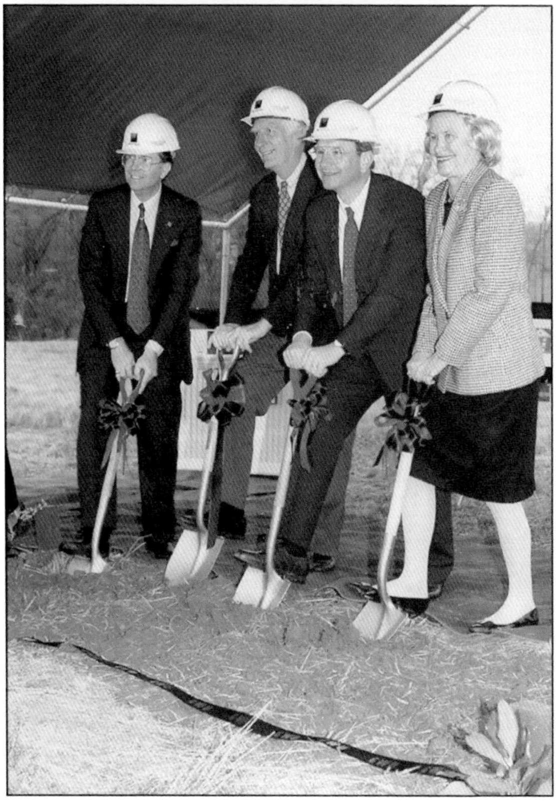

Representatives from *Cleveland Headline News* arrive for a planned interruption of a First National Board meeting to present an award to Brenda Page and the bank. They presented the "2002 Cleveland Award for Outstanding Service" to First National for its various activities in the community.

Three bank officials participated in the groundbreaking for new student apartments at Gardner-Webb University in Boiling Springs. From left to right are GWU Pres. M. Christopher White, FNB Board Chairman Ed Hamilton, FNB Senior Vice Pres. for Commercial Loans Joe Henderson, and bank CEO Adelaide Craver. Bank leaders regularly serve on boards of organizations in the community. Both George Blanton Jr. and Adelaide Craver have served on the board of trustees for Cleveland County's only four-year university.

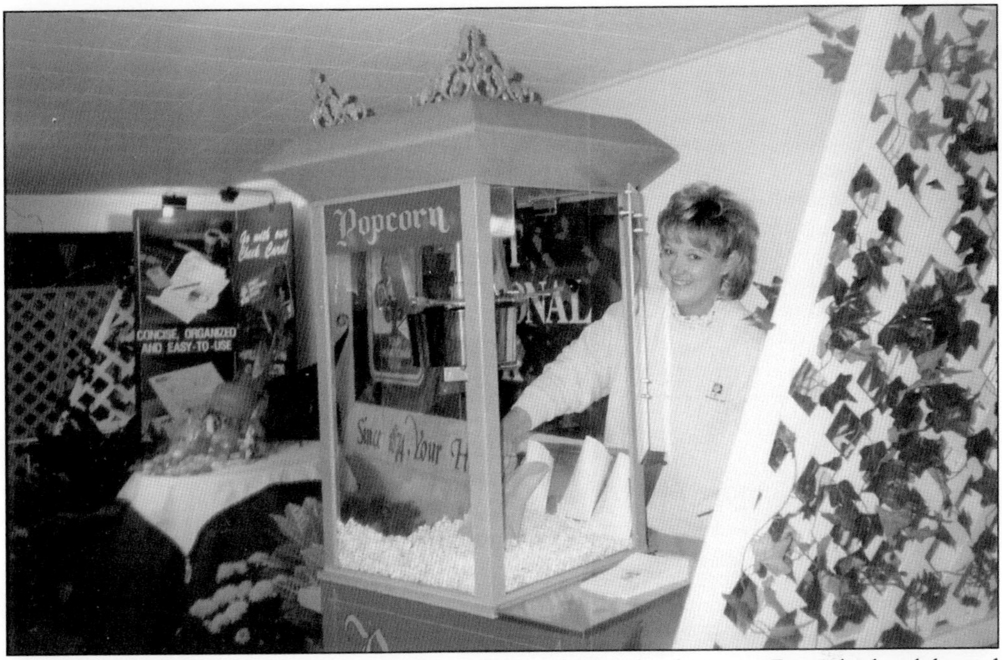

One of the largest county fairs in the South is the local Cleveland County Fair, which celebrated its 80th birthday this year. First National supports the fair and has a booth. Here Sharon Leigh is ready to serve popcorn to visitors.

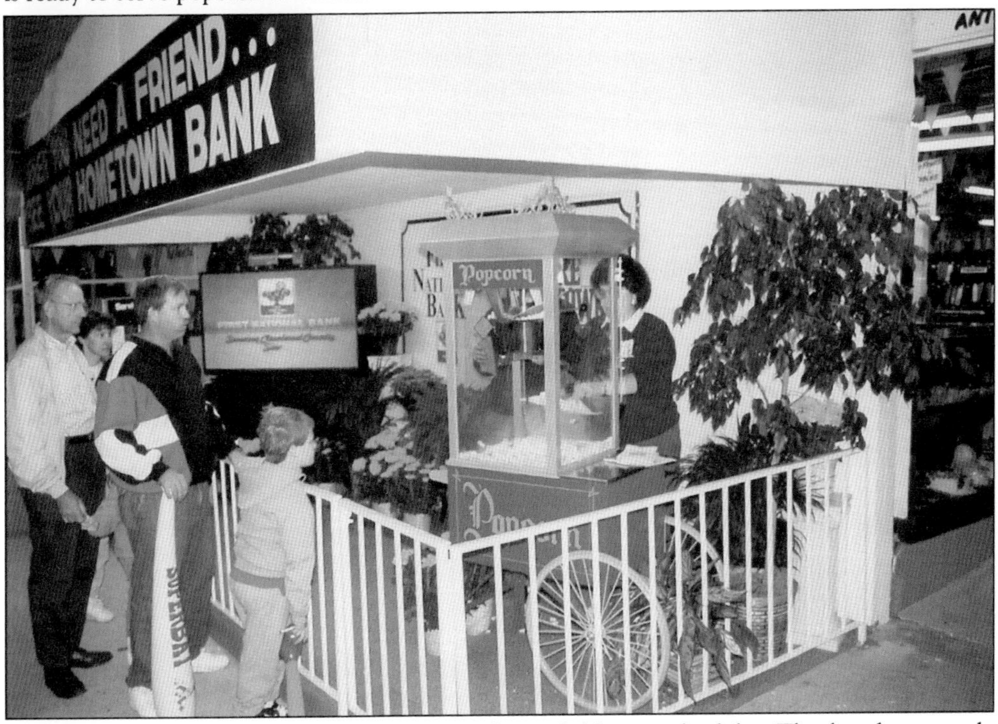

The Hometown Bank booth draws interest from children and adults. The booth not only provides popcorn, but also allows fair-goers to meet First National employees and learn about the bank's services.

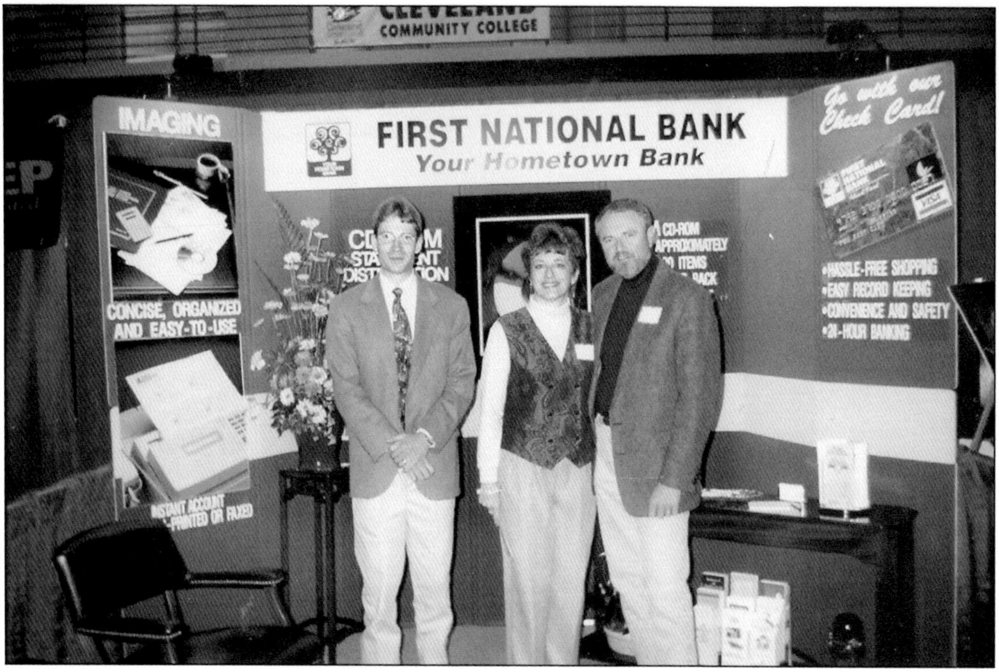

Helping the community includes marketing the bank's services to young people who are learning about money, checking, and credit. At Cleveland Community College's trade fair, "Your Hometown Bank" provides valuable information to students who need to learn about responsible banking.

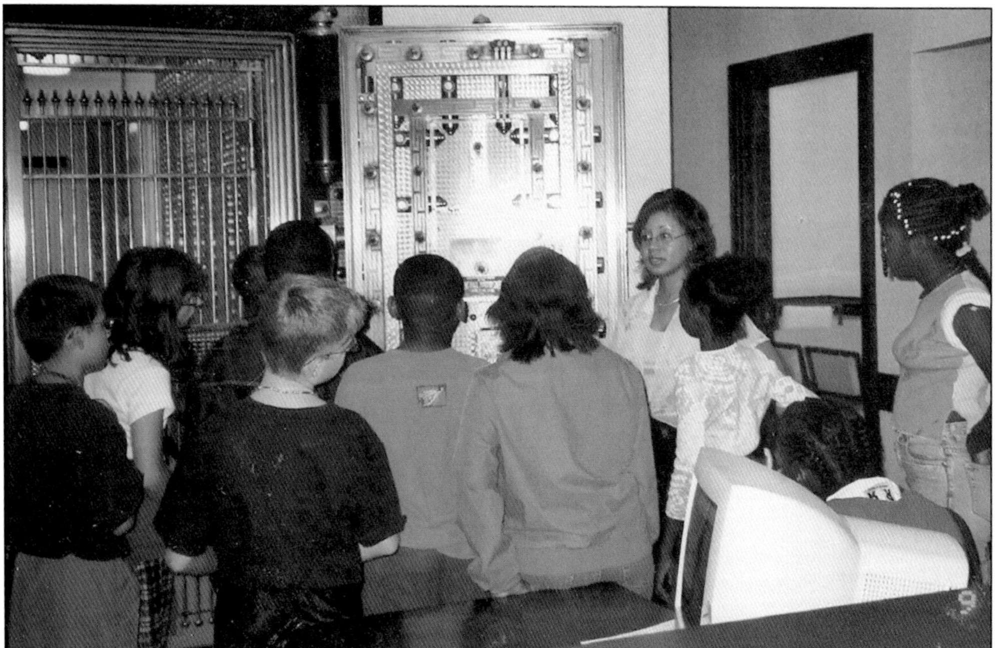

Even young children can learn about banking before they reach college. The bank has tours for students who learn about the nature of a bank and its activities. Here a group of students are impressed with one of the bank's vaults.

Five

The First National Team in 2004

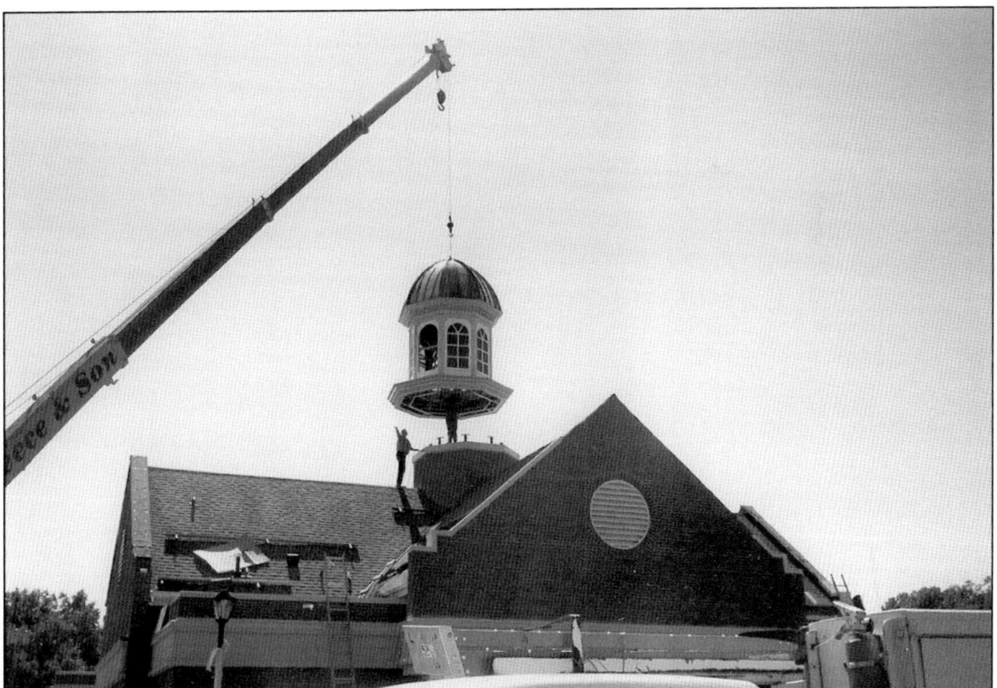

First National's expansion into areas outside of Shelby generated great community interest. In Boiling Springs Elementary School, students wrote essays for a bank contest. The winners' pictures and essays hang in the West Cleveland branch entryway.

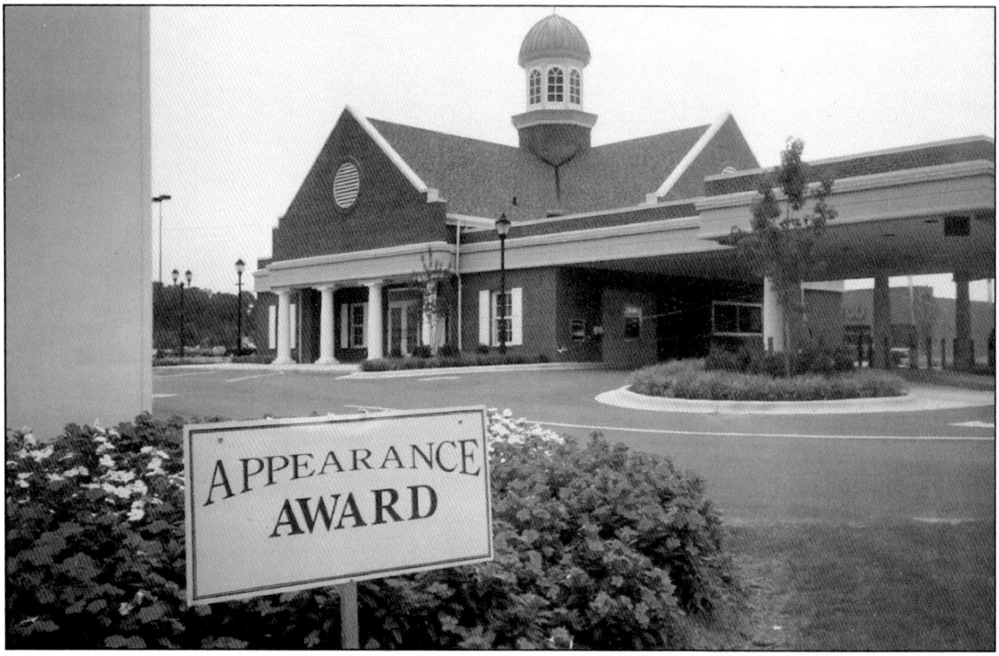

The bank seeks to have attractive facilities for its customers. This photograph shows the West Cleveland branch with its appearance award for its landscape. Note that the cupola has been installed on the bank's roof.

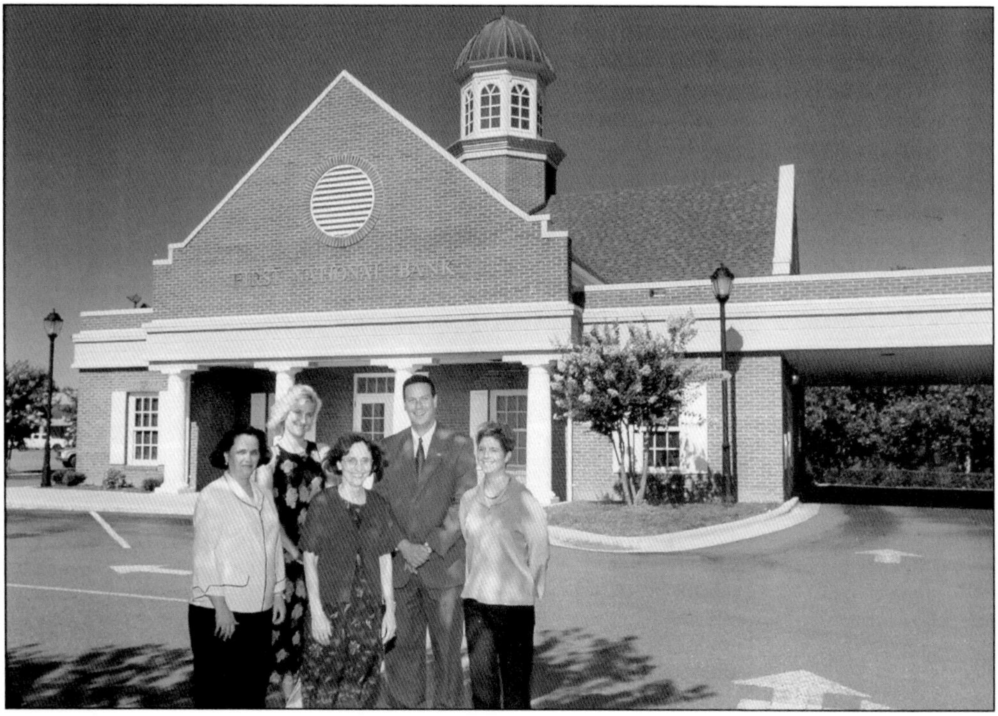

The West Cleveland branch is located in Boiling Springs. The 2004 staff, pictured here from left to right, includes Cindy Neason, Andrea Swink, Abby Hamrick, Jeff Triplett, Jamie Petty, and (not pictured) Pam Ledford.

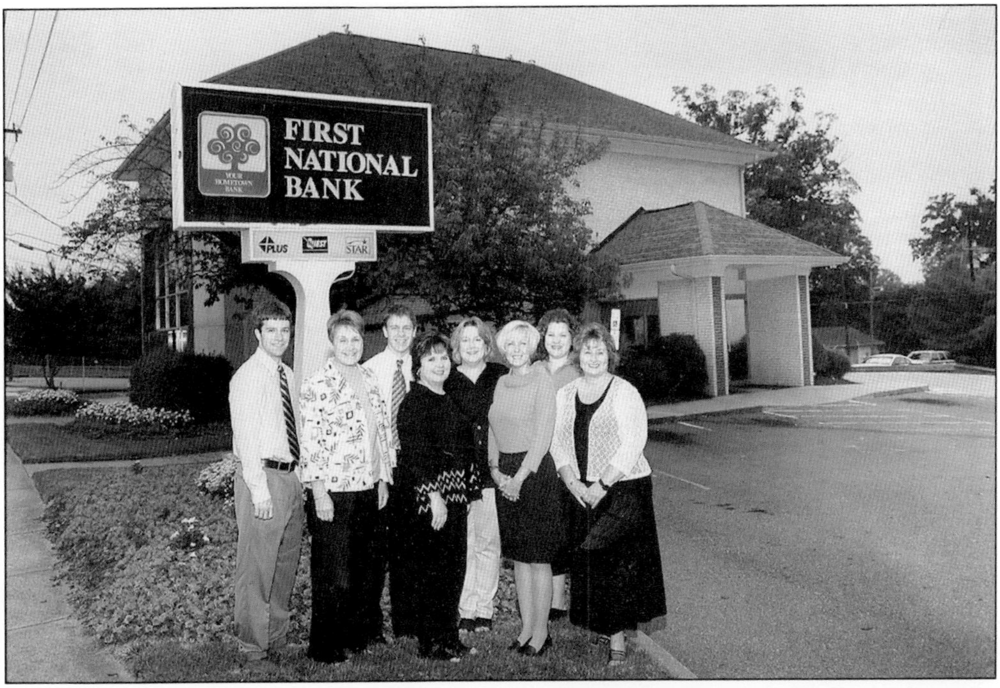

First National's oldest branch, South Branch on South Lafayette Street in Shelby, is almost 50 years old. Current employees, pictured from left to right, are Anderson Allen, Faye Hamrick, Nathaniel Blalock, Barbara Fitch, Karen Whitaker, Cathy Hunt, Meredith Baldree, and Cindy Jurich. Not pictured are Jan Tucker, Carolyn Wright, and Joan Standish.

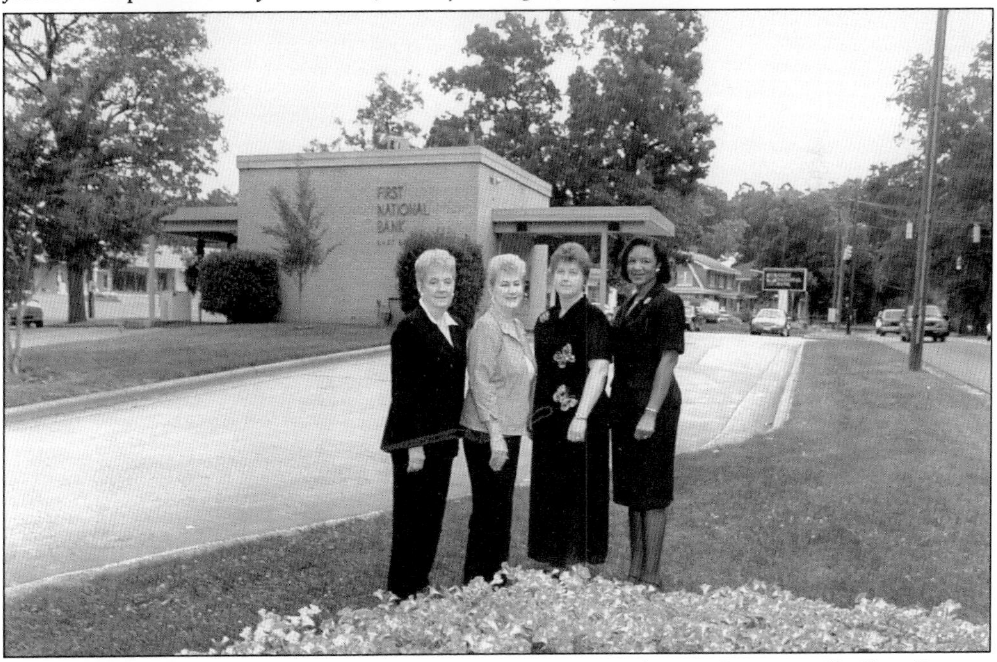

The East Branch is located on East Marion Street at Lineberger Street in Shelby. Current employees, shown here from left to right, are Martha Harrill, Mary Ivester, Martha Melton, and Tawanna Oates.

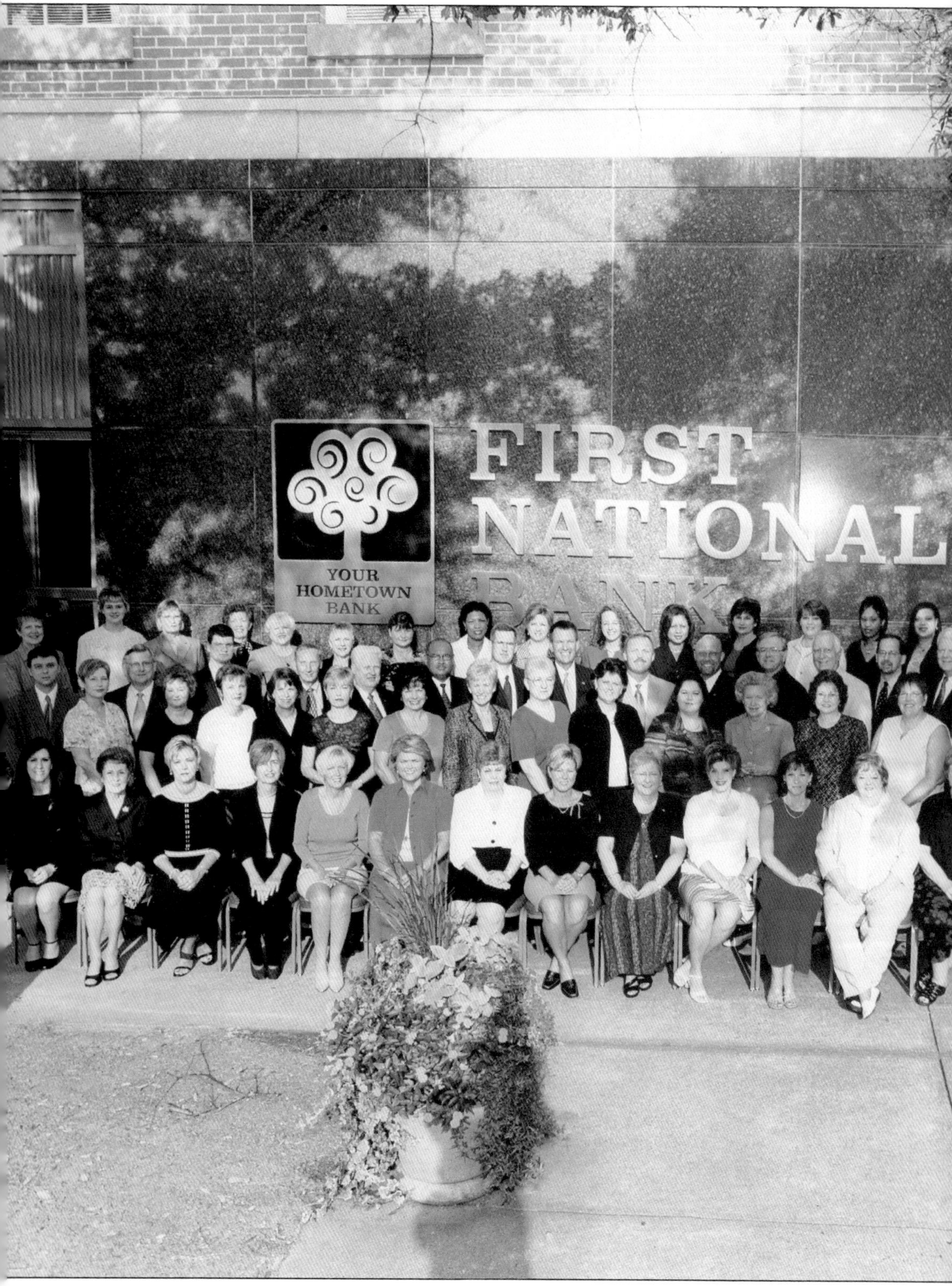
YOUR
HOMETOWN
BANK
FIRST
NATIONAL
BANK

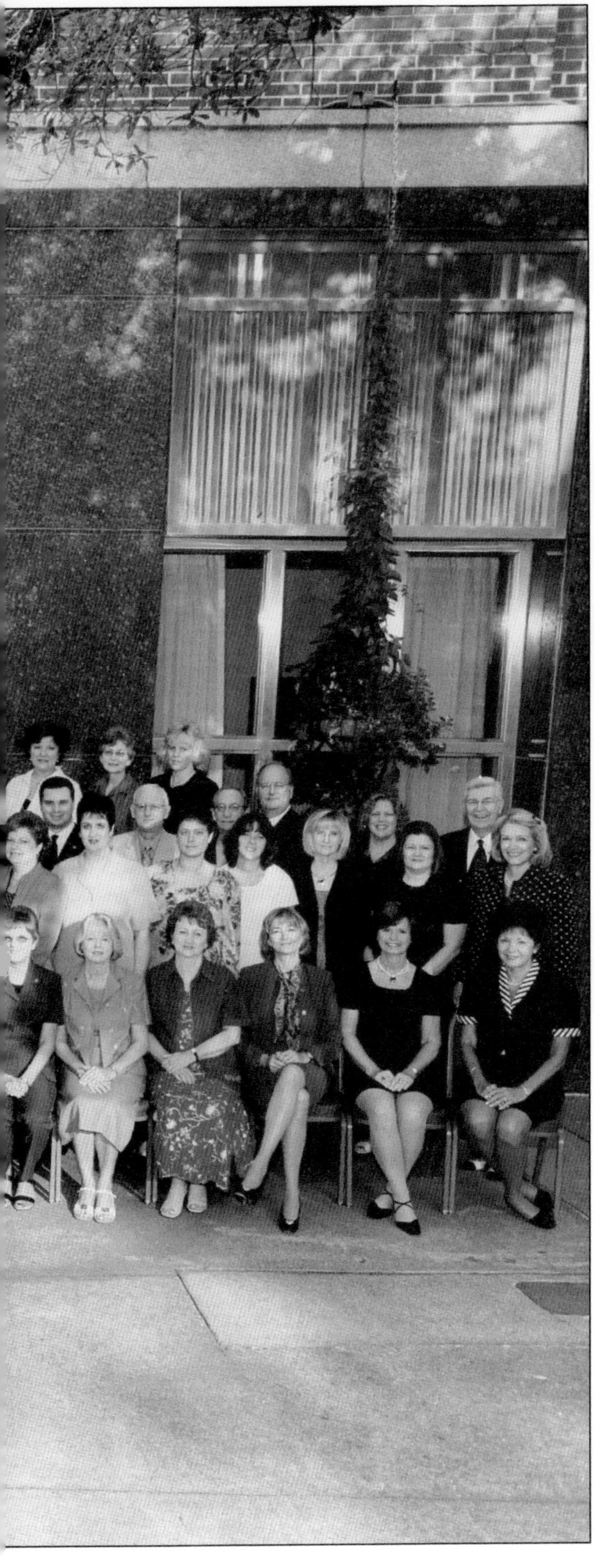

The First National Bank Center in Uptown Shelby has over 100 employees. Pictured, from left to right, are the following: (first row) Earlene Davis, Dot Pearson, Sharon Owens, Judy Edwards, Cathy Hunt, Rita Lowe, Rae Overstreet, Cindy Smart, Jeanette Capozzielli, Holly Wall, Tammy Sorendo, Donna Cloninger, Janie Ledbetter, Pat Willis, Carolyn Wince, Gailya Hamrick, Julie Greene, Penny Head, and Helen Jeffords; (second row) Vickie Melton, Patricia Phillips, Lynn Yarbro, Sandy Griffin, Pat Blaylock, Kay James, Billy Brown, Noel Powell, Rhonda Blackwood, Kris Champion, Adelaide Craver, Vickie Davis, Glenda Beck, Nina Price, Tammy Cogdell, Lisa Patrick, Bridgett Franklin, Skye Miller, Wendy Huskey, Lisa Rinehart, and Peggy Paksoy; (third row) Kevin Rhodes, Roger Humphries, Newton Craver, James Robbs, Phil Witherspoon, Mackie Ashe, Edwin White, Earl Lutz, Cecil Clark, Jim Wood, Lin Robinson, Ed Hamilton, William Martin, Bill Plowden, Dana Lundquist, Stever Tharrington, Carl Adams, Bob Eakins, David Thompson, Theresa Hamrick, and Bobby Smith; (fourth row) Carol Wood, Mary Van Horn, Janet Martin, Rachel Arndt, Diane Hines, Janie Doty, Becky Estes, Takischa Hopper, Myra Wright, Apryl McCraw, Annette Cherry, Mary Morrison, Denise McCoy, Paula Wilmer, Crystal Brown, Pam Goforth, Phyllis Monteith, Jeanette Harrill, and Sarah VanHoy; (not pictured) Lisa Alvino, Dawn Beam, Larry Beasley, Mabel Elliott, Faith Gantt, Amanda Gettys, Susan Pat Guffey, Karen Hall, Tom Harris, Joe Henderson, Billy Holland, Jack Horner, Vicky Huntsinger, Charles Jamerson, Sharon Leigh, Seal McSwain, Brenda Page, Julie Van Buren, Mike Weisman, Anthony Williams, and Cathy Williams.

The photograph of the Main Office staff has so many more employees than the other offices because it includes not only the tellers, Mary Van Horn, Wendy Huskey, Takischa Hopper, Jeanette Harrill, Joseph Henderson Jr., and Karen Hall; customer service representatives, Annette Cherry, Judy Edwards, Cathy Hunt, Rae Overstreet, and Sarah Vanhoy; loan officers, who were listed earlier; their assistants and senior management; and Administrative Officer Vickie Melton, but it also includes all of the bank's behind-the-scenes personnel.

These employees, whom you do not see everyday, are so important to the bank and its customers. They include Sharon Owens, who heads teller administration and personnel administration, and Rita Lowe, who heads customer service administration and assists Mrs. Owens in her functions and the bank's couriers. The audit department, loan administration, collection, marketing department, and the trust division, including brokerage, are also located and pictured with the main office, but they have been mentioned earlier in the book.

Also at the main office, Carol Wood, senior vice president, oversees the bank's information technology staff, which includes Jane Doty, check processing and electronic services; Pat Willis, deposit operations; Edwin White, computer operations; Cathy Williams, network operations; and Vickie Davis, special projects.

First National is the only bank in Cleveland County that processes its work locally. The bank is very proud of its cutting-edge technology that offers its customers the most up-to-date banking products, including check imaging, statements on CD-ROM, debit and ATM cards, and an interactive website, www.ibankatfnb.com, providing access to Internet banking and bill payment services for all customers and cash management services for commercial customers.

The financial services division of the bank under the leadership of the CFO provides financial reporting to bank management, regulatory authorities, stockholders, and other interested parties. This reporting includes budgeting, interest risk, liquidity management, and other monitoring analyses for internal and external use. Additionally, this division oversees the management and accounting for the investment portfolio. A capable team of financial accountants, including Lisa Alvino, Pat Guffey, and William Martin, are assisted by staff members Diane Hines, Nina Price, Myra Wright, Apryl McCraw, and Julie Greene. The call center, as an integral part of the bank's efforts to promote hometown banking, is provided so that all customers speak to a bank employee rather than to a machine.

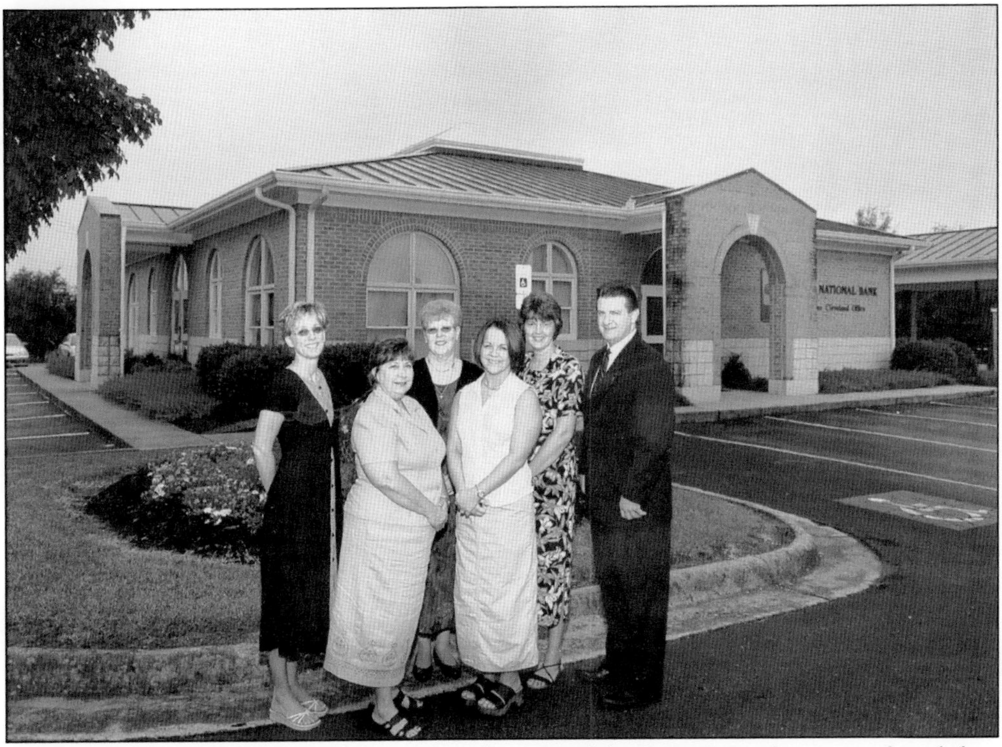

The bank's Upper Cleveland branch is located in Lawndale. Current employees are, from left to right, Sandy Jones, Judy Gray, Judy Brown, Kristin Green, Kim Laughlin, Ken Miller, and (not pictured) Teresa Garver.

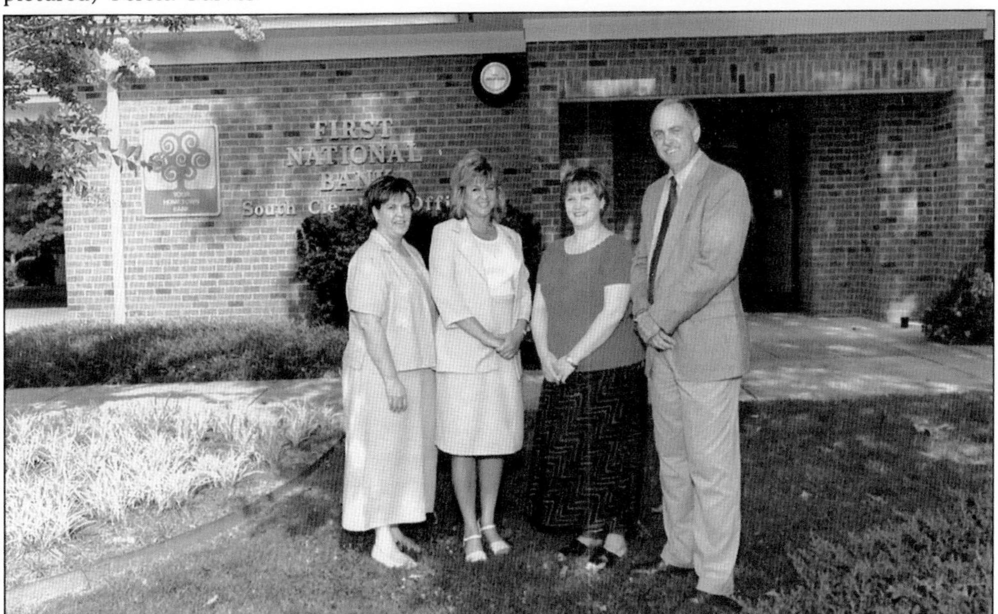

The South Cleveland office is located in the Patterson Springs and Earl vicinity. The current staff includes, from left to right, Carol Earls, Kelly Gregory, Lisa Frazier, Danny Denton, and (not pictured) Lujane Smith and Vicki Thomas.

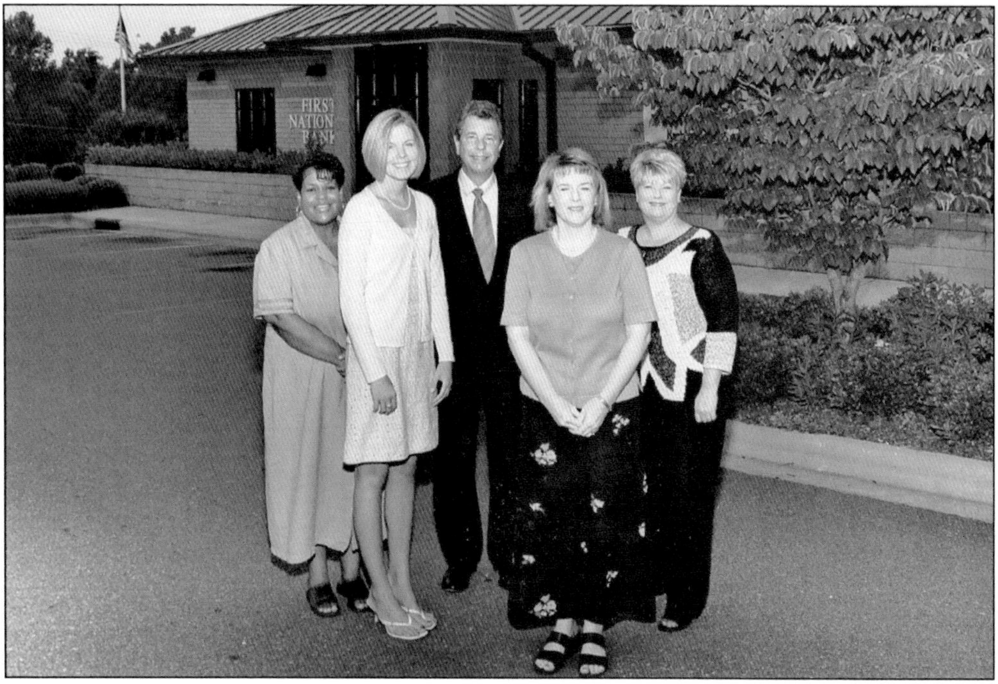

The Highland office is in the Highland Festival Shopping Center on East Marion Street in Shelby. The Highland staff, pictured here from left to right, includes Roslyn Crump, Ansley Barkley, Hill Hudson III, Robin Hawkins, and Carol Henry.

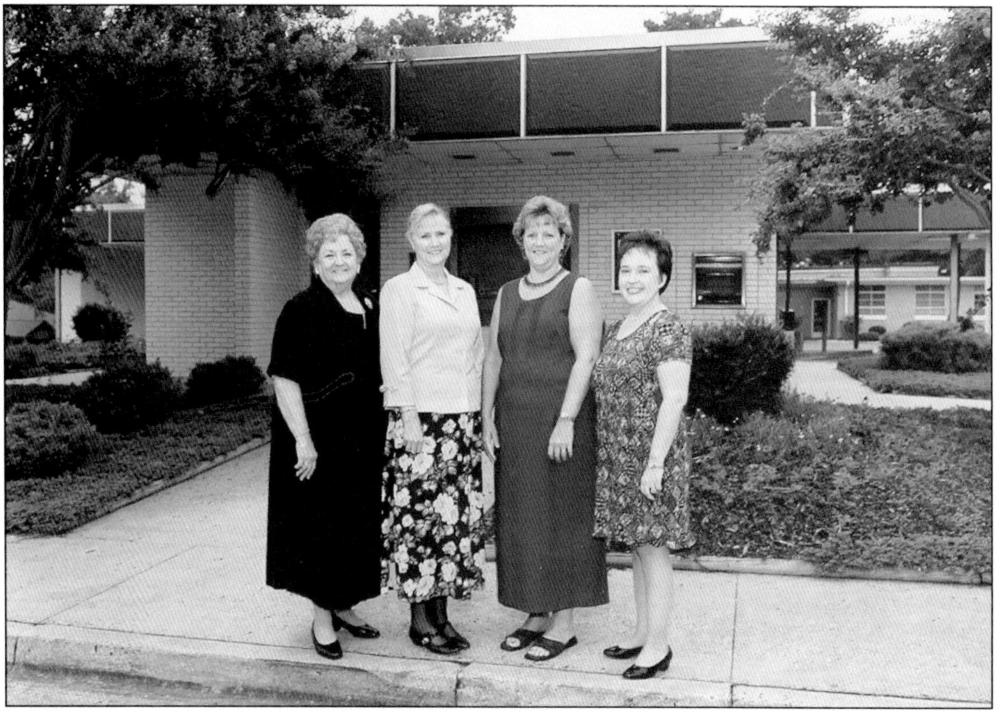

The North Branch is on North Lafayette Street in Shelby. Employees here are, from left to right, Betty Powell, Dot Fitch, Shirley Alexander, and Donna Sisk.

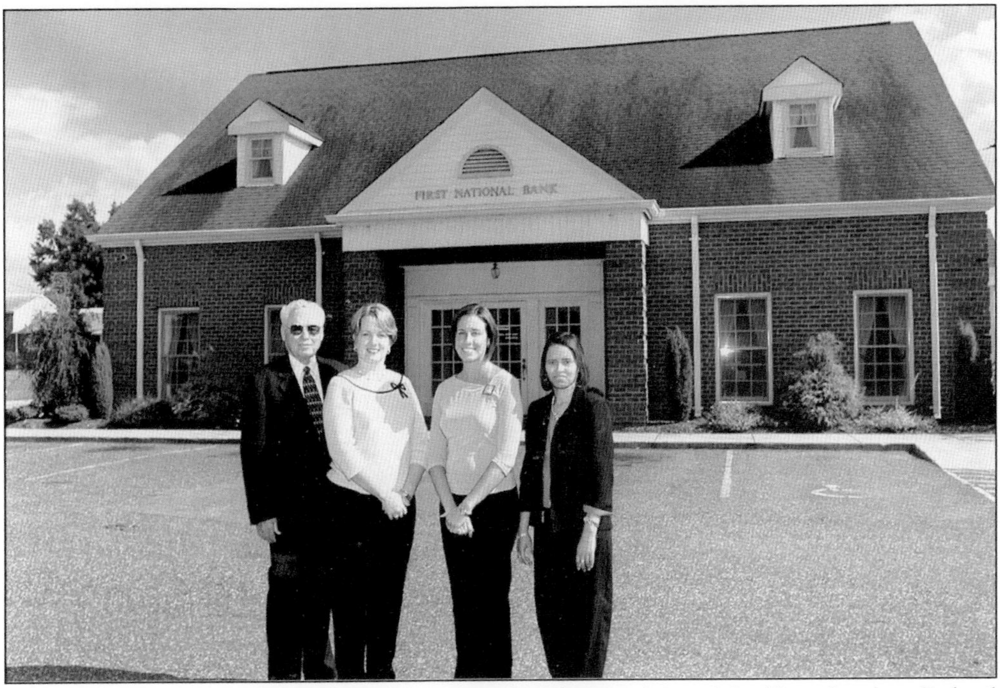

The East Dixon Boulevard branch was acquired in the purchase of the First Carolina Federal Savings Bank. The current staff includes, from left to right, Joe Cabaniss, Pam Toney, Crystal Lovelace, Contisha Browder, and (not pictured) Beth Blanton.

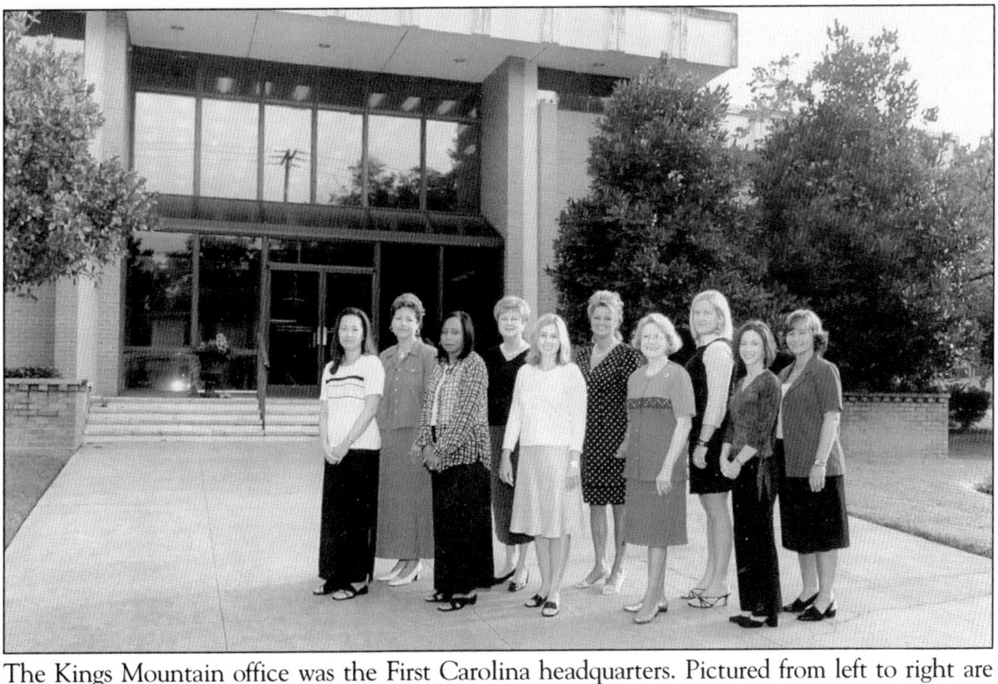

The Kings Mountain office was the First Carolina headquarters. Pictured from left to right are Jennifer McCall, Leslie Ramsey, Connie James, Brenda Lovelace, Julie Singalevitch, Cindy Wood, Carole Lee Ferguson, Elizabeth Ferguson, Kristin Anthony, and Tammy Rucker. Not pictured are Alison Gilbert, Carol Buchanan, Carolyn Hilpert, Brittni England, and Elaine Phifer.

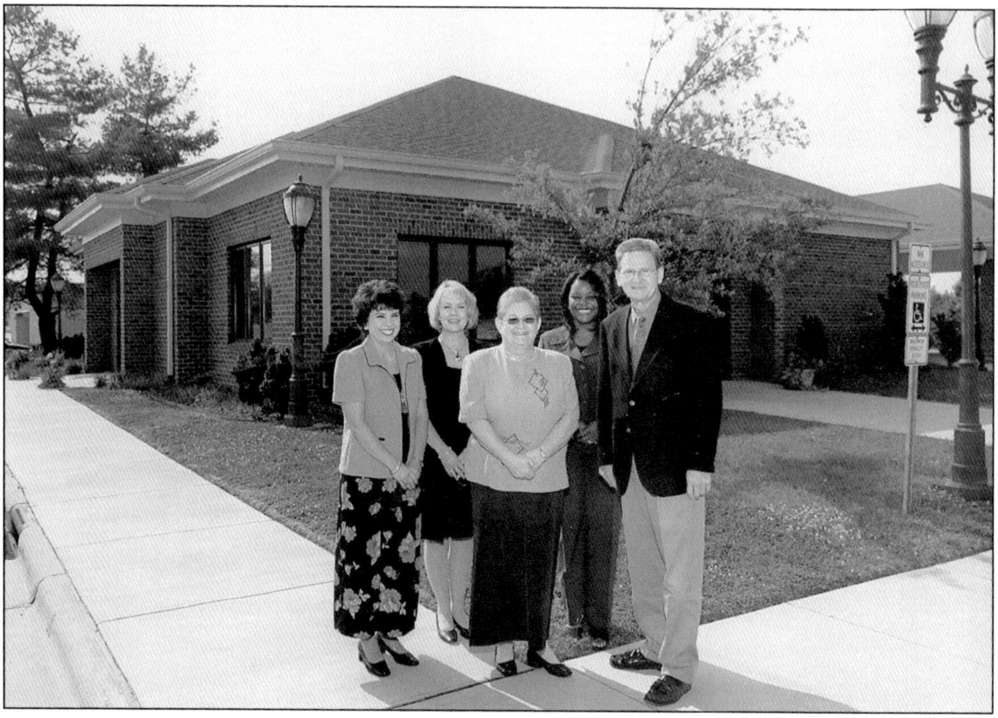

First National built the Bessemer City office just after the First Carolina purchase. The employees include, from left to right, Kim Collett, Stacy Ewart, JoAnn Hall, Patricia Scott, Allen Martin, and (not pictured) Carmen Pittman.

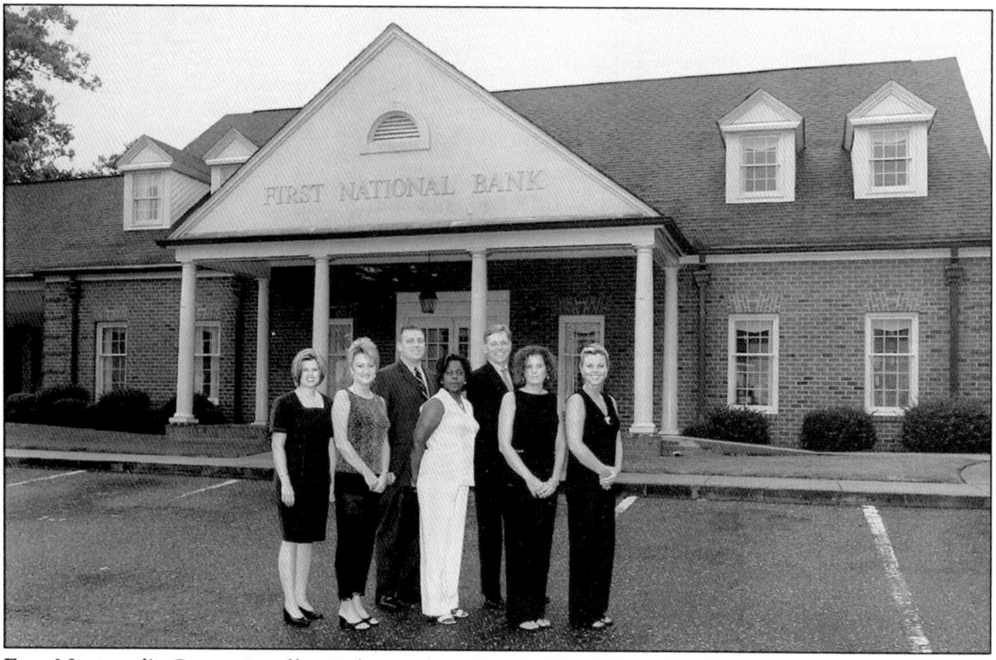

First National's Gastonia office is located on South New Hope Road. Current employees, seen here from left to right in front of the office, are Jody Goforth, Donna Sickenberger, Phillip Garrison, Shelia Wright, Bruce Hodge, Wendy Postell, and Jodi Parker.

Appendix

First National Bank Board of Directors, Advisors, and Bank Officers

First National Bank Board

Name	Elected to Board	Last Year Elected
Burwell Blanton	1903	1908
George Blanton, Sr.	1903	1959
Henry Franklin Schenck	1903	1915
Andrew Caleb Miller	1903	1930
John Dixon Lineberger	1903	1930
Orville Emberry Ford	1903	1923
Charles C. Blanton	1903	1940
Judge James L. Webb	1909	1930
Lawson A. Gettys	1913	1931
Forrest Eskridge	1916	1939
John F. Schenck, Sr.	1916	1945
John F. Schenck, Jr.	1945	1952
Hon. Clyde R. Hoey	1923	1936
Paul Webb	1923	1944
Hon. O. Max Gardner	1923	1934
J. F. Roberts	1923	1956
R. T. LeGrand, Sr.	1931	1961
Charles L. Eskridge	1931	1931
Hon. Lee B. Weathers	1932	1957
Clarence S. Mull	1935	1978
George Blanton, Jr.	1938	2000
John R. Dover, Jr.	1944	1963
O. M. Mull	1945	1962
D. W. Royster	1953	1973
Tom M. Cornwell	1955	1980
Don S. Carpenter	1955	1959
John F. Schenck, III	1955	1957
Fred W. Alexander	1956	1960
Horace H. Carter	1956	1980
Joseph C. Whisnant	1957	1990
Jean W. Schenck	1958	1978
Henry Lee Weathers	1958	2004
R. Patrick Spangler	1960	1987

R. T. LeGrand, Jr.	1962	2004
Charles I. Dover	1964	1990
Edgar B. Hamilton	1965	Still Active on Board
William E. Pearce	1966	1990
Robert R. Forney	1972	2002
C. Rush Hamrick, Jr.	1972	Still Active on Board
G. J. Vincent	1972	1990
Newlin P. Schenck	1979	2005
Lloyd C. Bost	1979	1996
Adelaide Austell Craver	1991	Still Active on Board
Kathleen D. Hamrick	1991	2002
Robert G. Laney, Jr.	1991	1991
David M. Roberts	1992	1996
Max J. Hamrick	1995	Still Active on Board
Helen A. Jeffords	1996	Still Active on Board
William E. Plowden, Jr.	1996	Still Active on Board
Martha R. Plaster	1997	Still Active on Board
John C. McGill, M.D.	1999	Still Active on Board (1956 First Carolina)
Glee E. Bridges	1999	Still Active on Board (1968 First Carolina)
Catherine Blanton Freedberg, Ph.D.	2000	Still Active on Board
Henry P. Neisler	2001	Still Active on Board
John O. Harris, III	2004	Still Active on Board
Kevin T. James, M.D.	2004	Still Active on Board
David W. Royster, III	2004	Still Active on Board
John E. Young	2004	Still Active on Board

First National Advisory Board

Martha ("Brownie") R. Plaster, Chair
Connie A. Allison
Samuel E. Blanton, DDS
F. Reid Bridges
Cary Caldwell, GWU Representative
Dennis E. Conner
F. Lawrence ("Larry") Fox
Robert Bryan Gamble
Katherine B. Gaston
Leonard R. Hollifield
Larry D. Hamrick Jr.
Charles N. Lineberger
J. Ben Morrow
George H. Norville
Jessie V. Putnam
Jeffrey T. Ross
David M. Schweppe, II
Frank A. Stewart
Susan B. Turner
Aaron Wood

Executive Officers

Adelaide Austell Craver	Chairman of the Board and CEO
Helen A. Jeffords	President, Chief Operating Officer and Chief Financial Officer
William E. Plowden Jr.	Vice Chairman and Senior Trust Officer
Edgar B. Hamilton	Chairman Emeritus

Executive Vice Presidents

Robert R. Eakins
Joseph B. Henderson Jr.
Brenda F. Page

Senior Vice Presidents

J. Thomas Harris
Cecil D. Clark
Brenda N. Lovelace
Earl H. Lutz Jr.
Kenneth H. Miller
Peggy M. Paksoy
Bobby G. Smith
Will Weill, III
Michael C. Weisman
Carol V. Wood

Vice Presidents

L. Michael Andrews
Carl R. Adams
J. Newton Craver II
Joseph E. Crews
Daniel L. Denton
Patsy P. Guffey
JoAnn J. Hall
W. Hill Hudson III
Mitchell P. Johnson
Dana K. Lundquist
James J. Wood
Edward G. Lunsford
Debra S. Martin
E. Allen Martin
William L. Martin Jr.
Sharon S. Owens
G. Lin Robinson
Holt D. Robinson
David G. Thompson
Jeffrey T. Triplett
Thomas L. Weaver

Senior Auditor

Perry K. Mardis

Auditor

Sonja A. Thomas

Assistant Vice Presidents

Tracy E. Barger
Rhonda G. Blackwood
Julie Greene Burch
Lisa P. Bryant
Karen L. Clark
Mary C. Davis
Victoria Q. Davis
Jane M. Doty
Rita H. Lowe
Linda H. Marsh
Bridgette G. Martin
Denise H. McCoy
Vickie B. Melton
Rae S. Overstreet
Dorothy W. Pearson
Wendy L. Postell

Judy B. Edwards
Barbara C. Fitch
Thomas S. Fletcher
David C. Garrett
Phillip R. Garrison
Alison C. Gilbert
Sandra H. Griffin
Jeffrey L. Halcomb
Roger T. Humphries
Phillip Hunt
Kay P. James
Sharon C. Leigh
Victoria M. Logan

Leslie S. Ramsey
Angela M. Roberts
Tammy W. Rucker
Karen H. Searcy
Julie L. Singalevitch
Donna S. Sisk
Nancy M. Taylor
Pamela L. Toney
Edwin W. White
Patricia H. Willis
Phillip W. Witherspoon
Myra P. Wright

Officers

Administrative Officer, Call Center	Rachel C. Arndt
Administrative Officer, Loan	Billie K. Brown
Branch Officer	Amy Brown
Branch Officer	Roslyn A. Crump
Branch Officer	Brittni J. England
Branch Officer/CSR	Carol J. Earls
Branch Officer	Vicky O. Franklin
Branch Officer	Lisa Frazier
Branch Officer/CSR	Judy F. Gray
Branch Officer	Kristen A. Gordon
Branch Officer/CSR/Loans	Cathy H. Hunt
Branch Officer	Tawanna D. Oates
Branch Officer	Janis E. Tucker
Customer Service Officer	Annette Cherry
Customer Service Officer	Sarah Vanhoy
Financial Services Officer	Diane H. Hines
Financial Services Officer	Nina H. Price
Financial Services Officer	Apryl W. McCraw
Loan Administrative Officer	Kris H. Champion
Loan Administrative Officer	Jodi E. Parker
Loan Administrative Officer	Anne Sale
Loan Officer	Susan A. Gibson
Marketing Officer	Cynthia H. Heinbach
Marketing Officer	Phyllis S. Monteith
Operations Officer, Electronics	Glenda P. Beck
Operations Officer, IT	Vicky Huntsinger
Operations Officer, Deposits	Cecelia P. McSwain
Security Officer	Mary V. Cabaniss
Training Officer	Holly D. Wall
Trust Officer, Retirement Plans and Investments	Theresa H. Hamrick